Android UI Development with Jetpack Compose

Bring declarative and native UI to life quickly and easily
on Android using Jetpack Compose and Kotlin

Thomas Künneth

BIRMINGHAM—MUMBAI

Android UI Development with Jetpack Compose

Group Product Manager: Rohit Rajkumar
Publishing Product Manager: Vaideeshwari Muralikrishnan
Senior Content Development Editor: Feza Shaikh
Technical Editor: Simran Ali
Copy Editor: Safis Editing
Project Coordinator: Aishwarya Mohan and Arul Viveaun S
Proofreader: Safis Editing
Indexer: Rekha Nair
Production Designer: Jyoti Kadam
DevRel Marketing Coordinators: Anamika Singh, Namita Velgekar, and Nivedita Pandey

First published: February 2022

Second edition: October 2023

Production reference: 1041023

Packt Publishing Ltd
Grosvenor House
11 St Paul's Square
Birmingham
B3 1R

ISBN 978-1-83763-425-5

www.packtpub.com

To my wonderful wife, Moni

Contributors

About the author

Thomas Künneth is a Google Developer Expert for Android and has been a speaker and panelist at multiple international conferences about Android. Currently, Thomas works as a senior Android developer at Snapp Mobile. He has authored countless articles as well as one of the top-selling German Android books (currently in its sixth edition). He also frequently contributes to various open source projects.

I want to thank the people who have been close to me and supported me, especially my wife, Moni.

About the reviewers

Guilherme Delgado is an accomplished mobile developer and team leader with a career spanning over a decade. Having joined Bliss Applications in 2012, the pioneering Portuguese company in mobile technology founded in 2009, Guilherme has been an integral part of the company's growth and evolution. Presently, as the mobile engineering manager, he orchestrates the entire mobile department's strategy and vision, guiding it toward new horizons of innovation. Beyond professional accomplishments, he is also an active open source contributor, generously sharing expertise with the global developer community. Currently, he's focused on studying and experimenting with Kotlin Multiplatform, showcasing his dedication to staying at the forefront of technology.

Jomar Tigcal is an Android developer with over 11 years of experience in mobile and software development. He worked on various stages of app development for organizations from small start-ups to large companies. Jomar has also given talks and conducted training and workshops on Android. He is one of the co-authors of *How to Build Android Apps with Kotlin* (first and second editions) and wrote *Simplifying Android Development with Coroutines and Flows*.

Table of Contents

3

Exploring the Key Principles of Compose 43

Part 2: Building User Interfaces

4

Laying Out UI Elements in Compose 69

5

Managing State of Your Composable Functions 89

9

Exploring Interoperability APIs   165

10

Testing and Debugging Compose Apps   181

11

Developing for Different Form Factors   203

12

Bringing Your Compose UI to Different Platforms   225

Index   247

Other Books You May Enjoy   254

Preface

Jetpack Compose is a paradigm shift in Android development and introduces a lot of new concepts that are essential for any Android developer to learn. It solves a lot of pain points that are associated with Android development, and it is touted to be the default way to build Android apps over the next few years.

Using practical examples, you will learn about the fundamental concepts of Jetpack Compose and how to use them when you build your own Android applications. The book starts with an in-depth explanation of the declarative approach, its differences, and its advantages over traditional UI frameworks. Having laid this foundation, we will get practical and write our first composable functions. After that, we will cover layouts, an important core component of every UI framework. Having mastered them, we will move on to more advanced topics such as animation, testing, and architecture best practices.

The second edition has been thoroughly updated to reflect all changes and additions that were made by Google since the initial stable release. All examples are based on Material 3 (also named Material You).

Who this book is for

This book is for Android developers with existing knowledge of the Kotlin programming language, who would like to learn how to build modern Android **user interfaces** (**UIs**) using Jetpack Compose.

What this book covers

Chapter 1, Building Your First Compose App, shows you how to build your first Compose app. Also, important key ideas such as composable functions and using previews are introduced. It is important to whet the appetite by offering early success, so we will build, preview, and run composable functions before digging too deep into details.

Chapter 2, Understanding the Declarative Paradigm, explains how Android UI development was done before Jetpack Compose and what the issues with this "old" approach are. Also, you will discover how composables are different from views and why this is both important and beneficial.

Chapter 3, Exploring the Key Principles of Compose, explores important terminology, concepts, and techniques. Their knowledge is essential to write well-behaving Compose apps.

Chapter 4, Laying Out UI Elements in Compose, examines how the way Jetpack Compose's layout system works is different compared to the classic Android UI toolkit. This chapter introduces some of the existing layouts. It also shows you how to implement custom layouts. These are needed if the built-in layouts cannot provide the required distribution of UI elements on screen.

Chapter 5, Managing State of Your Composable Functions, details why reacting to state changes is critical to how modern mobile apps work. Jetpack Compose tries to address this need by providing reactive state primitives. This chapter looks at how to use these state primitives and how they work under the hood.

Chapter 6, Building a Real-World App, revisits previously learned concepts and brings them together in one app. Seeing concepts in actual code will help you to understand them and make it easier to reuse in your own programs.

Chapter 7, Exploring App Architecture, further explores ViewModels and how they can help build a solid app architecture. You will learn how to inject objects such as repositories during ViewModel creation and why this is important. The chapter also introduces side effects as a means to trigger or react to changes outside the Compose world.

Chapter 8, Working with Animations, contains a detailed look at animations and transitions. Using them makes apps really shine. Jetpack Compose simplifies the process of adding animation effects greatly over the old view-based approach. This chapter introduces all the relevant APIs.

Chapter 9, Exploring Interoperability APIs, explains how to mix Jetpack Compose and old-fashioned views in one app. Although Jetpack Compose is the UI toolkit of choice for new apps, its powers can be leveraged in existing apps, too. This chapter discusses strategies to combine both declarative and imperative approaches in one app and offers a migration strategy to painlessly update existing UIs to Jetpack Compose.

Chapter 10, Testing and Debugging Compose Apps, explains why testing the UI of a Compose app works differently than testing a view-based UI. Compose uses a more declarative approach to testing. This chapter introduces basic testing scenarios for Compose apps.

Chapter 11, Developing for Different Form Factors, shows you how to write Compose apps that look great not only on smartphones but also on large-screen devices, such as tablets and foldables. It introduces the concept of Window Size Classes and shows you how they are used to organize screen content.

Chapter 12, Bringing Your Compose UI to Different Platforms, shows you how to bring Compose UIs to different platforms such as the desktop (Windows, Linux, or macOS) and the web. It offers a quick introduction to Compose Multiplatform and related technologies such as **Kotlin Multiplatform** (**KMP**). You will learn how to take one of the sample apps of the book to the desktop.

To get the most out of this book

Software/hardware covered in the book	Operating system requirements
Android Studio Giraffe or later versions	Windows, macOS, or Linux

If you are using the digital version of this book, we advise you to type the code yourself or access the code from the book's GitHub repository (a link is available in the next section). Doing so will help you avoid any potential errors related to the copying and pasting of code.

Download the example code files

You can download the example code files for this book from GitHub at https://github.com/PacktPublishing/Android-UI-development-with-Jetpack-Compose-Second-Edition. If there's an update to the code, it will be updated in the GitHub repository.

We also have other code bundles from our rich catalog of books and videos available at https://github.com/PacktPublishing/. Check them out!

Conventions used

There are a number of text conventions used throughout this book.

Code in text: Indicates code words in text, database table names, folder names, filenames, file extensions, pathnames, dummy URLs, user input, and Twitter handles. Here is an example: "Column() contains two children, Button() and Image(). The image is visible only when showImage is true."

A block of code is set as follows:

```
class MainActivity : AppCompatActivity() {
  override fun onCreate(savedInstanceState: Bundle?) {
    super.onCreate(savedInstanceState)
    setContent {
      MainView()
    }
  }
}
```

When we wish to draw your attention to a particular part of a code block, the relevant lines or items are set in bold:

```
TextField(
    value = name.value,
    onValueChange = {
        name.value = it
    },
    placeholder = {
        Text(text = stringResource(id = R.string.hint))
    },
```

Any command-line input or output is written as follows:

```
$ mkdir css
$ cd css
```

Bold: Indicates a new term, an important word, or words that you see on screen. For instance, words in menus or dialog boxes appear in **bold**. Here is an example: "To deploy a composable function to a real device or the Android Emulator, click on the **Run Preview** button."

> **Tips or important notes**
> Appear like this.

Get in touch

Feedback from our readers is always welcome.

General feedback: If you have questions about any aspect of this book, email us at customercare@packtpub.com and mention the book title in the subject of your message.

Errata: Although we have taken every care to ensure the accuracy of our content, mistakes do happen. If you have found a mistake in this book, we would be grateful if you would report this to us. Please visit www.packtpub.com/support/errata and fill in the form.

Piracy: If you come across any illegal copies of our works in any form on the internet, we would be grateful if you would provide us with the location address or website name. Please contact us at copyright@packt.com with a link to the material.

If you are interested in becoming an author: If there is a topic that you have expertise in and you are interested in either writing or contributing to a book, please visit authors.packtpub.com.

Share Your Thoughts

Once you've read, we'd love to hear your thoughts! Scan the QR code below to go straight to the Amazon review page for this book and share your feedback.

https://packt.link/r/1837634254

Your review is important to us and the tech community and will help us make sure we're delivering excellent quality content.

Download a free PDF copy of this book

Thanks for purchasing this book!

Do you like to read on the go but are unable to carry your print books everywhere?

Is your eBook purchase not compatible with the device of your choice?

Don't worry, now with every Packt book you get a DRM-free PDF version of that book at no cost.

Read anywhere, any place, on any device. Search, copy, and paste code from your favorite technical books directly into your application.

The perks don't stop there, you can get exclusive access to discounts, newsletters, and great free content in your inbox daily

Follow these simple steps to get the benefits:

1.   Scan the QR code or visit the link below

https://packt.link/free-ebook/9781837634255

2.   Submit your proof of purchase
3.   That's it! We'll send your free PDF and other benefits to your email directly

Part 1: Fundamentals of Jetpack Compose

In this part, you will get to know some important basic concepts of Jetpack Compose. An understanding of these is necessary to write well-behaving Compose apps.

We will cover the following chapters in this part:

- *Chapter 1, Building Your First Compose App*

- *Chapter 2, Understanding the Declarative Paradigm*

- *Chapter 3, Exploring the Key Principles of Compose*

1
Building Your First Compose App

When **Android** was introduced more than 10 years ago, it quickly gained popularity among developers because it was incredibly easy to write apps. All you had to do was define the **user interface** (**UI**) in an XML file and connect it to your *activity*. This worked flawlessly because apps were small, and developers needed to support just a handful of devices.

So much has changed since then.

With every new platform version, Android has gained new features. Through the years, device manufacturers introduced thousands of devices with different screen sizes, pixel densities, and form factors. While Google did its best to keep the Android *view* system comprehendible, the complexity of apps increased significantly; basic tasks such as implementing scrolling lists or animations require lots of boilerplate code.

It turned out that these problems were not specific to Android. Other platforms and operating systems faced them as well. Most issues stem from how UI toolkits used to work. They follow a so-called **imperative approach** (which I will explain in *Chapter 2, Understanding the Declarative Paradigm*). The solution was a paradigm shift. The React web framework was the first to popularize a declarative approach. Other platforms and frameworks (for example, Flutter and SwiftUI) followed.

Jetpack Compose is Google's declarative UI framework for Android. It dramatically simplifies the creation of UIs. As you will surely agree after reading this book, using Jetpack Compose is both easy and fun. But before we dive in, please note that Jetpack Compose is Kotlin-only. This means that all your Compose code will have to be written in **Kotlin**. To follow this book, you should have a basic understanding of the Kotlin syntax and the functional programming model. If you want to learn more about these topics, please refer to the *Further reading* section at the end of this chapter.

This chapter covers three main topics:

- Saying hello to composable functions
- Using the preview feature
- Running a Compose app

I will explain how to build a simple UI with Jetpack Compose. Next, you will learn to use the **preview** feature in Android Studio and how to run a Compose app. By the end of this chapter, you will have a basic understanding of how composable functions work, how they are integrated into your app, and how your project must be configured in order to use Jetpack Compose.

Technical requirements

All the code examples for this book can be found on GitHub at `https://github.com/ PacktPublishing/Android-UI-development-with-Jetpack-Compose-Second- Edition`. Please download the zipped version or clone the repository to an arbitrary location on your computer. The projects work best with Android Studio Giraffe or later versions. You can download the latest version at `https://developer.android.com/studio`. Please follow the detailed installation instructions at `https://developer.android.com/studio/install`.

To open a project, launch Android Studio, click the **Open** button in the upper-right area of the **Welcome to Android Studio** window, and select the base directory of the project in the folder selection dialog. This chapter has one project. It is called `Hello` and is located inside the `chapter_01` folder. Please make sure to not open the base directory of the repository, because Android Studio would not recognize the projects. Instead, you must pick the directory that contains the project you want to work with.

To run a sample app, you need a real device or an Android Emulator. Please make sure that developer options and USB debugging are enabled on the real device, and that the device is connected to your development machine via USB or WLAN. Please follow the instructions at `https://developer. android.com/studio/debug/dev-options`. You can also set up an Android Emulator. To get started, please follow the detailed instructions at `https://developer.android.com/ studio/run/emulator`.

Saying hello to composable functions

As you will see shortly, composable functions are the essential building blocks of Compose apps; these elements make up the UI.

To take a first look at them, I will walk you through a simple app called `Hello` (*Figure 1.1*). If you have already cloned or downloaded the repository of this book, its project folder is located inside `chapter_01`. Otherwise, please do so now. To follow this section, open the project in Android Studio and open `MainActivity.kt`. The use case of our first Compose app is very simple. After you have entered your name and clicked on the **Done** button, you will see a greeting message:

Figure 1.1 – The Hello app

Conceptually, the app consists of the following:

- The welcome text
- A row with an `EditText` equivalent and a button
- A greeting message

Let's look at how to create the app.

Showing a welcome text

Let's start with the welcome text, our first composable function:

```
@Composable
fun Welcome() {
    Text(
        text = stringResource(id = R.string.welcome),
        style = MaterialTheme.typography.bodyLarge
    )
}
```

Composable functions can be easily identified by the @Composable annotation. They do not need to have a particular return type but instead emit UI elements. This is usually done by invoking other composables (for the sake of brevity, I will sometimes omit the word "function"). *Chapter 3, Exploring the Key Principles of Compose*, will cover this in greater detail.

In this example, Welcome() summons a text. Text() is a built-in composable function and belongs to the androidx.compose.material3 package. To invoke Text() just by its name, you need to import it, as follows:

```
import androidx.compose.material3.Text
```

Note that you can save import lines by using the * wildcard. To use Text() and other Material Design elements, your build.gradle file must include an implementation dependency to androidx.compose.material3:material3.

> **Note**
>
> Jetpack Compose supports two versions of Material Design. The androidx.compose.material package represents the older one, Material 2. Android 12 introduced a new iteration named **Material You** (Material 3). This book uses Material You and the androidx.compose.material3 package.

Looking back at the welcome text code, the Text() composable inside Welcome() is configured through two parameters, text and style. The first, text, specifies what text will be displayed. R.string may look familiar; it refers to definitions inside the strings.xml files. Just as in view-based apps, you define text for UI elements there. The stringResource() is a predefined composable function. It belongs to the androidx.compose.ui.res package.

The style parameter modifies the visual appearance of text. Its value, MaterialTheme.typography.bodyLarge, causes the output to look like a large body text. You will learn more about Compose styling and theming in the *Styling a Compose app* section of *Chapter 6, Building a Real-World App*.

The next composable looks quite similar. Can you spot the differences?

```
@Composable
fun Greeting(name: String) {
    Text(
        text = stringResource(id = R.string.hello, name),
        textAlign = TextAlign.Center,
        style = MaterialTheme.typography.bodyLarge
    )
}
```

Here, `stringResource()` receives an additional parameter. This is very convenient for replacing placeholders with actual text. The string is defined in `strings.xml`, as follows:

```
<string name="hello">Hello, %1$s.\nNice to meet you.</string>
```

The `textAlign` parameter specifies how text is positioned horizontally. Here, each line is centered.

Using rows, text fields, and buttons

Next, let's turn to the text input field (**Your name**) and the **Done** button, which both appear on the same row. This is a very common pattern; therefore, Jetpack Compose provides a composable named `Row()`, which belongs to the `androidx.compose.foundation.layout` package. Just as with all composable functions, `Row()` can receive a comma-separated list of parameters inside ( ), and its children are put inside curly braces:

```
@Composable
fun TextAndButton(name: MutableState<String>,
                  nameEntered: MutableState<Boolean>) {
  Row(modifier = Modifier.padding(top = 8.dp)) {
      ...
  }
}
```

`TextAndButton()` requires two parameters, `name` and `nameEntered`. You will see what they are used for in the *Showing a greeting message* section. For now, please ignore their `MutableState` type.

`Row()` receives a parameter called `modifier`. Modifiers are a key technique in Jetpack Compose to influence both the look and behavior of composable functions. I will explain them in greater detail in *Chapter 3, Exploring the Key Principles of Compose*.

`padding(top = 8.dp)` means that the row will have a padding of eight density-independent pixels (`.dp`) at its upper side, thus separating itself from the welcome message above it.

Now, we will look at the text input field, which allows the user to enter a name:

```
TextField(
    value = name.value,
    onValueChange = {
        name.value = it
    },
    placeholder = {
        Text(text = stringResource(id = R.string.hint))
    },
    modifier = Modifier
        .alignByBaseline()
        .weight(1.0F),
    singleLine = true,
    keyboardOptions = KeyboardOptions(
        autoCorrect = false,
        capitalization = KeyboardCapitalization.Words,
    ),
    keyboardActions = KeyboardActions(onAny = {
        nameEntered.value = true
    })
)
```

TextField() belongs to the androidx.compose.material3 package. The composable can receive quite a few arguments; most of them are optional, though. Please note that the previous code fragment uses both the name and nameEntered parameters, which are passed to TextAndButton(). Their type is MutableState. MutableState objects carry changeable values, which you access as name.value or nameEntered.value.

The value parameter of a TextField() composable receives the current value of the text input field—for example, text that has already been input. onValueChange is invoked when changes to the text occur—for example, if the user enters or deletes something. But why is name.value used in both places? I will answer this question in the *Showing a greeting message* section.

> **Recomposition**
>
> Certain types trigger a so-called recomposition. For now, think of this as repainting an associated composable. MutableState is such a type. If we change its value, the TextField() composable is redrawn or repainted. Please note that neither term is entirely correct. We will cover recomposition in *Chapter 3, Exploring the Key Principles of Compose*.

Let's briefly look at the remaining code. With `alignByBaseline()`, we can nicely align the baselines of other composable functions in a particular `Row()`. `placeholder` contains the text that is shown until the user has entered something. `singleLine` controls whether the user can enter multiple lines of text. Finally, `keyboardOptions` and `keyboardActions` describe the behavior of the onscreen keyboard. For example, certain actions will set `nameEntered.value` to `true`. I will show you soon why we do this.

However, we need to take a look at the `Button()` composable first. It also belongs to the `androidx.compose.material` package:

```
Button(modifier = Modifier
    .alignByBaseline()
    .padding(8.dp),
  onClick = {
    nameEntered.value = true
  }) {
  Text(text = stringResource(id = R.string.done))
}
```

Some things will already look familiar. For example, we call `alignByBaseline()` to align the baseline of the button with the text input field, and we apply a padding of eight density-independent pixels to all sides of the button using `padding()`. Now, `onClick()` specifies what to do when the button is clicked. Here, too, we set `nameEntered.value` to `true`.

The next composable function, `Hello()`, finally shows you why this is done.

Showing a greeting message

The following code snippet shows the `Hello()` composable function. Depending on how the user has already interacted with the app, it either shows a greeting or a welcome message, a button, and some text:

```
@Composable
fun Hello() {
  val name = remember { mutableStateOf("") }
  val nameEntered = remember { mutableStateOf(false) }
  Box(
    modifier = Modifier
      .fillMaxSize()
      .padding(16.dp),
    contentAlignment = Alignment.Center
  ) {
    if (nameEntered.value) {
      Greeting(name.value)
```

```
    } else {
      Column(horizontalAlignment =
            Alignment.CenterHorizontally) {
        Welcome()
        TextAndButton(name, nameEntered)
      }
    }
  }
}
```

Hello() emits Box(), which (depending on nameEntered.value) contains either a Greeting() or a Column() composable that, in turn, includes Welcome() and TextAndButton(). The Column() composable is quite similar to Row() but arranges its siblings vertically. As with the latter one and Box(), it belongs to the androidx.compose.foundation.layout package.

Box() can contain one or more children. Children are stacked—that is, placed on top of each other along the *z* axis. They are positioned inside the box according to the contentAlignment parameter. We will be exploring this in greater detail in the *Combining basic building blocks* section of *Chapter 4, Laying Out UI Elements in Compose*.

Have you noticed remember and mutableStateOf? Both are very important for creating and maintaining **state**. Generally speaking, state in an app refers to a value that can change over time. While this also applies to domain data (for example, the result of a web service call), state usually refers to something being displayed or used by a UI element, such as the name in the Hello example. If a composable function has (or relies on) state, it is recomposed (for now, repainted or redrawn) when that state changes. To get an idea of what this means, recall this composable:

```
@Composable
fun Welcome() {
    Text(
        text = stringResource(id = R.string.welcome),
        style = MaterialTheme.typography.subtitle1
    )
}
```

Welcome() is said to be **stateless**; all values that might trigger a recomposition remain the same for the time being. Hello(), on the other hand, is **stateful**, because it uses the name and nameEntered variables. They change over time. This may not be obvious if you look at the source code of Hello(). Please recall that both name and nameEntered are passed to TextAndButton() and modified there.

Do you recall that, in the previous section, I promised to explain why `name.value` is used in two places, providing the text to display and receiving changes after the user has entered something? This is a common pattern often used with states; `Hello()` creates and remembers state by invoking `mutableStateOf()` and `remember`, and it passes the state to another composable (`TextAndButton()`), which is called **state hoisting**. You will learn more about this in *Chapter 5, Managing State of Your Composable Functions*.

So far, you have seen the source code of quite a few composable functions but not their output. Android Studio has a very important feature called **Compose preview**. It allows you to view a composable function without running the app. In the next section, I will show you how to use this feature.

Using the preview

The upper-right corner of the Android Studio code editor contains three buttons, **Code**, **Split**, and **Design** (*Figure 1.2*):

Figure 1.2 – Compose preview (Split mode)

They switch between the following different display modes:

- Code only (**Code**)
- Code and Preview (**Split**)
- Preview only (**Design**)

To use the Compose preview, your composable functions must contain an additional annotation, `@Preview`, which belongs to the `androidx.compose.ui.tooling.preview` package. This requires an implementation dependency to `androidx.compose.ui:ui-tooling-preview` in your `build.gradle` file.

Unfortunately, if you try to add `@Preview` to `Greeting()`, you will see an error message such as this:

```
Composable functions with non-default parameters are not supported in
Preview unless they are annotated with @PreviewParameter.
```

So, how can you preview composables that take parameters?

Preview parameters

The most obvious solution is a wrapper composable, as shown here:

```
@Composable
@Preview
fun GreetingWrapper() {
    Greeting("Jetpack Compose")
}
```

This means that you write another composable function that takes no parameters but invokes your existing one and provides the required parameter (in my example, a text). Depending on how many composable functions your source file contains, you might be creating quite a lot of boilerplate code. The wrappers don't add value besides enabling the preview.

Fortunately, there are other options. You can, for example, add default values to your composable, like so:

```
@Composable
fun AltGreeting(name: String = "Jetpack Compose") {
```

While this looks less hacky, it alters how your composable functions can be invoked (that is, without passing a parameter). This may not be desirable if you had a reason for not defining a default value in the first place.

With @PreviewParameter, you can pass values to a composable that affect only the preview. Unfortunately, this is a little verbose though, because you need to write a new class:

```
class HelloProvider : PreviewParameterProvider<String> {
    override val values: Sequence<String>
        get() =
            listOf("PreviewParameterProvider").asSequence()
}
```

The class must extend androidx.compose.ui.tooling.preview. PreviewParameterProvider because it will provide a parameter for the preview. Now, you can annotate the parameter of the composable with @PreviewParameter and pass your new class, as follows:

```
@Composable
@Preview
fun AltGreeting2(
    @PreviewParameter(HelloProvider::class)
    name: String) {
```

In a way, you are creating boilerplate code, too. So, which method you choose in the end is a matter of personal taste.

The `@Preview` annotation can receive quite a few parameters. They modify the visual appearance of the preview. Let's explore some of them.

Configuring previews

You can set a background color for a preview using `backgroundColor` =. The value is a Long type and represents an ARGB color. Please make sure to also set `showBackground` to `true`. The following snippet will produce a solid red background:

```
@Preview(showBackground = true, backgroundColor =
    0xffff0000)
```

By default, preview dimensions are chosen automatically. If you want to set them explicitly, you can pass `heightDp` and `widthDp`:

```
@Composable
@Preview(widthDp = 100, heightDp = 100)
fun Welcome() {
    Text(
        text = stringResource(id = R.string.welcome),
        style = MaterialTheme.typography.bodyLarge
    )
}
```

Figure 1.3 shows the result. Both values are interpreted as density-independent pixels, so you don't need to add `.dp` as you would do inside your composable function:

Figure 1.3 – Setting the width and height of a preview

To test different user locales, you can add the `locale` parameter. If, for example, your app contains German strings inside `values-de-rDE`, you can use them by adding the following:

```
@Preview(locale = "de-rDE")
```

The string matches the directory name after `values-`. Please recall that the directory is created by Android Studio if you add a language in the **Translations Editor**.

If you want to display the status and action bars, you can achieve this with `showSystemUi`:

```
@Preview(showSystemUi = true)
```

To get an idea of how your composables react to different form factors, aspect ratios, and pixel densities, you can utilize the `device` parameter. It takes a string. Pass one of the values from `Devices`—for example, `Devices.PHONE` or `Devices.FOLDABLE`.

In this section, you have seen how to configure a preview. Next, I will introduce you to preview groups. They are very handy if your source code file contains more than a few composable functions that you want to preview.

Grouping previews

Android Studio shows composable functions with a `@Preview` annotation in the order of their appearance in the source code. You can choose between **Vertical Layout** and **Grid Layout** (*Figure 1.4*):

Figure 1.4 – Switching between Vertical Layout and Grid Layout

Depending on the number of your composables, the preview pane may at some point feel crowded. If this is the case, just put your composables into different groups by adding a `group` parameter, like so:

```
@Preview(group = "my-group-1")
```

You can then show either all composable functions or just those that belong to a particular group (*Figure 1.5*):

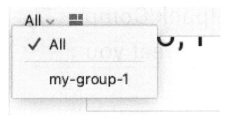

Figure 1.5 – Switching between groups

So far, I have shown you what the source code of composable functions looks like and how you can preview them inside Android Studio. In the next section, we will execute a composable on the Android Emulator or a real device, and you will learn how to connect composable functions to the other parts of an app. But before that, here is one more tip.

> **Exporting a preview as an image**
>
> If you click on a Compose preview with the secondary mouse button, you will see a small pop-up menu. Select **Copy Image** to put a bitmap of the preview on the system clipboard. Most graphics applications allow you to paste it into a new document.

Running a Compose app

If you want to see how a composable function looks and feels on the Android Emulator or a real device, you have two options:

- Deploying a composable function
- Running the app

The first option is useful if you want to focus on a particular composable rather than the whole app. Also, the time needed to deploy a composable may be significantly shorter than deploying a complete app (depending on the app size). So, let's start with this one.

Deploying a composable function

To deploy a composable function to a real device or the Android Emulator, click on the **Run Preview** button, which is a small image in the upper-right corner of a preview (*Figure 1.6*):

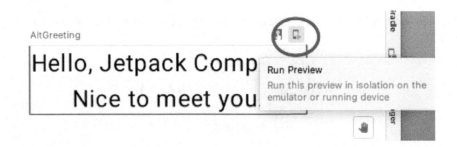

Figure 1.6 – Deploying a composable function

This will automatically create new launch configurations (*Figure 1.7*):

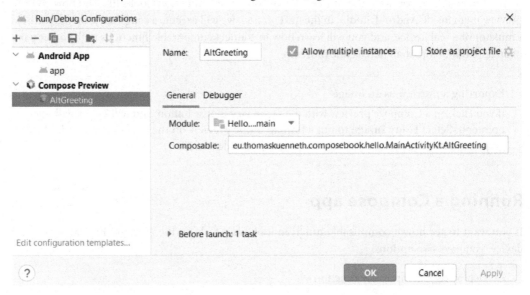

Figure 1.7 – Launch configurations representing Compose previews

You can modify or delete Compose preview configurations in the **Run/Debug Configurations** dialog. To access them, open the **Compose Preview** node. Then, you can—for example—change its name or deny parallel runs by unchecking **Allow parallel run**.

The goal of this chapter is to deploy and run your first Compose app on a real device or the Android Emulator. You are almost there; in the next section, I will show you how to embed composable functions in an activity, which is a prerequisite. You will finally be running the app in the *Pressing the Play button* section.

Using composable functions in activities

Activities have been one of the basic building blocks of Android apps since the first platform version. Practically every app has at least one activity. They are configured in the manifest file. To launch an activity from the home screen, the corresponding entry looks like this:

```
...
<activity
    android:name=".MainActivity"
    android:exported="true"
    android:label="@string/app_name">
    <intent-filter>
        <action android:name=»android.intent.action.MAIN»
            />
        <category
            android:name="android.intent.category.LAUNCHER" />
    </intent-filter>
</activity>
...
```

This is still true for Compose apps. An activity that wishes to show composable functions is set up just like one that inflates a traditional layout file. But what does its source code look like? The main activity of the `Hello` app is called `MainActivity`, shown in the next code block:

```
class MainActivity : ComponentActivity() {
    override fun onCreate(savedInstanceState: Bundle?) {
        super.onCreate(savedInstanceState)
        setContent {
            Hello()
        }
    }
}
```

As you can see, it is very short. The UI (the `Hello()` composable function) is displayed by invoking a function called `setContent`, which is an extension function to `androidx.activity.ComponentActivity` and belongs to the `androidx.activity.compose` package.

To render composables, your activity must extend either `ComponentActivity` or another class that has `ComponentActivity` as its direct or indirect ancestor. This is the case for `androidx.fragment.app.FragmentActivity` and `androidx.appcompat.app.AppCompatActivity`.

This is an important difference; while Compose apps invoke `setContent()`, View-based apps call `setContentView()` and pass either the ID of a layout (`R.layout.activity_main`) or the root view itself (which is usually obtained through some binding mechanism). Let's see how the older mechanism works. The following code snippet is taken from one of my open source apps (you can find it on GitHub at `https://github.com/tkuenneth/TKWeek` but it won't be discussed any further in this book):

```
class TKWeekActivity : TKWeekBaseActivity() {

    private var backing: TkweekBinding? = null
    private val binding get() = backing!!

    override fun onCreate(savedInstanceState: Bundle?) {
        super.onCreate(savedInstanceState)
        backing = TkweekBinding.inflate(
            layoutInflater,
            null,
            false
        )
        setContentView(binding.root)
    ...
```

If you compare both approaches, a striking difference is that with Jetpack Compose, there is no need to maintain references to the UI component tree or individual elements of it. I will explain in *Chapter 2, Understanding the Declarative Paradigm*, why this leads to code that is easily maintainable and less error-prone.

Let's now return to `setContent()`. It receives two parameters, `parent` (which can be `null`) and `content` (the UI). `parent` is an instance of `androidx.compose.runtime.CompositionContext`. It is used to logically link together two compositions. This is an advanced topic that I will be discussing in *Chapter 3, Exploring the Key Principles of Compose*.

> **Important note**
>
> Have you noticed that `MainActivity` does not contain any composable functions? They do not need to be part of a class. In fact, you should implement them as top-level functions whenever possible, as Jetpack Compose fully embraces a functional programming style. Jetpack Compose provides alternative means to access `android.content.Context`. You have already seen the `stringResource()` composable function, which is a replacement for `getString()`.

Now that you have seen how to embed composable functions in activities, it is time to look at the structure of Jetpack Compose-based projects. While Android Studio sets everything up for you if you create a Compose app using the project wizard, it is important to know which files are involved under the hood.

Looking under the hood

Jetpack Compose heavily relies on Kotlin. This means that your app project must be configured to use Kotlin. It does not imply, though, that you cannot use Java at all. In fact, you can easily mix Kotlin and Java in your project, as long as your composable functions are written in Kotlin. You can also combine traditional views and composables. I will be discussing this topic in *Chapter 9, Exploring Interoperability APIs*.

First, make sure to configure the Android Gradle plugin that corresponds to your version of Android Studio, as follows:

```
buildscript {
    ...
    dependencies {
        classpath 'com.android.tools.build:gradle:8.1.0'
        classpath
        'org.jetbrains.kotlin:kotlin-gradle-plugin:1.8.20'
        ...
    }
}
```

Second, the project must use a compatible version of Kotlin:

```
plugins {
    id 'com.android.application'
    id 'kotlin-android'
}
```

Next, please make sure that your app's minimum API level is set to 21 or higher and that Jetpack Compose is enabled. Lower API levels are not supported by Jetpack Compose. The following code snippet also sets the version for the Kotlin compiler plugin:

```
android {
    defaultConfig {
        ...
        minSdkVersion 28
    }
    buildFeatures {
        compose true
    }
    ...
    compileOptions {
        sourceCompatibility JavaVersion.VERSION_17
        targetCompatibility JavaVersion.VERSION_17
    }
```

```
    kotlinOptions {
        jvmTarget = "17"
    }
    composeOptions {
        kotlinCompilerExtensionVersion "1.4.6"
    }
}
```

Finally, declare dependencies. The following code snippet acts as a good starting point. Depending on which packages your app uses, you may need additional ones:

```
dependencies {
    implementation platform
        ('androidx.compose:compose-bom:2023.06.01')
    implementation "ndroid.compose.ui:ui"
    implementation "ndroid.compose.material3:material3"
    implementation "ndroid.compose.ui:ui-tooling-preview"
    debugImplementation
      "androidx.compose.ui:ui-tooling-android:1.6.0-alpha0"

    implementation
        'com.google.android.material:material:1.9.0'
    implementation 'androidx.core:core-ktx:1.10.1'
    implementation 'androidx.appcompat:appcompat:1.6.1'
    implementation
        'androidx.lifecycle:lifecycle-runtime-ktx:2.6.1'
    implementation
        'androidx.activity:activity-compose:1.7.1'
}
```

Jetpack Compose is not a monolithic library but consists of several individual pieces that can be worked on independently. These parts can even have independent version numbers. To make sure your app only uses versions of these sublibraries that work together well, Google encourages developers to rely on the Compose **Bill of Materials** (**BOM**). To do so, add a line to your `dependencies` section, like this:

```
implementation platform('androidx.compose:compose-bom:2023.06.01')
```

Each Compose part can then be referenced without a version number:

```
implementation "androidx.compose.ui:ui"
```

Once you have configured your project, building and running a Compose app works just like traditional view-based apps.

Pressing the play button

To run your Compose app, select your target device, make sure that the **app** module is selected, and press the green **play** button (*Figure 1.8*):

Figure 1.8 – Android Studio toolbar elements to launch an app

Congratulations! Well done. You have now launched your first Compose app, and you have achieved quite a lot. Let's recap.

Summary

In this chapter, we learned how to write our first composables: top-level Kotlin functions that have been annotated with @Composable. Composable functions are the core building blocks of Jetpack Compose-based UIs. You combined existing library composables with your own to create beautiful app screens.

To use Jetpack Compose in a project, both build.gradle files must be configured accordingly. In this chapter, I showed you what these files should look like for a Compose app.

We also looked at how to preview and test a composable function. To see a preview, we can add the @Preview annotation. We also saw how to deploy composable functions and Compose apps to the Android Emulator or real devices.

In *Chapter 2, Understanding the Declarative Paradigm*, we will take a closer look at the differences between the declarative approach of Jetpack Compose and the imperative nature of traditional UI frameworks such as Android's view-based component library.

Further reading

This book assumes you have a basic understanding of the syntax of Kotlin and Android development in general. If you would like to learn more about this, I suggest looking at *Android Programming with Kotlin for Beginners, John Horton, Packt Publishing, 2019, ISBN 9781789615401*.

Questions

Quiz time. Here are a couple of questions to test your Jetpack Compose knowledge:

1. What does the @Composable annotation do?
2. What do the Row(), Column(), and Box() composable functions do?
3. Which function is invoked to specify the root of a Compose UI?

2
Understanding the Declarative Paradigm

Jetpack Compose marks a fundamental shift in Android UI development. While the traditional view-based approach is centered on components and classes, the new framework follows a declarative approach.

In *Chapter 1, Building Your First Compose App*, I introduced you to composable functions, the basic building blocks of a Compose-based UI. In this chapter, we will briefly review how Android UIs are implemented with traditional classes and techniques. You will learn about some issues of this approach, and how a declarative framework helps overcome them.

The main sections of this chapter are set out as follows:

- Looking at the Android view system
- Moving from components to composable functions
- Examining architectural concepts

We'll start by looking at my second sample app, `HelloView`. It is a re-implementation of the `Hello` app from *Chapter 1, Building Your First Compose App*. `HelloView` uses views, an XML **layout file**, and **view binding**.

Next, we will cover key aspects of **components**, which are UI building blocks in the view-based world. You will learn about the similarities and differences of composable functions, and we will find out how composable functions can overcome some of the limitations of component-centric frameworks.

Finally, we will look at the different layers of the Android framework and how they relate to building UIs. By the end of this chapter, you will have gathered enough background information to explore the key principles of Jetpack Compose, which is the topic of the next chapter.

Technical requirements

Please refer to the *Technical requirements* section of *Chapter 1*, *Building Your First Compose App*, for information about how to install and set up Android Studio and how to get the sample apps. This chapter covers the `HelloView` and `Factorial` samples.

Looking at the Android view system

The traditional approach to building Android UIs is to define component trees and modify them during runtime. While this can be done completely programmatically, the preferred way is to create layout files. They use XML tags and attributes to define which UI elements should be presented on screen. Let's take a look:

```xml
<?xml version="1.0" encoding="utf-8"?>
<androidx.constraintlayout.widget.ConstraintLayout
xmlns:android="http://schemas.android.com/apk/res/android"
  xmlns:app="http://schemas.android.com/apk/res-auto"
  android:layout_width="match_parent"
  android:layout_height="match_parent">

  <TextView
    android:id="@+id/message"
    style="@style/TextAppearance.Material3.BodyLarge"
    android:layout_width="wrap_content"
    android:layout_height="wrap_content"
    android:textAlignment="center"
    app:layout_constraintBottom_toBottomOf="parent"
    app:layout_constraintBottom_toTopOf="@id/name"
    app:layout_constraintEnd_toEndOf="parent"
    app:layout_constraintHorizontal_bias="0.5"
    app:layout_constraintStart_toStartOf="parent"
    app:layout_constraintTop_toTopOf="parent"
    app:layout_constraintVertical_bias="0.5"
    app:layout_constraintVertical_chainStyle="packed" />
    ...
</androidx.constraintlayout.widget.ConstraintLayout>
```

Layout files define a hierarchical structure (a tree). In the previous XML snippet, the root node (`ConstraintLayout`) contains only one child (`TextView`). The complete XML file of `HelloView` has two more children, an `EditText` component and a `Button` component. Layout files of real-world apps can be quite nested, containing dozens of children.

Generally speaking, . . . Layout elements are responsible for sizing and positioning their children. While they may have a visual representation (for example, a background color or a border), they usually don't interact with the user. ScrollView is one of the exceptions to that rule. All other (non-. . . Layout) elements such as buttons, checkboxes, and editable text fields not only allow user interaction—it's their purpose.

Both layout and non-layout elements are called **components**. We will return to this term in the *Moving from components to composable functions* section. But before that, let's see how layout files are used in apps.

Inflating layout files

Activities are one of the core building blocks of an Android app. They implement a quite sophisticated lifecycle, which is reflected by a couple of methods we can override.

Typically, onCreate() is used to prepare the app and to show the UI by invoking setContentView(). This method can receive an ID representing a layout file—for example, R.layout.main. Because of this, you must define variables pointing to the UI elements you wish to access. This may look like the following:

```
private lateinit var doneButton: Button
...
val doneButton = findViewById(R.id.done)
```

It turned out that this doesn't scale well for bigger apps. There are two important issues to remember:

- You may face crashes during runtime if the variable is accessed before it has been initialized
- The code quickly becomes lengthy if you have more than a few components

Sometimes, you can prevent the first issue by using local variables, as follows:

```
val doneButton = findViewById<Button>(R.id.done)
```

This way, you can access the UI element immediately after the declaration. However, the variable exists only in the scope in which it has been defined—a block or a function. This may be problematic because you often need to modify a component outside onCreate(). That's because, in a component-based world, you modify the UI by modifying the properties of a component. It turned out that often the same set of changes are necessary for different parts of the app, so to avoid code duplication, they are refactored into methods, which need to know the component to change it.

To solve the second issue—that is, to spare the developer from the task of keeping references to components—Google introduced view binding. It belongs to Jetpack and debuted in Android Studio 3.6 (this version was released quite a while ago, in February 2020). Let's see how **view binding** is used:

```
class MainActivity : AppCompatActivity() {

  private lateinit var binding: MainBinding

  override fun onCreate(savedInstanceState: Bundle?) {
    super.onCreate(savedInstanceState)
    binding = MainBinding.inflate(layoutInflater)
    setContentView(binding.root)
    ...
    enableOrDisableButton()
  }
  ...
}
```

No matter how complex the UI of an activity is, we need to keep only one reference. This variable is usually called `binding`, which is initialized by invoking the `inflate()` function of a ...`Binding` instance. The `MainBinding` class in my example is automatically generated and updated when `main.xml` is modified. Every layout file gets a corresponding ...`Binding` class. To enable this mechanism, the `viewBinding` build option must be set to `true` in the module-level `build.gradle` file:

```
android {
  ...
  buildFeatures {
    viewBinding true
  }
}
```

So, after you have inflated a layout file by invoking ...`Binding.inflate()` and assigned it to an instance variable, you can access all its components via their IDs using this variable. IDs are set using the `android:id` XML attribute (for example, `android:id="@+id/message"`).

> **Important note**
>
> There is an important difference between the old-fashioned `findViewById()` function and view binding. If you use the latter one, you must pass the root component (`binding.root`) to `setContentView()`, rather than an ID representing the layout file (`R.layout.main`).

In this section, I have shown you how to obtain references to UI elements. The next section, *Modifying the UI*, will explain how to make use of this.

Modifying the UI

In this section, we will see how to make changes to a view-based UI. Let's start by looking at the enableOrDisableButton() function, which is invoked in onCreate(). Its name gives you a clue regarding its purpose—enabling or disabling a button. But why do we need this? HelloView is a reimplementation of the Hello app from *Chapter 1*, *Building Your First Compose App*, but it has one additional feature. As long as the user has not entered at least one non-blank character, **Done** can't be clicked:

```
private fun enableOrDisableButton() {
    binding.done.isEnabled = binding.name.text.isNotBlank()
}
```

binding.done refers to the button during runtime. It can be clicked only if isEnabled is true. The text input field is denoted by binding.name. Its text property reflects what the user has already entered. isNotBlank() tells us whether at least one non-whitespace character is present.

In the code I have shown you so far, enableOrDisableButton() is called only at the end of onCreate(). But we also need to invoke the function whenever the user has input something. Let's see how to do this (please note that the following code snippets belong inside onCreate() so that they are executed when the activity is created):

```
binding.name.run {
    setOnEditorActionListener { _, _, _ ->
        binding.done.performClick()
        true
    }
    doAfterTextChanged {
        enableOrDisableButton()
    }
    visibility = VISIBLE
}
```

Text input fields can modify certain aspects of the onscreen keyboard. For example, to have it show a **Done** key instead of the usual **Enter**, we add an android:imeOptions="actionDone" attribute to the layout file. To react to clicks on this key, we need to register the code by invoking setOnEditorActionListener(). Then, binding.done.performClick() simulates clicks on the **Done** button. You will see shortly why I do this.

The lambda function we pass to doAfterTextChanged() is invoked every time the user enters or deletes something in the text input field. When this happens, enableOrDisableButton() is called, which makes the button clickable if the text currently present in the input field is not blank.

Finally, visibility = VISIBLE occurs inside binding.name.run {, so it makes the text input field visible. This is the desired state when the activity is created.

Now, let's turn to code related to the **Done** button:

```
binding.done.run {
  setOnClickListener {
    val name = binding.name.text
    if (name.isNotBlank()) {
      binding.message.text = getString(R.string.hello,
                                       name)
      binding.name.visibility = GONE
      it.visibility = GONE
    }
  }
  visibility = VISIBLE
}
```

When **Done** is clicked, we test whether the text input field contains at least one character besides whitespace. If this is the case, the greeting message will be constructed and displayed. Also, both the button and the text input field are hidden; they need to disappear after the user has entered a name because then, only the greeting message should be visible. Making a component visible or invisible is done by modifying the visibility property: visibility = VISIBLE makes the **Done** button visible. This is the desired state when the activity is created.

Do you remember that I promised to explain why I invoke performClick() inside the lambda function for setOnEditorActionListener? This way, I can reuse the code inside the button listener without refactoring it into a separate function and calling it instead, which is certainly a viable alternative.

Before we move on, let's recap what have we seen so far:

- The UI is defined in an XML file
- At runtime, it is inflated to a component tree
- To change the UI, attributes of all related components must be modified
- Even if a UI element is not visible, it remains part of the component tree

This is why common UI frameworks are called **imperative**. Any change to the UI is done by deliberately modifying the attributes of all components involved. As you can see in my example, this works quite well for small apps. But the more UI elements an app has, the more demanding it will be to keep track of such changes. Let me explain. Changes in domain data (adding an item to a list, deleting text, or loading an image from a remote service) require changes in the UI. The developer needs to know which portion of domain data relates to which UI element and must then modify the component tree accordingly. The bigger an app becomes, the more difficult this is.

Also, without clear architectural guidance, the code for changing the component tree almost always eventually mixes with code that modifies the data the app is using. This makes it even more demanding and error-prone to maintain and further develop the app.

In the next section, we will turn to composable functions. You will learn how they differ from components and why this helps overcome weaknesses in the imperative approach.

Moving from components to composable functions

So far, I explained the word *component* by saying that it refers to UI elements. In fact, the term is used in quite a few other areas. Generally speaking, components structure systems by separating distinct portions or parts of them. The inner workings of a component are typically hidden from the outside (known as the **black box principle**).

> Tip
> To learn more about the black box principle, please refer to `https://en.wikipedia.`
> `org/wiki/Black_box`.

Components communicate with other parts of the system by sending and receiving messages. The appearance or behavior of a component is controlled through a set of attributes, or **properties**.

Consider `TextView`. We set text by modifying the `text` property and we control its visibility through `visibility`. What about sending and receiving messages? Let's look at `Button`. We can react to clicks (receive a message) by registering (sending a message) an `OnClickListener` instance. The same principle applies to `EditText`. We configure its appearance by setting properties (`text`), send a message by invoking `setOnEditorActionListener()`, and receive one through the lambda expression we passed as a parameter.

Message-based communication and configuration via properties make components very tool-friendly. In fact, most component-based UI frameworks work well with drawing board-like editors. The developer defines a UI using drag and drop. Components are configured using property sheets. *Figure 2.1* shows the **Layout Editor** in Android Studio. You can switch between a **Design** view, browse **Code** (an XML file), or a combination of both (**Split**):

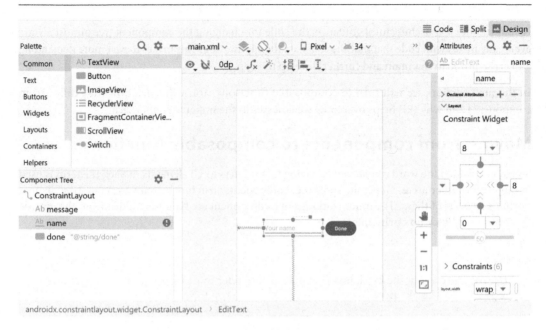

Figure 2.1 – The Layout Editor in Android Studio

We now have a more precise understanding of how the term *component* is used in the context of UIs. Building on this foundation, we will now look at component hierarchies.

Component hierarchies

If you compare the XML attributes of ConstraintLayout, TextView, and EditText, you will find unique attributes per tag, one example being android:inputType. On the other hand, android:layout_width and android:layout_height are present in all three tags, defining the size of the corresponding element. Size and position are relevant for all components.

Yet, specific attributes influence visual appearance or behavior; this is *not* relevant for all kinds of UI elements, only a subset. Here's an example: text fields and buttons will want to show or receive text. A FrameLayout UI element won't. Think of it this way: the *more specialized* an attribute is, the *less likely is its reuse* in another component. However, general ones (such as width, height, location, or color) will be needed in most UI elements.

Based on its attributes, each component has a level of specialization. For example, EditText is more specific than TextView because it can handle text input. Button is a general-purpose button; clicking on it triggers some action. On the other hand, a CheckBox component can be either checked or unchecked. This type of button can represent two states. A Switch component has two states, too. It's a toggle switch widget that can select between two options.

The degree of specialization can be modeled easily in **object-oriented programming** (**OOP**) languages through inheritance. A more specialized UI element (class) extends a general element. Therefore, many often-used UI frameworks have been implemented in Java, C++, or C# (OO languages). It is important to note, though, that component-like concepts can be achieved with other types of programming languages too. So, object orientation may be considered a benefit, but it's not a necessity.

At this point, you may be thinking, *Didn't he mix two different things? How are tags and attributes of Android layout files related to classes?* Allow me to explain. Earlier, I said that an XML file is **inflated** to a component tree. To be more precise, it becomes an *object* tree. The tags in the XML file represent class names and their attributes correspond to members of that class. `inflate()` creates a tree of objects based on this information.

So, Android layout files describe component trees outside of Java or Kotlin files using a different syntax (an XML syntax). But they are not declarative in the same way Jetpack Compose is because layout files define a UI regardless of the current state. For example, they do not take into account that a button should be disabled because a text field is empty. A Compose UI, on the other hand, is declared *based* on that.

The remaining part of this section will look closer at some of Android's UI components and how they are related. Before that, let's recap what we have learned so far:

- All Android views are classes
- Tags in layout files represent classes, and attributes are their members
- `inflate()` creates an object tree
- Changes to the UI are achieved by modifying this tree

Some of Android's UI elements are quite specific. `RatingBar`, for example, allows the user to rate something by selecting a certain number of stars. Others are way more general; for example, `ImageView` just displays image resources, and `FrameLayout` blocks out an area on the screen to display a stack of children.

To understand how Android's UI elements are related, let's look at the ones used in `HelloView` in a little more detail. We'll start with `ConstraintLayout`:

```
java.lang.Object
  ↳ android.view.View
    ↳ android.view.ViewGroup
      ↳ androidx.constraintlayout.widget.ConstraintLayout
```

The root of *all* classes in Java is `java.lang.Object`. Significant parts of the Android framework are based on Java and its class library. So, all views directly or indirectly extend `java.lang.Object`. The immediate parent of `ConstraintLayout` is `android.view.ViewGroup`, which in turn is a sibling of `android.view.View`.

Now, let's look at `android.widget.Button`:

```
java.lang.Object
   ↳ android.view.View
      ↳ android.widget.TextView
         ↳ android.widget.Button
```

Its direct ancestor is `android.widget.TextView`, which extends `android.view.View`. Are we seeing a pattern here? `android.view.View` seems to be the root of all Android UI elements. Let's check our hypothesis by examining another component:

```
java.lang.Object
   ↳ android.view.View
      ↳ android.widget.TextView
         ↳ android.widget.EditText
```

As you can see, components showing or receiving text usually extend `android.widget.TextView`, whose parent is `android.view.View`.

Important note

`android.view.View` is the root of all Android UI elements. All components that position and size their children extend `android.view.ViewGroup`.

So far, structuring UI elements in a hierarchy based on specialization seems to work well. Unfortunately, this approach does have limitations. We'll turn to them in the following section.

Limitations of component hierarchies

Buttons usually show text. Therefore, it seems natural to extend a more general text component. As we saw in the previous section, Android does just that. What if your app requires a button that has no text and shows an image instead? In such scenarios, you can use `ImageButton`:

```
java.lang.Object
   ↳ android.view.View
      ↳ android.widget.ImageView
         ↳ android.widget.ImageButton
```

The class extends `android.widget.ImageView`. This makes sense, as the purpose of this component is to show just an image, quite like `Button` and text. But what if we want to show a button that contains both text and image? The closest common ancestor of `ImageButton` and an ordinary text button is `android.view.View`, the root of the Android UI element hierarchy. Therefore, everything `Button` inherits from `TextView` is not immediately available to `ImageButton` (and vice versa).

The reason is that Java is based upon **single inheritance**: a class extends exactly one other class. If `Button` wanted to take advantage of the features of `TextView` and `ImageView`, it would need to extend both, which it can't. Does this mean that things would be different if Java supported **multiple inheritance**? We could combine the behavior of several components, but we still wouldn't be able to reuse functionality tied to *individual* attributes, methods, or sets of them. Let's see why this is important.

The `View` class knows about padding (providing space to the inside of its bounds) but not about margins (space to the outside of its bounds). Margins are defined in `ViewGroup`. Hence, if a component wants to use them, it must extend `ViewGroup`. But in doing so, it inevitably inherits all other features of this class (for example, the ability to lay out children), regardless of whether it needs them or not. The underlying issue is that in a component-centric framework, the combination of *individual features* of one or more components to create a more specialized UI element is not possible because you cannot cut out these features. The reason for this is that reuse happens at a component level.

To make individual features reusable, we need to put aside—or at least modify—the notion of components. That's what, for example, Flutter (the very successful cross-platform alternative to Jetpack Compose) does. Its UI framework is fully declarative and still class-based. Flutter relies on a simple principle called **composition over inheritance**. This means the look and the behavior of a UI element (and the complete UI) are defined by combining simple building blocks, such as `Container`, `Padding`, `Align`, or `GestureDetector`, rather than modifying a parent.

In Jetpack Compose, we combine simple building blocks too. Instead of classes, we use composable functions. Before we turn to them, I would like to briefly show you another potential issue with components.

As you have seen, in class-based UI component frameworks, specialization is modeled through inheritance. The specialized version of a class (which may have new features, a new look, or behave slightly differently than the ancestor) extends a more general version of the class. However, most OOP languages provide means to prohibit this; for example, if a Java class is marked `final` or a Kotlin class is not `open`, they cannot be extended.

So, the framework developer can make a deliberate decision to prevent further inheritance. `android.widget.Space`, a lightweight `View` subclass to create gaps between UI elements, is final. The same applies to `android.view.ViewStub`. It's an invisible, zero-sized `View` subclass used to lazily inflate layout resources at runtime. Fortunately, most of Android's UI elements can be extended. And for both examples, it seems unlikely that we would want to extend them. Hence, you may not face this potential issue at all. The point is that in a framework based on composition rather than inheritance, it doesn't matter.

Composing UIs with functions

Now, it's time to return to composable functions. In this section, we will look at my sample Factorial app (*Figure 2.2*). When the user picks a number between 0 and 9, its factorial (the product of it and all the integers below it greater than 0) is computed and output, like so:

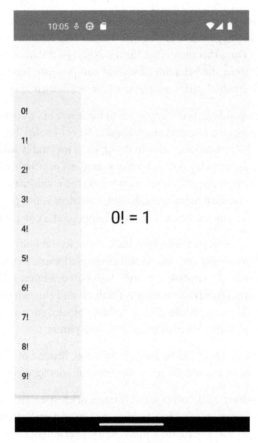

Figure 2.2 – The Factorial app

Here is the simple function that creates the output text:

```
fun factorialAsString(n: Int): String {
  var result = 1L
  for (i in 1..n) {
    result *= i
  }
  return "$n! = $result"
}
```

The factorial of an n non-negative integer value is the product of all positive integers less than or equal to n. So, the result can be computed easily by multiplying all integers between 1 and n. Please note that the maximum value of a Kotlin Long type is 9,223,372,036,854,775,807. Hence, my implementation does not work if `result` would need to be bigger than that.

Next, I'll show you how the UI is composed:

```
@Composable
fun Factorial() {
  var expanded by remember { mutableStateOf(false) }
  var text by remember {
    mutableStateOf(
      factorialAsString(0)
    )
  }
  Box(
    modifier = Modifier.fillMaxSize(),
    contentAlignment = Alignment.Center
  ) {
    Text(
      modifier = Modifier.clickable {
        expanded = true
      },
      text = text,
      style = MaterialTheme.typography.headlineMedium
    )
    DropdownMenu(
      expanded = expanded,
      onDismissRequest = {
        expanded = false
      }) {
      for (n in 0 until 10) {
        DropdownMenuItem(onClick = {
          expanded = false
          text = factorialAsString(n)
        },
          text = {
            Text("$n!")
          }
        )
      }
    }
  }
}
```

The Factorial() composable function contains one predefined composable, Box(), which in turn has two children, Text() and DropdownMenu(). I briefly introduced you to Text() and Box() in *Chapter 1, Building Your First Compose App*. So, let's concentrate on DropdownMenu().

A drop-down menu (the equivalent of a `Spinner` view) displays a list of entries in a compact way. It appears upon interaction with an element, such as the following:

- An icon or a button
- When the user performs a specific action

In my example, the `Text()` composable must be clicked.

The content of a menu can either be provided by a `forloop` statement or by adding it one by one. Often, but not necessarily, `DropdownMenuItem()` is used. If the menu is expanded (that is, open or visible), it is controlled by the `expanded` parameter. `onDismissRequest` is used to react to closing the menu without selecting something. `DropdownMenuItem()` receives a click handler via the `onClick` parameter. That code is executed when the item is clicked.

So far, I have presented quite a lot of information about composable functions to you. Before we move on, let's recap what we know so far:

- The entry point of a Compose UI is a composable function
- From there, other composable functions are called
- Often, composable functions receive *content* that is other composables
- The order of invocation controls where a UI element will be in relation to other UI elements

Let's continue with how `Factorial()` works. It defines two variables, `expanded` and `text`. But how are they used? While an Android layout file defines a component tree in its initial state, a composable UI is always declared using actual data. This means that there is no need to set up or prepare the UI before it can be displayed for the first time. Whenever it is displayed, it looks the way you want. Let's see how this works.

Most composable functions are configured by a set of parameters. Some of them are mandatory; others can be omitted. The important thing is that the composable is always called with actual values. On the other hand, components (that is, views) are initialized when they are created, and they remain this way until they are deliberately changed by altering the value of properties. That's why an app needs to keep references to all components (UI elements) it wishes to modify. But how is a Compose UI updated?

The process of updating a Compose UI is called **recomposition**. It takes place automatically whenever a composable function being part of the UI needs to be updated. This is the case when some of the values that influence its look or behavior (parameters) change. If you always pass the same text to `Text()`, there is no need to recompose it. If, on the other hand, you pass something Jetpack Compose knows it can change, the Compose runtime will initiate an update—a recomposition, when that change happens. Values that change over time are called **state**. You can create state, for example, using `mutableStateOf()`. To refer to state in a composable, you need to remember it in that composable function.

Both `expanded` and `text` contain state. When these variables are used as parameters for composable functions, those composables will be recomposed whenever the value of these variables changes. Setting `expanded` to `true` brings the drop-down menu on the screen immediately. This is done inside a lambda function passed to `clickable {}`. I will be discussing this in the next section. Giving `text` a new value changes the display of `Text()` because we pass the `text` variable as the value of the parameter of the same name. This happens, for example, inside the code block passed to `onClick`.

Getting rid of a component tree (that needs to be updated deliberately) in favor of declaring a UI based on state and thus getting updates upon state changes for free is possibly one of the most exciting advantages of the declarative approach. In the next section, I will explain a few more architectural principles of component-based and declarative UI frameworks.

Examining architectural aspects

In the *Component hierarchies* section, I showed you that component-based UI frameworks rely on specialization. General features and concepts are implemented in the root component or one of its immediate successors. Such general features include the following:

- Location and size on screen

- Basic visual aspects such as background (color)

- Simple user interactions (reacting to clicks)

Any component will provide these features, either in a specialized way or in its basic implementation. Android's view system is class-based, so changing functionality is done by overriding the methods of the parent.

Composable functions, on the other hand, do not have a shared set of properties. By annotating a function with `@Composable`, we make certain parts of Jetpack Compose aware of it. But besides not specifying a return type, composables seem to have few things in common. However, this would have been a pretty short-sighted architectural decision. In fact, Jetpack Compose makes providing a simple, predictable API really easy. The remaining part of this section illustrates this by showing you how to react to clicks, and how to size and position UI elements.

Reacting to clicks

Android's `View` class contains a method called `setOnClickListener()`. It receives a `View. OnClickListener` instance. This interface contains one method, `onClick(View v)`. The implementation of this method provides the code that should be executed when the view is clicked. Additionally, there is a view property called `clickable`. It is accessed through `setClickable()` and `isClickable()`. If `clickable` is set to `false` after the listener has been set, the click event will not be delivered (`onClick()` is not called).

Jetpack Compose can provide click handling in two ways. Firstly, composable functions that require it (because it is a core feature for them) have a dedicated `onClick` parameter. Secondly, composables that usually do not require click handling can be amended with a modifier. Let's start with the first one:

```
@Composable
@Preview
fun ButtonDemo(enabled: Boolean = true) {
  Box {
    Button(
      onClick = {
        println("clicked")
      },
      enabled = enabled
    ) {
      Text("Click me!")
    }
  }
}
```

`onClick` is mandatory; you must provide it. The `enabled` parameter controls if the button reacts to user interactions. If you want to show the button but the user should not be able to click it, just set it to `false`.

Figure 2.3 shows what the button looks like when `enabled` is `true` and `false`:

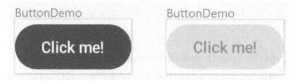

Figure 2.3 – A button with enabled = true and false

`Text()` doesn't have an `onClick` property. If you want to make it clickable (as I do in the Factorial app), you pass `clickable { ... }` to the `modifier` parameter, like so:

```
modifier = Modifier.clickable { ... }
```

Modifiers, as their name suggests, provide an infrastructure for influencing both the visual appearance and behavior of composable functions. I will show you another example of modifiers in the next section. *Chapter 3, Exploring the Key Principles of Compose,* covers them in much greater detail.

Sizing and positioning UI elements

In component-centric UI frameworks, size and location on screen (or relative to another component) are core properties. They are defined in the root component (on Android, the View class). Descendants of ViewGroup size and position their children by changing their corresponding properties. For example, RelativeLayout is based upon instructions such as toStartOf, toEndOf, or below. FrameLayout draws its children in a stack, and LinearLayout lays out children horizontally or vertically. So, . . . Layouts are containers with the ability to size and position their children.

Jetpack Compose has a very similar concept. You have already learned about Row() and Column(), which lay out their content horizontally or vertically. Box() is similar to FrameLayout. It organizes its content in the order it appears in code. The position inside the box is controlled by contentAlignment:

```
@Composable
@Preview
fun BoxDemo() {
  Box(contentAlignment = Alignment.Center) {
    Box(
      modifier = Modifier
        .size(width = 100.dp, height = 100.dp)
        .background(Color.Green)
    )
    Box(
      modifier = Modifier
        .size(width = 80.dp, height = 80.dp)
        .background(Color.Yellow)
    )
    Text(
      text = "Hello",
      color = Color.Black,
      modifier = Modifier.align(Alignment.TopStart)
    )
  }
}
```

The content may override this by using `modifier = Modifier.align()`, the result of which we can see in *Figure 2.4*:

Figure 2.4 – An invisible box containing two colored boxes and text

Modifiers can also be used to request a size. In some of my examples, you may have spotted `Modifier.fillMaxSize()`, which makes the composable as big as possible. `Modifier.size()` requests a particular size. Modifiers can be chained. The root of such a chain is the `Modifier` companion object. Subsequent modifiers are added using a dot.

Before closing this chapter, I would like to emphasize the benefits of the modifier concept with one more example. Did you notice the `background()` modifiers of the first and second content boxes? This modifier allows you to set a background color for any composable function. When you need something a composable function does not offer out of the box, you can add it with a modifier. As you can write custom modifiers, the possibilities to adjust a composable to your needs are almost endless. I will elaborate on this in the next chapter.

Summary

In this chapter, you have learned about key elements of component-centric UI frameworks. We saw some of the limitations of this approach and how the declarative paradigm can overcome them. For example, specialization takes place on a component level. If the framework is based on inheritance, the distribution of features to children may be too broad. Jetpack Compose tackles this with the modifier mechanism, which allows us to amend functionality at a very fine-grained level; this means that composables only get the functionality they need (for example, a background color).

The remaining chapters of this book are solely based on the declarative approach. In *Chapter 3*, *Exploring the Key Principles of Compose*, we will take an even closer look at composable functions and examine the concepts of composition and recomposition. And, as promised, we will also dive deep into modifiers.

Exercise

Android Studio offers an **Interactive Mode** for composable functions. This is great to see how they react to user input:

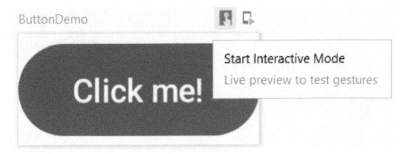

Figure 2.5 – Interactive Mode

Please give **Interactive Mode** a try and answer the following questions:

1.   What happens if you click inside the preview area when Interactive Mode is not active?

2.   What is the difference between *Interactive Mode* and *Run Preview*?

3

Exploring the Key Principles of Compose

In the first chapter of this book, we built and ran our first Jetpack Compose app. Then, in *Chapter 2, Understanding the Declarative Paradigm*, we explained the imperative nature of Android's traditional UI toolkit, illustrated some of its weaknesses, and saw how a declarative approach can overcome them.

In this chapter, we build upon these foundations by examining a few key principles Jetpack Compose relies on. This knowledge is essential for writing well-behaving Compose apps. This chapter introduces these key principles.

In this chapter, we will cover the following topics:

- Looking closer at composable functions
- Composing and recomposing the UI
- Modifying the behavior of composable functions

We will start by revisiting composable functions, the building blocks of a composable UI. This time, we will dig much deeper into their underlying ideas and concepts. By the end of the first main section, you will have established a thorough understanding of what composable functions are, how they are written, and how they are used.

The following section focuses on creating and updating the UI. You will learn how Jetpack Compose achieves what other UI frameworks call repainting. This mechanism, which is called **recomposition** in Compose, takes place automatically whenever something relevant to the UI changes. To keep this process fluent, your composable functions must adhere to a few best practices. I will explain them to you in this section.

We will close this chapter by expanding our knowledge of the concept of modifiers. We will take a close look at how modifier chains work and what you need to keep in mind to always get the intended results. You will also learn how to implement custom modifiers, which allow you to amend any composable function to look or behave in precisely the way you want it to.

Now, let's get started!

Technical requirements

Please refer to the *Technical requirements* section of *Chapter 1, Building Your First Compose App*, for information on how to install and set up Android Studio, as well as how to get the sample apps. This chapter covers the `ColoredTextDemo`, `ColorPickerDemo`, and `ModifierDemo` samples.

Looking closer at composable functions

The UI of a Compose app is built by writing and calling composable functions. We have already done both in the previous chapters, but my explanations regarding the structure of a composable, as well as its internals, have been quite basic—it's time to fix that.

Building blocks of composable functions

A **composable function** is a Kotlin function that has been annotated with `@Composable`. All composables *must* be marked this way because the annotation informs the Compose compiler that the function converts data into UI elements.

The signature of a Kotlin function consists of the following parts or building blocks:

- An optional visibility modifier (`private`, `protected`, `internal`, or `public`)
- The `fun` keyword
- A name
- A list of parameters (can be empty) or, optionally, a default value
- An optional return type
- A block of code

Let's explore these parts in greater detail.

The default visibility (if you omit the modifier) is `public`. This means that the (composable) function can be called from anywhere. If a function is meant to be reused (for example, a text styled to match your brand), it should be publicly available. On the other hand, if a function is tied to a particular **context** (the region of code, such as a class), it may make sense to restrict its access. There is an open debate on how rigidly the visibility of functions should be restrained. In the end, you and your team need to agree on a point of view and stick to it. For the sake of simplicity, my examples are usually public.

The name of a composable function uses `PascalCase` notation: it starts with an uppercase letter, whereas the remaining characters are lowercase. If the name consists of more than one word, each word follows this rule. The name should be a noun (`Demo`) or a noun that has been prefixed with a descriptive adjective (`FancyDemo`). Unlike other (ordinary) Kotlin functions, it should *not* be a verb or a verb phrase (`getDataFromServer`). The *API Guidelines for Jetpack Compose* file, which is available at `https://github.com/androidx/androidx/blob/androidx-main/compose/docs/compose-api-guidelines.md`, details these naming conventions.

All the data you want to pass to a composable function is provided through a comma-separated list, which is enclosed in parentheses. If a composable does not require values, the list remains empty. Here's a composable function that can receive two parameters:

```
@Composable
fun ColoredTextDemo(
  text: String = "",
  color: Color = Color.Black
) {
  Text(
    text = text,
    style = TextStyle(color = color)
  )
}
```

In Kotlin, function parameters are defined as `name: type`. Parameters are separated by a comma. You can specify a default value by adding `= ....`. This is used if no value is provided for a particular parameter when the function is being invoked. Default values are handy if you want to preview a composable function in Android Studio using the `@Preview` annotation.

The return type of a function is optional. In this case, the function returns `Unit`. `Unit` is a type with only one value: `Unit`. If, as in this example, it is omitted, the function body follows immediately after the list of arguments. Most composable functions you will be writing do not need to return anything, so do not need a return type. Situations that require it will be covered in the *Returning values* section.

If the code of a function contains more than one statement or expression, it will be enclosed in curly braces. Kotlin offers a nice abbreviation for if just one expression needs to be executed—Jetpack Compose itself uses this quite frequently:

```
@Composable
fun ShortColoredTextDemo(
    text: String = "",
    color: Color = Color.Black
) = Text(
    text = text,
    style = TextStyle(color = color)
)
```

As you can see, the expression follows an equals sign. This means that `ShortColoredTextDemo()` returns whatever `Text()` is returning.

Unlike Java, Kotlin does not know about the void keyword, so all the functions must return *something*. By omitting the return type, we implicitly tell Kotlin that the return type of a function is kotlin.Unit. This type has only one value: the Unit object. So, Unit corresponds to void in Java.

Let's test this by printing the result of invoking a composable function:

```kotlin
class ColorPickerDemoActivity : ComponentActivity() {
  override fun onCreate(savedInstanceState: Bundle?) {
    super.onCreate(savedInstanceState)
    setContent {
      Column(modifier = Modifier.fillMaxSize()) {
        println(
          ColoredTextDemo(
            text = stringResource(id =
                    R.string.colored_text_demo),
            color = Color.Blue
          )
        )
        ShortColoredTextDemo(
          text = stringResource(id =
                  R.string.short_colored_text_demo),
          color = Color.Black
        )
      }
    }
  }
}
```

If you run the app, the following line will be printed:

```
2023-05-28 13:09:15.964  7347-7347 System.out eu....h.composebook.
coloredtextdemo  I  kotlin.Unit
```

While this may not look too exciting, its implications are profound. Think of it: although the ColoredTextDemo() composable function returns nothing interesting, some text is shown on the screen. This happens because it invokes another composable, called Text(). So, whatever may be needed to show text must happen inside Text(), and it cannot have anything to do with the return value of a composable.

In the previous chapter, I said that composable functions *emit* UI elements. I will explain what this means in the next section.

Emitting UI elements

A Compose UI is created by nesting calls to composable functions, which can be provided by the Jetpack Compose libraries, code of other developers, or your app.

Let's find out what happens once `ColoredTextDemo()` has called `androidx.compose.material3.Text()`. To see the source code of (among others) composable functions in Android Studio, you can click on their names while holding down the *Ctrl* key (on a Mac, it's the *cmd* key).

> **Note**
>
> I will only show you the important steps because otherwise, I would need to copy too much code. To get the best learning experience, please follow the call chain directly in your IDE.

`Text()` defines two local variables, `textColor` and `mergedStyle`, and passes them to `androidx.compose.foundation.text.BasicText()`. Although you can use `BasicText()` in your code, you should stick to `androidx.compose.material3.Text()` because it consumes style information from a `MaterialTheme`. Please refer to *Chapter 6, Building a Real-World App*, for more information about themes.

`BasicText()` initializes and remembers quite a few variables. There is no need to explain them here. The important piece is the invocation of another composable function: `Layout()`; it belongs to the `androidx.compose.ui.layout` package. Its different implementations are the core composable functions for the layout, with their purpose being to size and position children. *Chapter 4, Laying Out UI Elements in Compose*, covers this in great detail. Right now, we still need to find out what *emitting UI elements* means. So, let's see what `Layout()` does:

```kotlin
inline fun Layout(
    modifier: Modifier = Modifier,
    measurePolicy: MeasurePolicy
) {
    val density = LocalDensity.current
    val layoutDirection = LocalLayoutDirection.current
    val viewConfiguration = LocalViewConfiguration.current
    val materialized = currentComposer.materialize(modifier)
    ReusableComposeNode<ComposeUiNode, Applier<Any>>(
        factory = ComposeUiNode.Constructor,
        update = { this: Updater<ComposeUiNode>
            set(measurePolicy, ComposeUiNode.SetMeasurePolicy)
            set(density, ComposeUiNode.SetDensity)
            set(layoutDirection, ComposeUiNode.SetLayoutDirection)
            set(viewConfiguration, ComposeUiNode.SetViewConfiguration)
            set(materialized, ComposeUiNode.SetModifier)
        },
    )
}
```

Figure 3.1 – Source code of Layout()

Layout() invokes ReusableComposeNode(), which belongs to the androidx.compose.
runtime package. This composable function *emits* a so-called **node**, a UI element hierarchy. Nodes
are created using a factory, which is passed through the factory argument. The update parameter
receives code that performs updates on the node.

> **Note**
>
> BasicText() calls a variation of Layout() for leaf nodes. There are also more general
> ones that receive different or additional parameters.
>
> Also, when we speak of composable functions *emitting* UI elements, we mean that **nodes** are
> added to data structures that are internal to Jetpack Compose. This will eventually lead to UI
> elements being visible.

To complete the call chain, let's briefly look at ReusableComposeNode():

```
@Composable inline fun <T : Any, reified E : Applier<*>> ReusableComposeNode(
    noinline factory: () -> T,
    update: @DisallowComposableCalls Updater<T>.() -> Unit
) {
    if (currentComposer.applier !is E) invalidApplier()
    currentComposer.startReusableNode()
    if (currentComposer.inserting) {
        currentComposer.createNode { factory() }
    } else {
        currentComposer.useNode()
    }
    Updater<T>(currentComposer).update()
    currentComposer.endNode()
}
```

Figure 3.2 – Source code of ReusableComposeNode()

currentComposer is a top-level variable inside androidx.compose.runtime.Composables.
kt. Its type is Composer, which is an interface. Composer is targeted by the Jetpack Compose
Kotlin compiler plugin and used by code generation helpers; your code should not call it directly.
ReusableComposeNode determines if a new node should be created (currentComposer.
createNode { factory() }) or whether an existing one should be reused (currentComposer.
useNode()). It then performs updates (Updater<T>(currentComposer).update()) and
finishes by invoking currentComposer.endNode().

Based on what you know by now, let me elaborate a little more on nodes. Layout() passes
ComposeUiNode.Constructor to ReusableComposeNode as the factory argument,
which is used to create a node. So, the features of a node are defined by the ComposeUiNode interface:

```
@PublishedApi
internal interface ComposeUiNode {
    var measurePolicy: MeasurePolicy
    var layoutDirection: LayoutDirection
    var density: Density
    var modifier: Modifier
    var viewConfiguration: ViewConfiguration

    Object of pre-allocated lambdas used to make use
    with ComposeNode allocation-less.

    companion object {
        val Constructor: () -> ComposeUiNode = LayoutNode.Constructor
        val VirtualConstructor: () -> ComposeUiNode = { LayoutNode(isVirtual = true) }
        val SetModifier: ComposeUiNode.(Modifier) -> Unit = { this.modifier = it }
        val SetDensity: ComposeUiNode.(Density) -> Unit = { this.density = it }
        val SetMeasurePolicy: ComposeUiNode.(MeasurePolicy) -> Unit =
            { this.measurePolicy = it }
        val SetLayoutDirection: ComposeUiNode.(LayoutDirection) -> Unit =
            { this.layoutDirection = it }
        val SetViewConfiguration: ComposeUiNode.(ViewConfiguration) -> Unit =
            { this.viewConfiguration = it }
    }
}
```

Figure 3.3 – Source code of ComposeUiNode

A node has five properties, as defined by the following classes or interfaces:

- `MeasurePolicy` defines the measure and layout behavior of a layout
- `LayoutDirection` is a class for defining layout directions
- `Density` is used for the conversions between pixels, `Dp`, `Int`, and `TextUnit`
- `Modifier` is an ordered, immutable collection of elements
- `ViewConfiguration` contains methods to standard constants used in the UI for timeouts, sizes, and distances

In essence, a node is an element in a Compose hierarchy. You will not be dealing with them in your code because nodes are part of the inner workings of Jetpack Compose that are not exposed to apps. However, you will see `MeasurePolicy`, `LayoutDirection`, `Density`, `Modifier`, and, to a much lesser extent, `ViewConfiguration` throughout this book. They represent important data structures and concepts that are relevant to apps.

This concludes our investigation of how UI elements are emitted (nodes are added to data structures that are internal to Jetpack Compose). In the next section, we will look at composable functions that return values.

Returning values

Most of your composable functions will not need to return something, so they will not specify a return type. This is because the main purpose of a composable is to compose the UI. As you saw in the previous section, this is done by emitting UI elements or element hierarchies. But when do we need to return something different than `Unit`?

Some of my examples invoke `remember {}` to retain state for future use and `stringResource()` to access strings that are stored in the `strings.xml` file. To be able to perform their tasks, both must be composable functions.

Let's look at `stringResource()` to see why. Remember that you can *Ctrl*-click on a name to see its source code. The function is pretty short; it does just two things:

```
val resources = resources()
return resources.getString(id)
```

`resources()` is a composable too. It returns `LocalContext.current.resources`. `LocalContext` is a top-level variable in `AndroidCompositionLocals.android.kt` that belongs to the `androidx.compose.ui.platform` package. It returns an instance of `StaticProvidableCompositionLocal`, which holds an `android.content.Context` object. This object provides access to resources.

Even though the returned data has nothing to do with Jetpack Compose, the code that obtains it must conform to Jetpack Compose mechanics because, in the end, it will be called from a composable function. The important thing to remember is that if you need to return something that is part of the composition and recomposition mechanic, you must make your function composable by annotating it with `@Composable`. Also, such functions do not follow the naming conventions for composable functions but follow the `camelCase` style (they begin with a small letter, with subsequent words starting in uppercase) and consist of verb phrases (`rememberScrollState`).

In the next section, we will return to composing user interfaces at the app level. You will learn more about the terms *composition* and *recomposition*.

Composing and recomposing the UI

Unlike imperative UI frameworks, Jetpack Compose does not depend on the developer proactively modifying a component tree when changes in the app data require changes to be made to the UI. Instead, Jetpack Compose detects such changes on its own and updates only the affected parts.

As you know by now, a Compose UI is declared *based on* the current app data. In my previous examples, you have seen quite a few conditional expressions (such as `if` or `when`) that determine which composable function is called or which parameters it receives. So, we are describing the *complete* UI in our code. The branch that will be executed depends on the app data (state) during runtime. The web framework React has a similar concept called **Virtual DOM**. But doesn't this contradict my saying *Compose detects such changes on its own and updates only the affected parts*?

Conceptually, Jetpack Compose regenerates the entire UI when changes need to be applied. This, of course, would waste time, battery, and processing power, and it might be noticeable by the user as screen flickering. Therefore, the framework puts a lot of effort into making sure only those parts of the UI element tree requiring an update are regenerated. You saw some of these efforts in the previous section, where I briefly mentioned `update`.

To ensure fast and reliable **recompositions** (the Jetpack Compose term for updating, regenerating, or repainting), you need to make sure your composable functions follow a few simple rules. I will introduce them to you by walking you through the code of an app called `ColorPickerDemo`:

Figure 3.4 – The ColorPickerDemo app

The app aims to set a color by specifying its **red, green, and blue** (**RGB**) portions. This color is used as the background color of a text (which displays the value of the color as a hexadecimal string). The foreground color is complementary to the selected one.

In the next few sections, we look at its code. You will learn how sliders communicate changes in their values.

Sharing state among composable functions

Sometimes, you may want to use a state in more than one composable function. For example, you may wish to use the color portion that's been set by one slider to create the full color, which, in turn, becomes the background color of a text. So, how can you share state? Let's start by looking at `ColorPicker()` —it groups three sliders vertically in a `Column()`:

```
@Composable
fun ColorPicker(color: MutableState<Color>) {
  val red = color.value.red
  val green = color.value.green
  val blue = color.value.blue
  Column {
    Slider(
      value = red,
      onValueChange = { color.value = Color(it, green,
                                            blue) })
    Slider(
      value = green,
      onValueChange = { color.value = Color(red, it,
                                            blue) })
    Slider(
      value = blue,
      onValueChange = { color.value = Color(red, green,
                                            it) })
  }
}
```

The composable receives one parameter: `MutableState<Color>`. The `value` property of `color` contains an instance of `androidx.compose.ui.graphics.Color`. Its `red`, `green`, and `blue` properties contain a `Float` type based on the so-called **color space**, which is used to identify a specific organization of colors. Each color space is characterized by a color model, which, in turn, defines how a color value is represented. If not specified otherwise, this is `ColorSpaces.Srgb`. This causes the values for red, green, and blue to be between `0F` and `1F`.

The first three lines assign the red, green, and blue portions of the color to local variables named `red`, `green`, and `blue`. They are used for the `Slider()` functions; let's see how: each slider in my example receives two parameters, `value` and `onValueChange`. The first specifies the value that the slider will display. It must be between `0F` and `1F` (which fits nicely with `red`, `green`, and `blue`). If needed, you can supply an alternative range through the optional `valueRange` parameter. `onValueChange` is invoked when the user drags the slider handle or clicks on the thin line underneath.

The code of the three lambda expressions is quite similar: a new `Color` object is created and assigned to `color.value`. Color portions that are being controlled by other sliders are taken from the corresponding local variables. They have not been changed. The new color portion of the current slider can be obtained from `it` because it is the new slider value, which is passed to `onValueChange`.

By now, you may be wondering why `ColorPicker()` receives the color wrapped inside a `MutableState<Color>` instance. Wouldn't it suffice to pass it directly, using `color: Color`? As shown in *Figure 3.4*, the app shows the selected color as a text with complementary background and foreground colors. But `ColorPicker()` does not emit text. This happens somewhere else (as you will see shortly, inside a `Column()`). To show the correct color, the text must receive it too. As the color change takes place inside `ColorPicker()`, we must inform the caller about it. An ordinary `Color` instance being passed as a parameter can't do that because Kotlin function parameters are immutable.

Now, let's learn how the color is passed to the text:

```
Column(
  modifier = Modifier.width(min(400.dp, maxWidth)),
  horizontalAlignment = Alignment.CenterHorizontally
) {
  val color = remember { mutableStateOf(Color.Magenta) }
  ColorPicker(color)
  Text(
    modifier = Modifier
      .fillMaxWidth()
      .background(color.value),
    text =
      "#${color.value.toArgb().toUInt().toString(16)}",
    textAlign = TextAlign.Center,
    style = MaterialTheme.typography.displayMedium.merge(
      TextStyle(
        color = color.value.complementary()
      )
    )
  )
}
```

`ColorPicker()` and `Text()` are laid out vertically (being centered horizontally) inside a `Column()`. The width of the column is either `400` density-independent pixels or `maxWidth`, depending on which value is smaller. `maxWidth` is defined by the predefined `BoxWithConstraints()` composable (you will learn more about it in the *Controlling size* section). The color for both `ColorPicker()` and `Text()` is defined like this:

```
val color = remember { mutableStateOf(Color.Magenta) }
```

When `Column()` is composed for the first time, `mutableStateOf(Color.Magenta)` is executed. This creates **state**. State represents app data (in this case, a color) that may change over time. You will learn more about state in *Chapter 5, Managing State of Your Composable Functions*. For now, it suffices to understand that the state is *remembered* and assigned to `color`.

But what does `remember` mean? Any subsequent composition, which is called **recomposition**, will lead to `color` receiving the value created by `mutableStateOf`—that is, a reference to a `MutableState<Color>` instance (state hoisting). The lambda expression that's passed to `remember` is called a **calculation**. It will only be evaluated once. Recompositions always return the same value.

If the reference remains the same, how can the color be changed? The actual color is accessed through the `value` property. You saw this in the code of `ColorPicker()`. `Text()` does not modify the color—it only works with it. Therefore, we pass `color.value` (which is the color), not the mutable state (`color`), to some of its parameters, such as `background`. Note that this is a modifier. You will learn more about them in the *Modifying the behavior of composable functions* section. It sets the background color of a UI element that's emitted by a composable function.

Also, have you noticed the call of `complementary()` inside `TextStyle()`? This is what it does:

```
fun Color.complementary() = Color(
   red = 1F - red,
   green = 1F - green,
   blue = 1F - blue
)
```

`complementary()` is an extension function of `Color`. It computes the complementary color to the one it receives. This is done to make the text (the hexadecimal RGB value of the color that was selected using the three sliders) readable, regardless of the currently selected color (which is used as the background of the text).

This has been quite a bit of information to digest. So, let's recap: we defined a mutable state and passed it to a composable function because the state needs to be modified inside the composable. At this point, you may be asking yourself if this is the only way to achieve changeability. An alternative approach would be using global properties. But this is not recommended for Jetpack Compose. Composables should not use global variables at all.

It is a best practice to pass all data that influences the look or behavior of a composable function as parameters. If that data is modified inside the composable, you can use `MutableState`, just as in my example. But there is an even more elegant solution. Have a look:

```
@Composable
fun ColorPicker(color: Color,
                colorChanged: (Color) -> Unit) {
   val red = color.red
   val green = color.green
```

```
    val blue = color.blue
    Column {
      Slider(
        value = red,
        onValueChange = { colorChanged(Color(it, green,
                                        blue)) })
      Slider(
        value = green,
        onValueChange = { colorChanged(Color(red, it,
                                        blue)) })
      Slider(
        value = blue,
        onValueChange = { colorChanged(Color(red, green,
                                        it)) })
    }
}
```

Unlike in the first version, we now pass the color as an ordinary `Color`. Remember that earlier I said we can't change that value because it is immutable? That is why we pass a second parameter, `colorChanged: (Color) -> Unit`. When a slider is moved, its `onValueChange` lambda is invoked. My implementation creates a new `Color` instance (with the corresponding red, green, or blue value being changed) and invokes `colorChanged`, the second parameter of the new `ColorPicker()` version.

Here's how it is used inside `Column()`:

```
Column(...) {
  var color by remember { mutableStateOf(Color.Magenta) }
  ColorPicker(
    color = color,
    colorChanged = { color = it }
  )
  Text(
    modifier = ...,
    text = "#${color.toArgb().toUInt().toString(16)}",
    textAlign = ...,
    style = ...
  )
}
```

The important thing to note is the slightly different definition of `color`, using `var color by remember`. The by keyword tells Kotlin that we want to assign the value of our mutable state, not the state itself. The benefit is that we no longer need to add `.value`, which enhances the readability of our code. The assignment of the new values happens inside `{ color = it }`.

Moving state to a composable's caller is called **state hoisting**. As you have just seen, a good alternative to passing `MutableState` and applying changes inside a composable is to pass the change logic as a lambda expression. If possible, you should follow this practice in your apps.

> **Important note**
>
> Try to make your composables idempotent. Having a side-effect-free function means calling it repeatedly with the same set of arguments will always produce the same result. Besides getting all the relevant data from the caller, being free of side effects also requires not relying on global properties or calling functions that return unpredictable values. There are a few scenarios where you want side effects. I will cover these in *Chapter 7, Exploring App Architecture*.

In this section, I talked about some very important Jetpack Compose concepts. Let's recap what we've learned so far:

- A Compose UI is defined by nesting calls to composable functions
- Composable functions emit UI elements or UI element hierarchies
- Building the UI for the first time is called **composition**
- Rebuilding the UI upon changes being made to app data is called **recomposition**
- Recomposition happens automatically

> **Important note**
>
> There is no way for your app to predict when or how often recomposition will take place. If animations are involved, this may happen in each frame. Therefore, it is of utmost importance to make your composables as fast as possible. You may never do time-consuming calculations, load or save data, or access the network. Any such code must be executed outside of composable functions. They only receive ready data. Also, please note that the order of recomposition is unspecified. This means that the first child of, say, a `Column()`, might be recomposed later than a sibling that appears after it in the source code. Recomposition can occur in parallel, and it may be skipped. Therefore, never rely on a particular order of recomposition, and never compute something in a composable that is needed somewhere else.

In the next section, we will finish our walkthrough of the `ColorPickerDemo` app. I will show you how to specify and limit the dimensions of composable functions.

Controlling size

Most of my examples contain code such as `fillMaxSize()` or `fillMaxWidth()`. Both so-called **modifiers** control the size of a composable function. `fillMaxSize()` uses all the available horizontal and vertical space, while `fillMaxWidth()` maximizes only the horizontal expansion.

However, `fillMaxWidth()` may not be the right choice for sliders. In my opinion, large sliders are awkward to use due to the distance you would need to drag their handles to reach the minimum or maximum value. So, the question is, how can we limit its width? The most straightforward solution is to use the `width()` modifier, which sets the preferred width of a composable to a particular size. I want sliders to be 400 density-independent pixels wide at most. If the screen is smaller, its width should be used instead. Here's how you achieve this:

```
modifier = Modifier.width(min(400.dp, maxWidth)),
```

The modifier belongs to the `Column()` property that contains both `ColorPicker()` and `Text()`.

`maxWidth` is provided by the `BoxWithConstraints()` composable:

```
BoxWithConstraints(
  contentAlignment = Alignment.Center,
  modifier = Modifier.fillMaxSize()
                     .padding(32.dp)
) {
  Column ...
}
```

Its content receives an instance of a `BoxWithConstraintsScope` scope, which provides access to `constraints`, `minWidth`, `minHeight`, `maxWidth`, and `maxHeight`. `BoxWithConstraints()` defines its content according to the available space, based on incoming constraints. You will learn more about this in *Chapter 4, Laying Out UI Elements in Compose*.

`padding(32.dp)` adds an empty area to the top, bottom, left, and right. This makes sure that, even on small screens, the sliders won't come too close to the screen borders.

This concludes our walkthrough of the `ColorPickerDemo` app. In the next section, we take a closer look at how a composable hierarchy is displayed in an `Activity`.

Displaying a composable hierarchy inside an Activity

In the previous section, we built a UI element hierarchy consisting of three sliders and some text. We embedded it in an `Activity` using `setContent`, an extension function of `androidx.activity.ComponentActivity`. This implies that you cannot invoke `setContent` on *any* activity, but only ones that extend `ComponentActivity`. This is the case for `androidx.appcompat.app.AppCompatActivity`.

However, this class inherits quite a lot of functionality that is relevant to the old View-based world, such as support for toolbars and the options menu. Jetpack Compose handles these differently. You will learn more about this in *Chapter 6, Building a Real-World App*. Therefore, you may want to avoid using `AppCompatActivity`, and instead extend `ComponentActivity` if possible. For combining View-based and Compose UIs, please refer to *Chapter 9, Exploring Interoperability APIs*.

Let's return to setContent. It expects two parameters, as follows:

- parent, an optional CompositionContext class

- content, a composable function for declaring the UI

You will likely omit parent most of the time. CompositionContext is an abstract class that belongs to the androidx.compose.runtime package. It is used to logically connect two compositions. This refers to the inner workings of Jetpack Compose that you do not need to worry about in your app code. Yet, to get an idea of what this means, let's look at the source code of setContent:

```
public fun ComponentActivity.setContent(
    parent: CompositionContext? = null,
    content: @Composable () -> Unit
) {
    val existingComposeView = window.decorView View
        .findViewById<ViewGroup>(android.R.id.content) ViewGroup!
        .getChildAt( index: 0) as? ComposeView

    if (existingComposeView != null) with(existingComposeView) { this: ComposeView
        setParentCompositionContext(parent)
        setContent(content)
    } else ComposeView( context: this).apply { this: ComposeView
        // Set content and parent **before** setContentView
        // to have ComposeView create the composition on attach
        setParentCompositionContext(parent)
        setContent(content)
        // Set the view tree owners before setting the content view so that the inflation process
        // and attach listeners will see them already present
        setOwners()
        setContentView( view: this, DefaultActivityContentLayoutParams)
    }
}
```

Figure 3.5 – Source code of setContent

First, findViewById() is used to find out whether the activity already contains content that is an instance of androidx.compose.ui.platform.ComposeView. If so, the setParentCompositionContext() and setContent() methods of this view will be invoked.

Let's look at setParentCompositionContext() first. It belongs to AbstractComposeView, the immediate parent of ComposeView. It sets a CompositionContext instance that should be the parent of the view's composition. If that context is null, it will be determined automatically: AbstractComposeView contains a private function called ensureCompositionCreated(). It invokes another implementation of setContent (an internal extension function of AbstractComposeView that's defined in Wrapper.android.kt) and passes the result of a call to resolveParentCompositionContext() as a parent.

Now, let's return to the version of `setContent()` that's shown in the preceding screenshot. Once `setParentCompositionContext()` has been called, it invokes yet another version of `setContent()`. This implementation belongs to `ComposeView`. It sets the content of the view.

If `findViewById()` does not return a `ComposeView` instance, a new instance is created and passed to `setContentView`, after `setParentCompositionContext()`, `setContent()`, and `setOwners()` have been invoked.

In this section, we continued looking at some of the inner workings of Jetpack Compose. You now know that `ComposeView` is the missing link to the old-fashioned View-based world. We will revisit this class in *Chapter 9, Exploring Interoperability APIs*.

In the next section, we will return to modifiers; you will learn how they work under the hood and how you can write your own.

Modifying the behavior of composable functions

Unlike components in traditional imperative UI frameworks, composable functions do not share a basic set of properties. They also do not automatically (in the sense of inheriting) reuse functionality. This must be done explicitly by calling other composables. Their visual appearance and behavior can be controlled through parameters, modifiers, or both. In a way, modifiers pick up the idea of properties in a component but enhance it—unlike properties of components, modifiers can be used completely at the discretion of the developer.

You have already seen quite a few modifiers in my examples, such as the following:

- `width()`
- `fillMaxWidth()`
- `fillMaxSize()`

These control the width and size of the corresponding UI element.

`background()` can set a background color and shape, while `clickable {}` allows the user to interact with the composable function by clicking on the UI element. Jetpack Compose provides an extensive list of modifiers, so it may take some time to make yourself familiar with most of them. Conceptually, these modifiers can be assigned to one of several categories, such as *Actions* (`draggable()`), *Alignment* (`alignByBaseline()`), or *Drawing* (`paint()`). You can find a list of modifiers grouped by category at `https://developer.android.com/jetpack/compose/modifiers-list`.

To further familiarize yourself with modifiers, let's look at the `ModifierDemo` example. It contains several composable functions:

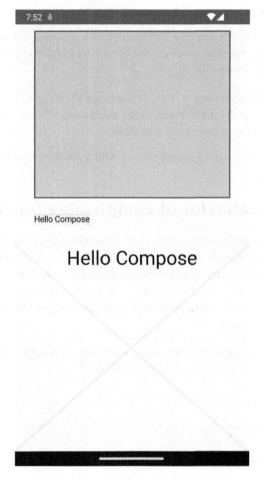

Figure 3.6 – The ModifierDemo app

Let's look at `OrderDemo()` first. The composable produces a gap of 32 density-independent pixels on all its sides, followed by a 2-density-independent pixels-wide blue border. The inner rectangle is painted in light gray.

Here's what the code looks like:

```
@Composable
fun OrderDemo() {
  var color by remember { mutableStateOf(Color.Blue) }
  Box(
    modifier = Modifier
```

```
    .fillMaxSize()
    .padding(32.dp)
    .border(BorderStroke(width = 2.dp, color = color))
    .background(Color.LightGray)
    .clickable {
      color = if (color == Color.Blue)
        Color.Red
      else
        Color.Blue
    }
  )
}
```

Box() is clickable—doing so changes the border color from blue to red and back. If you click inside the gaps, nothing will happen. If, however, you move .clickable { } before .padding(32. dp), clicks work inside the gaps too. This is intentional. Here's what happens: you define a modifier chain by combining several modifiers with .. In doing so, you specify the order in which the modifiers are used. The location of a modifier in the chain determines when it is executed. As clickable {} only reacts to clicks inside the bounds of a composable, the padding is not considered for clicks when it occurs before clickable {}.

In the next section, I will show you how Jetpack Compose handles modifiers and modifier chains internally.

Understanding how modifiers work

Composable functions that accept modifiers should receive them via the modifier parameter and assign it a default value of Modifier. modifier should be the first optional parameter and thus appear after all the required ones, except for trailing lambda parameters. Please refer to the next link provided for a detailed explanation.

Let's see how a composable can receive a modifier parameter:

```
@Composable
fun TextWithYellowBackground(
  text: String,
  modifier: Modifier = Modifier
) {
  Text(
    text = text,
    modifier = modifier.background(Color.Yellow)
  )
}
```

This way, the composable can receive a modifier chain from the caller. If none is provided, `Modifier` acts as a new, empty chain. In both cases, the composable can add additional modifiers, such as `background()` in the previous code snippet.

If a composable function accepts a modifier that will be applied to a specific part or child of its corresponding UI element, the name of this part or child should be used as a prefix, such as `titleModifier`. Such modifiers follow the rules I mentioned previously. They should be grouped and appear after the parent's modifier. Please refer to `https://developer.android.com/reference/kotlin/androidx/compose/ui/Modifier` for additional information regarding the definition of modifier parameters.

Now that you know how to define a `modifier` parameter in a composable function, let's focus a little more on the idea of chaining. `Modifier` is both an interface and a companion object. The interface belongs to the `androidx.compose.ui` package. It defines several functions, such as `foldIn()` and `foldOut()`. You won't need them, though. The important one is `then()`. It concatenates two modifiers. As you will see shortly, you need to invoke it in your modifiers. The `Element` interface extends `Modifier`. It defines a single element contained within a `Modifier` chain. Finally, the `Modifier` companion object is the empty, default modifier, which contains no elements.

> **Note**
>
> A modifier is an ordered, immutable collection of modifier elements.

Next, let's see how the `background()` modifier is implemented:

```kotlin
fun Modifier.background(
    color: Color,
    shape: Shape = RectangleShape
) = this.then(
    Background(
        color = color,
        shape = shape,
        inspectorInfo = debugInspectorInfo { this: InspectorInfo
            name = "background"
            value = color
            properties["color"] = color
            properties["shape"] = shape
        }
    )
)
```

Figure 3.7 – Source code of the background() modifier

`background()` is an extension function of `Modifier`. It receives a `Modifier` instance. It invokes `then()` and returns the result (a concatenated modifier). `then()` expects just one parameter: the *other* modifier that should be concatenated with the current one. In the case of `background()`, *other* is an instance of `Background`. This class extends `InspectorValueInfo` and implements the `DrawModifier` interface, which, in turn, extends `Modifier.Element`. As `InspectorValueInfo` is primarily used for debugging purposes, I will not elaborate on it any further. `DrawModifier`, on the other hand, is very interesting. Implementations can draw into the space of a UI element. We will make use of this in the final section.

Implementing custom modifiers

Although Jetpack Compose contains an extensive list of modifiers, you may want to implement your own. Let me show you how to do this. My example, `drawYellowCross()`, draws two thick yellow lines behind the content, which is some `Text()` here:

Figure 3.8 – A custom modifier

The modifier is invoked like this:

```
@Composable
@Preview(widthDp = 400, heightDp = 200)
fun TextWithYellowCross() {
  Text(
    text = "Hello Compose",
    modifier = Modifier
      .fillMaxSize()
      .drawYellowCross(),
    textAlign = TextAlign.Center,
    style = MaterialTheme.typography.headlineLarge
  )
}
```

As you can see, the modifier integrates nicely into an existing modifier chain. Now, let's look at the source code:

```
fun Modifier.drawYellowCross() = then(
  object : DrawModifier {
    override fun ContentDrawScope.draw() {
      drawLine(
        color = Color.Yellow,
        start = Offset(0F, 0F),
        end = Offset(size.width - 1, size.height - 1),
        strokeWidth = 10F
      )
      drawLine(
        color = Color.Yellow,
        start = Offset(0F, size.height - 1),
        end = Offset(size.width - 1, 0F),
        strokeWidth = 10F
      )
      drawContent()
    }
  }
)
```

drawYellowCross() is an extension function of Modifier. This means we can invoke then() and simply return the result. then() receives an instance of DrawModifier. After that, we need to implement only one function, called draw(), which is an extension function of ContentDrawScope. This interface defines one function (drawContent()) and extends DrawScope; this way, we gain access to quite a few drawing primitives, such as drawLine(), drawRect(), and drawImage(). drawContent() draws the UI element, so depending on when it is invoked, the element appears in front of, or behind, the other drawing primitives. In my example, it is the last instruction, so the UI element (for example, Text()) is the topmost one.

Jetpack Compose also includes a modifier called drawBehind { }. It receives a lambda expression that can contain drawing primitives, just as in my example. To learn even more about the internals of Jetpack Compose, you may want to take a look at its source code. To see it, just click on drawBehind() in your code while pressing the *Ctrl* key.

This concludes my explanations of modifiers. As you have seen, they are a very elegant way to control both the visual appearance and behavior of composable functions.

Summary

This chapter introduced you to the key principles of Jetpack Compose. We closely looked at the underlying ideas and concepts of composable functions, and you now know how they are written and used. We also focused on how to create and update the UI, as well as how Jetpack Compose achieves what other frameworks call repainting or updating the screen. When relevant app data changes, the UI changes, or so-called recomposition, takes place automatically; this is one of the advantages over the traditional View-based approach, where the developer must imperatively change the component tree.

sWe then expanded our knowledge of the concept of modifiers. We looked at how modifier chains work and what you need to keep in mind to always get the intended results. For example, to receive clicks inside padding, `padding {}` must occur after `clickable {}` in the `modifier` chain. Finally, you learned how to implement custom modifiers.

In *Chapter 4, Laying Out UI Elements in Compose*, we will examine how to lay out UI elements and introduce you to the **single-pass measurement** Jetpack Compose uses. We will explore built-in layouts, but also write a custom compose layout.

Questions

- Composable functions usually do not specify a return type. Please list three that do.
- What does state hoisting mean?
- What are the key differences between properties in class-based UI frameworks and modifiers?

Part 2:
Building User Interfaces

This part takes a practical approach to teach you how to write fast, robust, and beautiful Jetpack Compose apps. The many examples we will examine will provide you with a solid understanding of how the library works.

We will cover the following chapters in this part:

- *Chapter 4, Laying Out UI Elements in Compose*
- *Chapter 5, Managing State of Your Composable Functions*
- *Chapter 6, Building a Real-World App*
- *Chapter 7, Exploring App Architecture*

4

Laying Out UI Elements in Compose

In the previous chapters, you learned how to build simple UIs. Although they consisted of just a few UI elements, they needed to arrange their buttons, text fields, and sliders in a particular order, direction, or hierarchy. **Layouts** position and size their content in a way specific to this layout, such as horizontally (`Row()`) or vertically (`Column()`). This chapter explores layouts in greater detail.

In this chapter, we will cover the following topics:

- Using predefined layouts
- Understanding the single measure pass
- Creating custom layouts

We will start by exploring the predefined layouts of `Row()`, `Column()`, and `Box()`. You will learn how to combine them to create beautiful UIs. Next, I'll introduce you to `ConstraintLayout`. It places composables that are relative to others on the screen and uses attributes to flatten the UI element hierarchy. This is an alternative to nesting `Row()`, `Column()`, and `Box()`.

The second main section will explain why the layout system in Jetpack Compose is more performant than the traditional View-based approach. We will once again go under the covers and look at some of the internals of the Compose runtime. This will prepare you for the final main section of this chapter, *Creating custom layouts*.

In this final section, you will learn how to create a custom layout and thus gain precise control over the rendering of its children. This is helpful if the predefined layouts do not offer enough flexibility for a particular use case.

Now, let's get started!

Technical requirements

Please refer to the *Technical requirements* section of *Chapter 1, Building Your First Compose App*, for information about how to install and set up Android Studio, as well as how to get the sample apps. This chapter covers the `ColumnWithTextsDemo`, `ConstraintLayoutDemo`, `CustomLayoutDemo`, and `PredefinedLayoutsDemo` samples.

Using predefined layouts

When you create a UI, you must define where its elements appear and how big they are. Jetpack Compose provides a couple of basic layouts, which arrange their content along one main axis. There are three axes to consider:

- Horizontal
- Vertical
- Stacked

Each axis is represented by a layout. `Row()` arranges its content horizontally, while `Column()` does so vertically. `Box()` and `BoxWithConstraints()` stack their contents on top of each other. By combining these axes-orientated building blocks, you can create great-looking UIs easily.

Combining basic building blocks

The following `PredefinedLayoutsDemo` sample app shows three checkboxes that toggle a red, a green, and a blue rectangle, respectively. The boxes appear only if the corresponding checkbox is checked:

Figure 4.1 – Sample PredefinedLayoutsDemo app

Let's see how this is done. First, I will show you how to create a checkbox with an accompanying label:

```
@Composable
fun CheckboxWithLabel(
  label: String,
```

```
    checked: Boolean,
    onClicked: (Boolean) -> Unit
) {
    Row(
      modifier = Modifier.clickable {
        onClicked(!checked)
      }, verticalAlignment = Alignment.CenterVertically
    ) {
      Checkbox(
        checked = checked,
        onCheckedChange = {
          onClicked(it)
        }
      )
      Text(
        text = label,
        modifier = Modifier.padding(start = 8.dp)
      )
    }
}
```

Jetpack Compose has a built-in `Checkbox()`. It receives the current state (`checked`) and a lambda expression (`onCheckedChange`), which is invoked when the checkbox is clicked. At the time of writing, you cannot pass a label. However, we can achieve something similar by putting `Checkbox()` and `Text()` inside a `Row()`. We need to make the row clickable because we want to change the state of the checkbox when the text is clicked too. To make the checkbox with a label more visually appealing, we can center `Checkbox()` and `Text()` vertically inside the row by setting `verticalAlignment` to `Alignment.CenterVertically`.

Besides the label, `CheckboxWithLabel()` receives two additional parameters:

- `checked` indicates if `Checkbox()` is currently checked
- `onClicked` will be called from `clickable { }` and `onCheckedChange`

While we could have passed a `MutableState<Boolean>` instance instead, the recommended approach is to use immutable values and callbacks for value changes.

Next, let's see how `CheckboxWithLabel()` is invoked. Here's the first part:

```
@Composable
@Preview
fun PredefinedLayoutsDemo() {
  var red by remember { mutableStateOf(true) }
  var green by remember { mutableStateOf(true) }
  var blue by remember { mutableStateOf(true) }
  Column(
    modifier = Modifier
      .fillMaxSize()
      .padding(16.dp)
  ) {
    …
```

`PredefinedLayoutsDemo()` arranges its content vertically by putting it inside a `Column()`. The column fills all the available space (`fillMaxSize()`) and has a padding of 16 density-independent pixels on all 4 sides (`padding(16.dp)`). Three mutable `Boolean` states are assigned to their corresponding variables `red`, `green`, and `blue` using the by keyword. This way, their values can be passed to `CheckboxWithLabel()` without having to add `.value`.

Here's what these invocations look like:

```
CheckboxWithLabel(
  label = stringResource(id = R.string.red),
  checked = red,
  onClicked = { red = it }
)
CheckboxWithLabel(
  label = stringResource(id = R.string.green),
  checked = green,
  onClicked = { green = it }
)
CheckboxWithLabel(
  label = stringResource(id = R.string.blue),
  checked = blue,
  onClicked = { blue = it }
)
```

They are almost the same, differing only in the following aspects:

- The value (red, green, or blue) being assigned to `checked =`
- The label string (`R.string.red`, `R.string.green`, or `R.string.blue`)
- The variable (red, green, or blue) being set inside `onClicked`

Finally, let's find out how the stacked colored boxes are created:

```
Box(
  modifier = Modifier
    .fillMaxSize()
    .padding(top = 16.dp)
) {
  if (red) {
    Box(
      modifier = Modifier
        .fillMaxSize()
        .background(Color.Red)
    )
  }
  if (green) {
    Box(
      modifier = Modifier
        .fillMaxSize()
        .padding(32.dp)
        .background(Color.Green)
    )
  }
  if (blue) {
    Box(
      modifier = Modifier
        .fillMaxSize()
        .padding(64.dp)
        .background(Color.Blue)
    )
  }
}
```

The three colored boxes are put inside another `Box()`, which fills all the available space. To create a gap between it and the last checkbox, I specified a top padding of 16 density-independent pixels.

A colored box is only added if its corresponding variable is `true` (for example, `if (red) { ...}`). All colored boxes fill the available space. As they will be stacked on top of each other, only the last (top) one will be visible. To fix this, the green and blue boxes receive paddings that differ in size: the padding for the blue box (the last one) is 64 density-independent pixels, so in the areas of the padding, the green box becomes visible. The green box has a padding of 32 density-independent pixels, so in this area, the first box (the red one) can be seen.

As you have seen, by combining basic layouts such as Box() and Row(), you can easily create great-looking UIs. In the next section, I will introduce you to an alternative approach where we will define a UI based on constraints.

Creating layouts based on constraints

Defining UIs based on constraints has been the most recent preferred approach in Android's traditional View world because older layouts such as RelativeLayout or LinearLayout could impact performance when they're used in large, multiply nested layouts. ConstraintLayout avoids this by flattening the View hierarchy. As you will see in the *Understanding the single measure pass* section, this is no issue for Jetpack Compose. However, for more complex layouts in a Compose app, you may still want to limit the nesting of Box(), Row(), and Column() to make your code simpler and clearer. This is where ConstraintLayout() can help.

The ConstraintLayoutDemo sample app is a reimplementation of PredefinedLayoutsDemo based on ConstraintLayout(). By comparing the two versions, you get a thorough understanding of how this composable function works. To use ConstraintLayout() in your app, you need to add a dependency to your module-level build.gradle file. Please note that the version number shown here is just an example. You can find the latest version at https://developer.android.com/jetpack/androidx/versions/all-channel:

```
implementation "androidx.constraintlayout:constraintlayout-compose-
android:1.1.0-alpha10"
```

So, how do we define a layout based on constraints? Let's find out by examining the reimplementation of CheckboxWithLabel(). It places text next to a checkbox:

```
@ExperimentalComposeUiApi
@Composable
fun CheckboxWithLabel(
  label: String,
  checked: Boolean,
  onClicked: (Boolean) -> Unit,
  modifier: Modifier = Modifier
) {
  ConstraintLayout(modifier = modifier.clickable {
    onClicked(!checked)
  }) {
    val (checkbox, text) = createRefs()
    Checkbox(
      checked = checked,
      onCheckedChange = {
        onClicked(it)
      },
```

```
        modifier = Modifier.constrainAs(checkbox) {
        }
    )
    Text(
        text = label,
        modifier = Modifier.constrainAs(text) {
            start.linkTo(checkbox.end, margin = 8.dp)
            top.linkTo(checkbox.top)
            bottom.linkTo(checkbox.bottom)
        }
    )
    }
}
```

`ConstraintLayout()` uses a **domain-specific language** (**DSL**) to define the location and size of a UI element relative to other ones. Therefore, each composable in a `ConstraintLayout()` must have a reference associated with it, which is created using `createRefs()`. Constraints are provided using the `constrainAs()` modifier. Its lambda expression receives a `ConstrainScope`. It includes properties such as `start`, `top`, and `bottom`. These are called **anchors** because they define a location that can be linked (using `linkTo()`) to the location of another composable.

Let's look at `Text()`. Its `constrainAs()` modifier contains `bottom.linkTo(checkbox.bottom)`. This means that the bottom of the text is constrained to the bottom of the checkbox. As the top of the text is linked to the top of the checkbox, the height of the text is equal to the height of the checkbox. The following line means that the start of the text is constrained by the end of the checkbox, with an additional margin of 8 density-independent pixels:

```
start.linkTo(checkbox.end, margin = 8.dp)
```

So, in the direction of reading, the text comes after the checkbox. Next, let's look at `ConstraintLayoutDemo()`:

```
@ExperimentalComposeUiApi
@Composable
@Preview
fun ConstraintLayoutDemo() {
    var red by remember { mutableStateOf(true) }
    var green by remember { mutableStateOf(true) }
    var blue by remember { mutableStateOf(true) }
    ConstraintLayout(
        modifier = Modifier
            .fillMaxSize()
            .padding(16.dp)
    ) {
```

```
    val (cbRed, cbGreen, cbBlue, boxRed, boxGreen, boxBlue)
        = createRefs()
CheckboxWithLabel(
    label = stringResource(id = R.string.red),
    checked = red,
    onClicked = { red = it },
    modifier = Modifier.constrainAs(cbRed) {
        top.linkTo(parent.top)
    }
)
...
```

Once we have created the references that are needed to define constraints using `createRefs()`, we add our first `CheckboxWithLabel()`. Its top is linked to (constrained by) the top of `parent`, which is `ConstraintLayout()`. So, the first checkbox with a label is the topmost one. Here's how the second one, which toggles the green box, is invoked:

```
CheckboxWithLabel(
    label = stringResource(id = R.string.green),
    checked = green,
    onClicked = { green = it },
    modifier = Modifier.constrainAs(cbGreen) {
        top.linkTo(cbRed.bottom)
    }
)
```

Its top is constrained by the bottom of the first checkbox with a label (which toggles the red box).

Finally, here's how we need to constrain the third `CheckboxWithLabel()`:

```
modifier = Modifier.constrainAs(cbBlue) {
    top.linkTo(cbGreen.bottom)
}
```

To conclude this section, let me show you how to define the colored boxes. Let's start with the red one:

```
if (red) {
  Box(
    modifier = Modifier
        .background(Color.Red)
        .constrainAs(boxRed) {
            start.linkTo(parent.start)
            end.linkTo(parent.end)
            top.linkTo(cbBlue.bottom, margin = 16.dp)
            bottom.linkTo(parent.bottom)
```

```
            width = Dimension.fillToConstraints
            height = Dimension.fillToConstraints
        }
    )
}
```

Both `start` and `end` are linked to the corresponding anchors of `parent` (which is `ConstraintLayout()`). `top` is constrained by `bottom` of the last checkbox, so the red box appears below it. `bottom` of the red box is constrained by `bottom` of `parent`. Please note that we must set `width` and `height` to the value that we obtained from `Dimension.fillToConstraints`. Otherwise, the box won't have the correct size.

Next, let's look at the constraints of the green box:

```
constrainAs(boxGreen) {
    start.linkTo(parent.start, margin = 32.dp)
    end.linkTo(parent.end, margin = 32.dp)
    top.linkTo(cbBlue.bottom, margin = (16 + 32).dp)
    bottom.linkTo(parent.bottom, margin = 32.dp)
    width = Dimension.fillToConstraints
    height = Dimension.fillToConstraints
}
```

This code is practically the same. One important difference is that all the sides receive a `margin` of 32 density-independent pixels. This is necessary because we want the red box, which is below the green one, to be visible at the locations of the margin. As the red box already has a `top` margin of 16, we must add this value to the `top` margin. You may be wondering why I am not linking to `boxRed` instead. That is because the red box will not be present if its corresponding checkbox is not checked. In this case, the anchor would not be there.

Here's what the constraints for the blue box will look like:

```
constrainAs(boxBlue) {
    start.linkTo(parent.start, margin = 64.dp)
    end.linkTo(parent.end, margin = 64.dp)
    top.linkTo(cbBlue.bottom, margin = (16 + 64).dp)
    bottom.linkTo(parent.bottom, margin = 64.dp)
    width = Dimension.fillToConstraints
    height = Dimension.fillToConstraints
}
```

The only thing I needed to change is the margin on all four sides (`64.dp`) because, otherwise, the box below (the green one) would not be visible.

In a nutshell, this is how ConstrainLayout() works:

- You constrain a composable by linking its anchors to other ones.

- The linking is based on references. To set up these references, you must call createRefs().

The main advantage of combining Box(), Row(), and Column() (that is, using ConstraintLayout() instead) is that you flatten your UI element hierarchy. Think of it like this: in PredefinedLayoutsDemo, I needed to stack the colored boxes in a Box() parent. In ConstrainLayoutDemo, the boxes and the three CheckboxWithLabel() share the same parent (a ConstrainLayout()). This reduces the number of composables and makes the code cleaner.

In the next section, we will once again peek inside the internals of Jetpack Compose. We will learn how the layout process works and why it is more efficient than the traditional View-based approach.

Understanding the single measure pass

Laying out a UI element hierarchy means determining the sizes of all the elements and positioning them on the screen based on the layout strategy of their parent. At first, getting the size of, say, some text doesn't sound too complicated. After all, isn't it determined by the font and the text to be output? Here's an example, with two pieces of text laid out in a Column():

```
@Composable
@Preview
fun ColumnWithTexts() {
  Column {
    Text(
      text = "Android UI development with Jetpack Compose",
      style = MaterialTheme.typography.headlineMedium,
    )
    Text(
      text = "Hello Compose",
      style = MaterialTheme
        .typography.headlineSmall
              .merge(TextStyle(color = Color.Red))
    )
  }
}
```

If you run the preview on a simulated or real device, you will notice that, in portrait mode, the first text requires more space vertically than in landscape mode. The second text always fits into one line. The size that a composable takes onscreen partially depends on the conditions that have been imposed from *outside*. Here, the maximum width of the column (the parent) influences the height of the first piece of text. Such conditions are called **constraints**. You will see them in action in the *Creating custom layouts* section. Please note that they are not the same as the constraints you use in ConstraintLayout().

Once a layout has obtained and measured the size of its content, the layout will position its children (the content). Let's see how this works by looking at the source code of Column():

```
71    @Composable
72    inline fun Column(
73        modifier: Modifier = Modifier,
74        verticalArrangement: Arrangement.Vertical = Arrangement.Top,
75        horizontalAlignment: Alignment.Horizontal = Alignment.Start,
76        content: @Composable ColumnScope.() -> Unit
77    ) {
78        val measurePolicy = columnMeasurePolicy(verticalArrangement, horizontalAlignment)
79        Layout(
80            content = { ColumnScopeInstance.content() },
81            measurePolicy = measurePolicy,
82            modifier = modifier
83        )
84    }
```

Figure 4.2 – Source code of Column()

The composable is very short. Besides assigning a value to measurePolicy, it only invokes Layout(), passing content, measurePolicy, and modifier. We briefly looked at the source code of Layout() in the *Emitting UI elements* section of *Chapter 3*, *Exploring the Key Principles of Compose*, to understand what it means to emit UI elements. Now, we'll focus on the layout process. The measurePolicy variable references an implementation of the MeasurePolicy interface. In this case, it's the result of a call to columnMeasurePolicy().

Defining measure policies

Depending on the values of verticalArrangement and horizontalAlignment, the call to columnMeasurePolicy() returns either DefaultColumnMeasurePolicy (an internal immutable variable) or the result of rowColumnMeasurePolicy(). DefaultColumnMeasurePolicy calls rowColumnMeasurePolicy. Therefore, this function defines the measure policy for any Column(). It returns a MeasurePolicy.

> **Tip**
>
> Please remember that you can look at the source code of a policy by pressing the *Ctrl* key (on a Mac, it's *cmd*) and clicking on a name, such as `columnMeasurePolicy`.

`MeasurePolicy` belongs to the `androidx.compose.ui.layout` package. It defines how a layout is measured and laid out, so it is the main building block for both predefined (for example, `Box()`, `Row()`, and `Column()`) and custom layouts. Its most important function is `measure()`, which is an extension function of `MeasureScope`. This function receives two parameters, `List<Measurable>` and `Constraints`. The elements of the list represent the children of the layout. They can be measured using `Measurable.measure()`. This function returns an instance of `Placeable`, a representation of the size a child wants to span.

`MeasureScope.measure()` returns an instance of `MeasureResult`. This interface defines the following components:

- The size of a layout (`width` and `height`)
- Alignment lines (`alignmentLines`)
- Logic to position the children (`placeChildren()`)

You can find an implementation of `MeasureResult` in the *Creating custom layouts* section.

Alignment lines define an offset line that can be used by parent layouts to align and position their children. For example, text baselines are alignment lines.

Depending on the complexity of the UI, a layout may find that its children do not fit nicely in its boundaries. The layout may want to remeasure the children, passing different measurement configurations. Remeasuring children is possible in the Android `View` system, but this can lead to decreased performance. Therefore, in Jetpack Compose, a layout may measure its content only once. If it tries again, an exception will be thrown.

A layout can, however, query the **intrinsic size** of its children and use it for sizing and positioning. `MeasurePolicy` defines four extension functions of `IntrinsicMeasureScope`. `minIntrinsicWidth()` and `maxIntrinsicWidth()` return the minimum and maximum width of a layout, given a particular height, so that the content of the layout can be painted completely. `minIntrinsicHeight()` and `maxIntrinsicHeight()` return the minimum and maximum height of a layout given a particular width so that the content of the layout can be painted completely. To get an idea of how they work, let's briefly look at one of them:

```
                    The function used to calculate IntrinsicMeasurable.minIntrinsicWidth. It represents the minimum
                    width this layout can take, given a specific height, such that the content of the layout can be painted correctly.

98   ●↓     fun IntrinsicMeasureScope.minIntrinsicWidth(
99              measurables: List<IntrinsicMeasurable>,
100             height: Int
101     ): Int {
102             val mapped = measurables.fastMap {
103                 DefaultIntrinsicMeasurable(it, IntrinsicMinMax.Min, IntrinsicWidthHeight.Width)
104             }
105             val constraints = Constraints(maxHeight = height)
106             val layoutReceiver = IntrinsicsMeasureScope( density: this, layoutDirection)
107             val layoutResult = layoutReceiver.measure(mapped, constraints)
108             return layoutResult.width
109     }
```

Figure 4.3 – Source code of minIntrinsicWidth()

`IntrinsicMeasureScope.minIntrinsicWidth()` receives two parameters: height and a list of children (measurables). The `IntrinsicMeasurable` interface defines four functions that obtain the minimum or maximum values for a particular element (`minIntrinsicWidth()`, `maxIntrinsicWidth()`, `minIntrinsicHeight()`, and `maxIntrinsicHeight()`).

Each element of `measurables` is converted into an instance of `DefaultIntrinsicMeasurable`. As this class implements the `Measurable` interface, it provides an implementation of `measure()`. It returns `FixedSizeIntrinsicsPlaceable`, which provides the smallest possible width for a given `height`. The converted children are then measured by an instance of `IntrinsicsMeasureScope`.

We'll finish looking at the internals of the Compose layout process by turning to `Constraints`. They are, for example, passed to `MeasureScope.measure()`. The class belongs to the `androidx.compose.ui.unit` package. It stores four values: `minWidth`, `minHeight`, `maxWidth`, and `maxHeight`. They define the minimum and maximum values the children of a layout must honor when measuring themselves. So, their width must be no smaller than `minWidth` and no larger than `maxWidth`. Their height must lie within `minHeight` and `maxHeight`.

The companion object defines the `Infinity` constant. It is used to signal that the constraint should be considered infinite. To create a `Constraints` instance, you can invoke the top-level `Constraints()` function.

This was a lot of information. Before moving on, let's recap what we have learned:

- The `Layout()` composable receives three parameters: the content, the measure policy, and a modifier

- The measure policy defines how a layout is measured and laid out

- The intrinsic size of a layout determines the minimum or maximum dimension for the corresponding input

In the traditional View system, a parent view may call the `measure()` method more than once on its children (please refer to `https://developer.android.com/guide/topics/ui/how-android-draws` for details). On the other hand, Jetpack Compose requires that children must be measured *exactly once* before they are positioned. This results in a more performant measurement.

In the next section, we will make use of this knowledge by implementing a simple custom layout. It will position its children from left to right and from top to bottom. When one row is filled, the next one will be started below it.

Creating custom layouts

Sometimes, you may want to lay children out one after another in a row and start a new row when the current one has been filled. The `CustomLayoutDemo` sample app, as shown in the following screenshot, shows you how to do this. It creates 43 randomly colored boxes that vary in width and height:

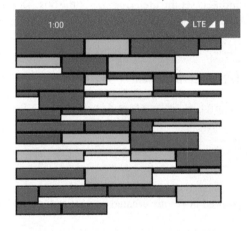

Figure 4.4 – Sample CustomLayoutDemo app

Let's start by looking at the composable function that creates colored boxes:

```
@Composable
fun ColoredBox() {
  Box(
    modifier = Modifier
      .border(
        width = 2.dp,
        color = Color.Black
      )
      .background(randomColor())
      .width((40 * randomInt123()).dp)
      .height((10 * randomInt123()).dp)
  )
}
```

A colored box consists of a `Box()` with a black, two density-independent pixels wide border. The `width()` and `height()` modifiers set the preferred size of the box. This means that the layout could override it. For simplicity, my example doesn't. `randomInt123()` randomly returns either 1, 2, or 3:

```
private fun randomInt123() = Random.nextInt(1, 4)
```

`randomColor()` randomly returns red, green, or blue:

```
private fun randomColor() = when (randomInt123()) {
    1 -> Color.Red
    2 -> Color.Green
    else -> Color.Blue
}
```

Next, I'll show you how the colored boxes are created and set as the content of my custom layout:

```
@Composable
@Preview
fun CustomLayoutDemo() {
    SimpleFlexBox {
        for (i in 0..42) {
            ColoredBox()
        }
    }
}
```

`SimpleFlexBox()` is our custom layout. It is used like any predefined layout. You can even provide a modifier (which has not been done here for simplicity). So, how does the custom layout work? Let's find out:

```
@Composable
fun SimpleFlexBox(
  modifier: Modifier = Modifier,
  content: @Composable () -> Unit
) {
  Layout(
    modifier = modifier,
    content = content,
    measurePolicy = simpleFlexboxMeasurePolicy()
  )
}
```

Custom layouts should receive at least two parameters—`content` and `modifier` with a default value of `Modifier`. Additional parameters may influence the behavior of your custom layout. For example, you may want to make the alignment of children configurable. For simplicity, the example does not do so.

As you know from the previous section, measurement and positioning are defined through a measure policy. I will show you how to implement one in the next section.

Implementing a custom measure policy

At this point, I have shown you almost all the code for the custom layout. The only thing that's missing is the measure policy. Let's see how it works:

```
private fun simpleFlexboxMeasurePolicy(): MeasurePolicy =
  MeasurePolicy { measurables, constraints ->
    val placeables = measurables.map { measurable ->
      measurable.measure(constraints)
    }
    layout(
      constraints.maxWidth,
      constraints.maxHeight
    ) {
      var yPos = 0
      var xPos = 0
      var maxY = 0
      placeables.forEach { placeable ->
        if (xPos + placeable.width >
          constraints.maxWidth
```

```
        ) {
            xPos = 0
            yPos += maxY
            maxY = 0
        }
        placeable.placeRelative(
            x = xPos,
            y = yPos
        )
        xPos += placeable.width
        if (maxY < placeable.height) {
            maxY = placeable.height
        }
    }
  }
}
```

`MeasurePolicy` implementations must provide implementations of `MeasureScope.measure()`. This function returns an instance of the `MeasureResult` interface. You do not need to implement this on your own. Instead, you must invoke `layout()`. This function belongs to `MeasureScope`.

We pass the measured size of the layout and `placementBlock`, which is an extension function of `Placeable.PlacementScope`. This means that you can invoke functions such as `placeRelative()` to position a child in its parent's coordinate system.

A measure policy receives the content, or children, as `List<Measurable>`. As you know from the *Understanding the single measure pass* section, children must be measured exactly once before they are positioned. We can do this by creating a map of `placeables`, invoking `measure()` on each `measurable`. My example doesn't constrain child views further, instead measuring them with the given constraints.

`placementBlock` iterates over the `placeables` map, calculating the location of a placeable by increasing `xPos` and `yPos` along the way. Before invoking `placeRelative()`, the algorithm checks whether a placeable completely fits into the current row. If this is not the case, `yPos` will be increased and `xPos` will be reset to 0. How much `yPos` will be increased depends on the maximum height of all the placeables in the current row. This value is stored in `maxY`.

As you have seen, implementing simple custom layouts is straightforward. Advanced topics such as alignment lines (which help position composables in relation to others) are beyond the scope of this book. You can find more information about them at `https://developer.android.com/jetpack/compose/layouts/alignment-lines`.

Summary

This chapter explored the predefined layouts of Row(), Column(), and Box(). You learned how to combine them to create beautiful UIs. You were also introduced to ConstraintLayout, which places composables that are relative to others on the screen and flattens the UI element hierarchy.

The second main section explained why the layout system in Jetpack Compose is more performant than the traditional View-based approach. We looked at some of the internals of the Compose runtime, which prepared us for the final main section of this chapter, *Creating custom layouts*, where you learned how to create a custom layout and thus gain precise control over the rendering of its children.

The next chapter, *Chapter 5, Managing State of Your Composable Functions*, will deepen your knowledge of state. We will look at advanced use cases and learn more about Jetpack Compose's reactive state primitives.

Questions

1. Using Jetpack Compose, it's perfectly OK to nest layouts. Why is that?

2. Which building blocks are needed to create a custom Compose layout?

3. Which parameters may custom layouts want to receive at least?

5
Managing State of Your Composable Functions

In *Chapter 4, Laying Out UI Elements in Compose*, I showed you how to set the red, green, and blue portions of a color by dragging sliders. We used **state** to store the color portions and passed simple values and callbacks that are invoked when value changes are due to composable functions. Quite a few other sample apps of the previous chapters dealt with state too. In fact, reacting to state changes is critical to how modern mobile apps work.

So far, I have described state as data that can change over time. You learned about a few important functions – for example, `remember { }` and `mutableStateOf()`. I also briefly touched on a concept called **state hoisting**.

This chapter builds on these foundations. For example, you will understand the difference between stateless and stateful composables, and when to choose which. Also, I will show you how events should flow in a well-behaved Compose app.

The main sections of this chapter are the following:

- Understanding stateful and stateless composable functions
- Hoisting state and passing events
- Surviving configuration changes

We will start by exploring the differences between stateful and stateless composable functions. You will learn their typical use cases and understand why you should try to keep your composables stateless. Hoisting state is a tool to achieve that; we will cover this important topic in the second main section. Also, I will show you that you can make your composable functions reusable by passing logic as parameters, rather than implementing it inside the composable.

Finally, the *Surviving configuration changes* section will explore the integration of a Compose UI hierarchy in activities, concerning how to retain user input. If a user changes from portrait to landscape mode (or vice versa), activities are destroyed and recreated. Of course, input should not be lost. We will look at several ways that a Compose app can achieve this.

Technical requirements

Please refer to the *Technical requirements* section in *Chapter 1, Building Your First Compose App*, for information about how to install and set up Android Studio, as well as how to get the sample apps. This chapter covers the FlowOfEventsDemo, StateDemo, and ViewModelDemo samples.

Understanding stateful and stateless composable functions

In this section, I will show you the difference between stateful and stateless composable functions. To understand why this is important, let's first focus on the term **state**.

In the previous chapters, I described state as *data that can change over time. Where* the data is held (e.g., a SQLite database, a file, or a value inside an object) does not matter. What is important is that the UI must always show the current data. Therefore, if a value changes, the UI must be notified. To achieve this, we use **observable** types. This is not specific to Jetpack Compose and is a common pattern in many frameworks, programming languages, and platforms. For example, Kotlin supports observables through **property delegates**. Let's see how they work.

Please note that the following code snippet is not an Android app. While you could execute it in Android Studio using a **Scratch File**, there's a much easier way – Kotlin LaunchPad. You can find it at https://play.kotlinlang.org/. Just enter the following few lines there:

```
import kotlin.properties.Delegates.observable

fun main() {
  for (i in 0..3) counter = i
}

var counter by observable(-1) { _, oldValue, newValue ->
  println("$oldValue -> $newValue")
}
```

observable() returns a delegate for a property that can be read and written to. In the previous code snippet, the initial value is set to -1. The property calls a specified function when its value is changed (counter = i). My example prints the old and new values.

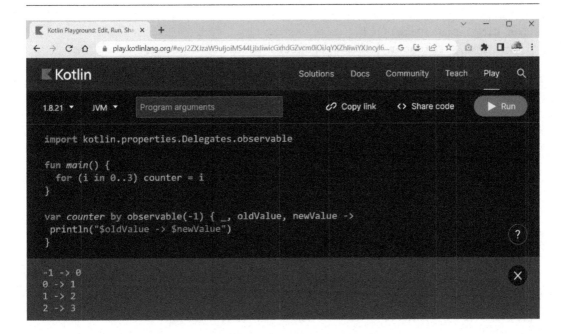

Figure 5.1 – Kotlin LaunchPad

In an imperative UI framework, state changes require modifying the component tree. Such code can be put in the callback function. Fortunately, Jetpack Compose doesn't require this because state changes automatically trigger a recomposition of the relevant UI elements. Let's see how this works.

The `androidx.compose.runtime.State` base interface defines a **value holder**, an object that stores a value of a particular type in a property named `value`. If this property is read during the execution of a composable function, the composable will be recomposed whenever `value` changes because, internally, the current `RecomposeScope` interface will be subscribed to changes of that value.

Please note that to be able to change the value, state must be an implementation of `MutableState`; unlike its immediate predecessor (`State`), this interface defines `value` using `var` instead of `val`.

The easiest way to create `State` instances is to invoke `mutableStateOf()`. This function returns a new `MutableState` instance, initialized with the value that was passed in. The next section explains how to use `mutableStateOf()` to create a stateful composable function.

Using state in a composable function

A composable function is said to be **stateful** if it maintains (remembers) some value. We achieve this by invoking `remember {}`. Let's take a look:

```
@Composable
@Preview
```

```
fun SimpleStateDemo1() {
  val num = remember { mutableStateOf(Random.nextInt(0,
    10)) }
  Text(text = num.value.toString())
}
```

SimpleStateDemo1() creates a mutable state that holds a random integer number. By invoking remember {}, we save the state, and by using =, we assign it to num. We get the random number through num.value. Note that although we defined num with the val keyword, we can change the value with num.value = ... because num holds the reference to a mutable value holder (whose value property is writeable), not the value itself. Think of it as modifying an item in a list, not changing to another list.

We can slightly alter the code, as shown in the following snippet. Can you spot the difference?

```
@Composable
@Preview
fun SimpleStateDemo2() {
  val num by remember { mutableStateOf(Random.nextInt(0,
    10)) }
  Text(text = num.toString())
}
```

SimpleStateDemo2() creates a mutable state that holds a random integer number too. Using by, we do not assign the state itself to num but the value it stores (the random number). This spares us from using .value, which makes the code a little shorter and hopefully more understandable. However, if we want to change num, we must change val to var. Otherwise, we will see a Val cannot be reassigned error message.

You may wonder what remember {} does under the hood. Let's peek into its code and find out:

```
     Remember the value produced by calculation.
     calculation will only be evaluated during the
     composition. Recomposition will always return the value
     produced by composition.
23   @Composable
24   inline fun <T> remember(crossinline calculation: @DisallowComposableCalls () -> T): T =
25       currentComposer.cache( invalid: false, calculation)
26
```

Figure 5.2 – The source code of remember {}

The read-only, top-level `currentComposer` property belongs to the `androidx.compose.runtime` package. It references an instance of `Composer`. This interface is targeted by the Compose Kotlin compiler plugin and used by code generation helpers. You should not call it directly because the runtime assumes that calls are generated by the compiler and, therefore, do not contain much validation logic. The `Composer.cache()` extension function stores a value in the composition data of a composition. So, `remember {}` creates internal state. Therefore, composable functions that contain `remember {}` are stateful.

The `calculation` argument represents a lambda expression that creates the value to be remembered. It is evaluated only once, during the composition (think of it as the first time a composable function is invoked). Subsequent calls to `remember {}` (during recompositions – that is, subsequent calls of the composable containing `remember`) always return this value. The expression is not evaluated again.

However, what if we need to reevaluate the calculation – that is, remember a new value? After all, isn't state data that can change over time? Here's how you can do this:

```
@Composable
@Preview
fun RememberWithKeyDemo() {
  var key by remember { mutableStateOf(false) }
  val date by remember(key) { mutableStateOf(Date()) }
  Column(horizontalAlignment =
  Alignment.CenterHorizontally) {
    Text(date.toString())
    Button(onClick = { key = !key }) {
      Text(text = stringResource(id = R.string.click))
    }
  }
}
```

The preview of `RememberWithKeyDemo()` is shown in *Figure 5.3*. You can observe what happens upon button clicks by starting the interactive preview mode.

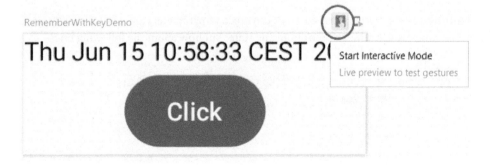

Figure 5.3 – A preview of RememberWithKeyDemo()

`RememberWithKeyDemo()` emits `Column()` with two horizontally centered children:

- `Text()` shows the string representation of a remembered `Date` instance
- `Button()` toggles a Boolean value (`key`)

Have you noticed that I pass `key` to `remember { mutableStateOf(Date()) }`? Here's what happens – when `remember {}` is invoked for the first time, the result of the calculation (`mutableStateOf(Date())`) is remembered and returned. During recompositions, the calculation is not reevaluated unless `key` is *not* equal to the previous composition. In this case, a new value is calculated, remembered, and returned.

> **Tip**
>
> You can pass any number of keys to `remember {}`. If one of them has changed since the previous composition, the calculation is reevaluated, and the new value is remembered and returned.

Passing keys to `remember {}` allows you to change remembered values. However, keep in mind that this makes the composable function less predictable. Therefore, you should carefully consider whether such logic needs to be composable or whether you can pass all state to it.

In the next section, we will turn to stateless composables.

Writing stateless composable functions

`remember {}` makes a composable function stateful. Conversely, a stateless composable doesn't hold any state. Here's an example:

```
@Composable
@Preview
fun SimpleStatelessComposable1() {
  Text(text = "Hello Compose")
}
```

`SimpleStatelessComposable1()` doesn't receive parameters and always calls `Text()` with the same parameters. Clearly, it doesn't hold any state. But how about the following one?

```
@Composable
fun SimpleStatelessComposable2(text: State<String>) {
  Text(text = text.value)
}
```

While it receives state through the `text` parameter, it doesn't store it, and it doesn't remember other state. Consequently, `SimpleStatelessComposable2()` is stateless too. It behaves the same way when called with the same argument multiple times. Such functions are said to be **idempotent**. This makes `SimpleStatelessComposable2()` a good blueprint for your own composable functions. They should be as follows:

- **Fast**: Your composable must not do heavy (that is, time-consuming) computations. Never invoke a web service or do any other I/O. Data that is used by a composable should be passed to it.

- **Free of side-effects**: Do not modify global properties or produce unintended observable effects (modifying state that has been passed to a composable is certainly intentional).

- **Idempotent**: Do not use `remember {}`, do not access global properties, and do not call unpredictable code. For example, `SimpleStateDemo1()` and `SimpleStateDemo2()` use `Random.nextInt()`, which, by definition, is (practically) not predictable.

Such composable functions are both easy to reuse and test because they don't rely on anything that isn't passed in as parameters.

When developing reusable composables, you may want to expose both a stateful and a stateless version. Let's see how this looks:

```
@Composable
fun TextFieldDemo(
  value: String,
  onValueChange: (String) -> Unit
) {
  TextField(
    value = value,
    onValueChange = onValueChange,
    placeholder = { Text("Hello") },
    modifier = Modifier.fillMaxWidth()
  )
}
```

Now, what do you think? Is this version stateful or stateless?

It is stateless because it receives a value and a callback that it invokes upon value changes. And it does not remember anything. Stateless versions are necessary for callers that need to control state or hoist it themselves:

```
@Composable
@Preview
fun TextFieldDemo() {
  val state = remember { mutableStateOf("") }
```

```
TextFieldDemo(
    value = state.value,
    onValueChange = { state.value = it }
)
}
```

This version is stateful because it remembers the state it creates. Stateful versions are convenient for callers that don't care about state.

In summary, try to make your composables stateless by not relying on `remember {}` or other functions that remember state (for example, `rememberLazyListState()` or `rememberSaveable()`). Instead, pass state to the composable, or, as shown in the previous code snippet, pass values that represent the current state and lambda expressions that will react to value changes.

You will see more use cases in the next section.

Hoisting state and passing events

So, state is any value that can change over time. As Jetpack Compose is a declarative UI framework, the only way to update a composable is to call it with new arguments. This happens automatically when state that a composable is using changes. State hoisting is a pattern of moving state up to make a composable function stateless.

Besides making a composable more easily reusable and testable, moving state up is necessary to use it in more than one composable function. You have already seen this in quite a few of my sample apps. For example, in the *Composing and recomposing the user interface* section of *Chapter 3*, *Exploring the Key Principles of Compose*, we used three sliders to create and display a color.

While state controls the visual representation of a composable function (that is, how it looks on screen), **events** notify a part of a program that something has happened. Let's focus a little more on this. My sample `FlowOfEventsDemo` app is a simple temperature converter. The user enters a value, specifies whether it represents degrees Celsius or Fahrenheit, and then hits the **Convert** button:

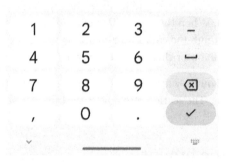

Figure 5.4 – A sample FlowOfEventsDemo app

The user interface consists of Column() with four children – a text input field, a group of radio buttons with text, a button, and result text. Let's look at the text input field first:

```
@Composable
fun TemperatureTextField(
    temperature: String,
    onValueChange: (String) -> Unit,
    modifier: Modifier = Modifier,
    callback: () -> Unit
) {
    TextField(
        value = temperature,
```

```
    onValueChange = onValueChange,
    placeholder = {
      Text(text = stringResource(id =
          R.string.placeholder))
    },
    modifier = modifier,
    keyboardActions = KeyboardActions(onAny = {
      callback()
    }),
    keyboardOptions = KeyboardOptions(
      keyboardType = KeyboardType.Number,
      imeAction = ImeAction.Done
    ),
    singleLine = true
  )
}
```

The text input field receives the current temperature as `String`. When the text is changed, the new value is passed to `onValueChange`. The virtual keyboard is configured to show a **Done** button (`imeAction = ImeAction.Done`) and to allow the input of numbers (`keyboardType = KeyboardType.Number`). When the virtual **Done** button on the soft keyboard is pressed, code passed to the composable through the `callback` lambda will be executed. As you will see a little later, that same code will run if a user clicks on the **Convert** button.

In the next section, I'll show you how to create radio buttons and put them into groups so that only one button is selected at a time. The section also covers the button and result text, which you can see in *Figure 5.4*.

Creating radio button groups

The app converts between degrees Celsius and Fahrenheit. Therefore, a user must choose the target scale. Such selections can be implemented easily in Jetpack Compose using `androidx.compose.material3.RadioButton()`. This composable doesn't show a descriptive text, but it is easy to add one. Here's how:

```
@Composable
fun TemperatureRadioButton(
  selected: Boolean,
  resId: Int,
  onClick: (Int) -> Unit,
  modifier: Modifier = Modifier
) {
  Row(
    verticalAlignment = Alignment.CenterVertically,
```

```
    modifier = modifier
) {
    RadioButton(
        selected = selected,
        onClick = {
            onClick(resId)
        }
    )
    Text(
        text = stringResource(resId),
        modifier = Modifier
            .padding(start = 8.dp)
    )
    }
}
```

RadioButton() and Text() are simply added to Row() and vertically centered. TemperatureRadioButton() receives a lambda expression with the onClick parameter. That code is executed when the radio button is clicked. My implementation passes the resId parameter to the lambda expression, which will be used to determine the button in a group. Here's how:

```
@Composable
fun TemperatureScaleButtonGroup(
    selected: Int,
    radioButtonClicked: (Int) -> Unit,
    modifier: Modifier = Modifier
) {
    Row(modifier = modifier) {
        TemperatureRadioButton(
            selected = selected == R.string.celsius,
            resId = R.string.celsius,
            onClick = { radioButtonClicked(R.string.celsius) }
        )
        TemperatureRadioButton(
            selected = selected == R.string.fahrenheit,
            resId = R.string.fahrenheit,
            onClick = { radioButtonClicked(R.string.fahrenheit) },
            modifier = Modifier.padding(start = 16.dp)
        )
    }
}
```

Two `TemperatureRadioButton()` composables are put in `Row()`. The first one is configured to represent degrees Celsius, and the second one degrees Fahrenheit. Both receive an `onClick` lambda that does almost the same thing – it invokes the `radioButtonClicked` lambda and passes an integer value (either `R.string.celsius` or `R.string.fahrenheit`) to it.

So, what is happening here? Clicks on a radio button are not handled inside `TemperatureRadioButton()` but passed to the parent, `TemperatureScaleButtonGroup()`. The event, a button click, is said to **bubble up**. This way, the parent can orchestrate its children and notify its parent. As you will see shortly, in my example, this means changing some state.

Next, let's see what happens when the user clicks the **Convert** button. This happens inside `FlowOfEventsDemo()`. Here's the overall structure of this composable function:

```
@Composable
@Preview
fun FlowOfEventsDemo() {
  ...
  val calc = {
    val temp = temperature.toFloat()
    convertedTemperature = if (scale == R.string.celsius)
      (temp * 1.8F) + 32F
    else
      (temp - 32F) / 1.8F
  }
  val result = remember(convertedTemperature) {
    if (convertedTemperature.isNaN())
      ""
    else
      "${convertedTemperature}${
        if (scale == R.string.celsius)
          strFahrenheit
        else strCelsius
      }"
  }
  val enabled = temperature.isNotBlank()
  Column( ... ) {
    TemperatureTextField(
      temperature = temperature,
      onValueChange = { temperature = it },
      modifier = Modifier.padding(bottom = 16.dp),
      callback = calc
    )
    TemperatureScaleButtonGroup(
```

```
        selected = scale,
        radioButtonClicked = { scale = it },
        modifier = Modifier.padding(bottom = 16.dp)
    )
    Button(
      onClick = calc,
      enabled = enabled
    ) {
      Text( ... )
    }
    if (result.isNotEmpty()) {
      Text(text = result, …
        )
      }
    }
  }
}
```

The conversion logic is assigned to a read-only variable called `calc`. It is passed to `TemperatureTextField()` and `Button()`. Passing the code that will be executed in response to an event to a composable function, rather than hardcoding it inside makes the composable more easily reusable and testable.

The text that is displayed after conversion is remembered and assigned to `result`. It is reevaluated when `convertedTemperature` changes. This happens inside the `calc` lambda expression. Note that I need to pass a key to `remember { }`; otherwise, the result will also be changed if a user picks another scale.

In the next section, we will look at how state can be persisted. To be more precise, we will turn to configuration changes. If a user rotates a device, the UI should not be reset. Unfortunately, this is what happens with all the sample apps I have shown you so far. It's time to fix this.

Surviving configuration changes

Recall that our definition of state as data that may change over time is quite broad. For example, we do not specify *where* the data is stored. If it resides in a database, a file, or some backend in the cloud, the app should include a dedicated persistence layer. However, until Google introduced Android Architecture Components back in 2017, there had been practically no guidance for developers on how to structure their apps. Consequently, persistence code, UI logic, and domain logic were often crammed into one activity. Such code was difficult to maintain and often prone to errors. To make matters a little more complicated, there are situations when an activity is destroyed and recreated shortly after. For example, this happens when a user rotates a device. Certainly, data should then be remembered.

The `Activity` class has a few methods to handle this. For example, `onSaveInstanceState()` is invoked when the activity is (temporarily) destroyed. Its counterpart `onRestoreInstanceState()` method is called only when such an instance state has been saved before. Both methods receive an instance of `Bundle`, which has getters and setters for various data types. However, the concept of instance state has been designed for the traditional view system. Most activities held references to UI elements and, therefore, could be accessed easily inside `onSaveInstanceState()` and `onRestoreInstanceState()`.

Conversely, composables are usually implemented as top-level functions. So, how can their state be set or queried from inside an activity? To temporarily save state in a Compose app, you can use `rememberSaveable {}`. This composable function remembers the value produced by a factory function. It behaves similarly to `remember {}`. The stored value will survive the activity or process recreation. Internally, the `savedInstanceState` mechanism is used.

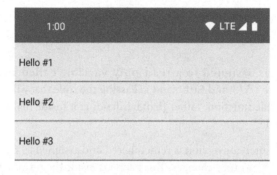

Figure 5.5 – The ViewModelDemo app

The sample `ViewModelDemo` app (*Figure 5.5*) shows you how to use `rememberSaveable {}`. Let's have a look at its main activity first:

```
class ViewModelDemoActivity : ComponentActivity() {
  override fun onCreate(savedInstanceState: Bundle?) {
    super.onCreate(savedInstanceState)
    setContent {
      ViewModelDemo()
    }
  }
}
```

Apparently, we don't need to override `onSaveInstanceState()` to temporarily save the state used with composables. Here's how to achieve this:

```
@Composable
@Preview
fun ViewModelDemo() {
  ...
  val state1 = remember {
    mutableStateOf("Hello #1")
  }
  val state2 = rememberSaveable {
    mutableStateOf("Hello #2")
  }
  ...
  state3.value?.let {
    Column(modifier = Modifier.fillMaxWidth()) {
      MyTextField(state1.value) { state1.value = it }
      MyTextField(state2.value) { state2.value = it }
      ...
    }
  }
}
```

The app shows three text input fields that receive their values from states assigned to `state1`, `state2`, and `state3`. For now, we will focus on the first two. `state3` will be the subject of the *Using ViewModel* section. `state1` invokes `remember {}`, whereas `state2` uses `rememberSaveable {}`. If you ran `ViewModelDemo`, changed the content of the text input fields, and rotated the device, the first one would be reset to the original text, whereas the second one would keep your changes.

MyTextField is a very simple composable. It looks like this:

```
@Composable
fun MyTextField(
  value: String?,
  onValueChange: (String) -> Unit
) {
  value?.let {
    TextField(
      value = it,
      onValueChange = onValueChange,
      modifier = Modifier.fillMaxWidth()
    )
  }
}
```

Have you noticed that value is of type String?? Why would I need a nullable value and, therefore, need to check with value?.let {} that it isn't null? You will find the answer to this question in the following section when we reuse the composable. However, note that for both state1 and state2, this would not have been necessary.

Using ViewModel

While temporarily storing state with rememberSaveable {} works great, an app must still get data that is persisted for a longer time (for example, in a database or file) and make it available as state that can be used in composables. Android Architecture Components include ViewModel and LiveData. Both can be used seamlessly with Jetpack Compose.

Before I show you how, note that there is a heated discussion in the Android community about whether LiveData should still be used at all. Most Compose apps use Kotlin Flows, and in the following chapters, we will do exactly that. However, if you plan to use Jetpack Compose in an existing app, ViewModels using LiveData may just already be there. I genuinely feel a book teaching Jetpack Compose should cover such scenarios too.

First, you need to add a few implementation dependencies to the module-level build.gradle file:

```
dependencies {
  implementation platform('androidx.compose:compose-
    bom:2023.05.01')
  implementation "androidx.compose.ui:ui"
  implementation "androidx.compose.runtime:runtime-
    livedata"
  ...
  implementation 'androidx.lifecycle:lifecycle-runtime-
```

```
    ktx:2.6.1'
  implementation 'androidx.lifecycle:lifecycle-viewmodel-
    compose:2.6.1'
  ...
}
```

The next step is to define a `ViewModel` class. It extends `androidx.lifecycle.ViewModel`. A `ViewModel` class stores and manages UI-related data in a lifecycle-conscious way. This means that data will survive configuration changes, such as screen rotations. `MyViewModel` exposes one property called `text` and a method named `setText()` to set it:

```
class MyViewModel : ViewModel() {

  private val _text: MutableLiveData<String> =
    MutableLiveData<String>("Hello #3")

  val text: LiveData<String>
    get() = _text

  fun setText(value: String) {
    _text.value = value
  }
}
```

My example shows a `ViewModel` class using `LiveData`. Depending on the architecture of an app, you can utilize other mechanisms to work with observable data. However, going into more detail is beyond the scope of this book. You can find additional information in *Guide to app architecture* at `https://developer.android.com/jetpack/guide#fetching_data`.

To access the `ViewModel` class from inside a composable function, we invoke the composable `viewModel()`. It belongs to the `androidx.lifecycle.viewmodel.compose` package:

```
val viewModel: MyViewModel = viewModel()
```

`LiveData` is made available as state like this:

```
val state3 = viewModel.text.observeAsState()
```

Let's take a quick look at the `observeAsState()` source code:

```
40    @Composable
41    fun <T> LiveData<T>.observeAsState(): State<T?> = observeAsState(value)
42
```

Figure 5.6 – The parameterless observeAsState() composable function

observeAsState() is an extension function of LiveData. It passes the value property of its LiveData instance to a variant of observeAsState() that takes parameters. This version is shown in *Figure 5.7*.

```
57    @Composable
58    fun <R, T : R> LiveData<T>.observeAsState(initial: R): State<R> {
59        val lifecycleOwner = LocalLifecycleOwner.current
60        val state = remember {
61            @Suppress( ...names: "UNCHECKED_CAST") /* Initialized values of a LiveData<T> must be a T */
62            mutableStateOf(if (isInitialized) value as T else initial) ^remember
63        }
64        DisposableEffect( key1: this, lifecycleOwner) { this: DisposableEffectScope
65            val observer = Observer<T> { state.value = it }
66            observe(lifecycleOwner, observer)
67            onDispose { removeObserver(observer) } ^DisposableEffect
68        }
69        return state
70    }
```

Figure 5.7 – The observeAsState() composable function

Two important things happen here:

- Either the current (if (isInitialized) ...) LiveData value or an initial value that was passed as a parameter is remembered

- The LiveData value is observed inside DisposableEffect(); whenever it changes, the state is updated (state.value = it)

Have you noticed that the return type of the parameterless version of observeAsState() is State<T?>? That is why I defined MyTextField() in the previous section to receive State<String?>. To be able to use State<String> as with remember {} and rememberSaveable {}, we would need to define state3 like this:

```
val state3 =
  viewModel.text.observeAsState(viewModel.text.value) as
  State<String>
```

In my opinion, this is less favorable than using State<String?> because we use an unchecked cast.

To reflect changes in state in the ViewModel class, we need code like this:

```
MyTextField(state3) {
  viewModel.setText(it)
}
```

Unlike using `MutableState`, we must explicitly invoke the `setText()` method of `MyViewModel` and pass the changed text.

To conclude, `rememberSaveable {}` is simple and easy to use. It is a good choice to save primitive types and objects that implement either `Serializable` or `Parcelable`. However, as it uses the `savedInstanceState` mechanism internally, it comes with the same limitations regarding, for example, size.

For more complex scenarios than those presented in this chapter, you can provide `androidx.compose.runtime.saveable.Saver` implementations, which make your data objects simpler and convert them to something saveable. Bigger apps should use `ViewModel` classes, as recommended for quite a while now by Google. The combination of `ViewModel` and `LiveData` classes can be integrated nicely into composable apps using `observerAsState()`.

Summary

This chapter aimed to provide a more detailed look at state in Compose apps. We started by exploring the differences between stateful and stateless composable functions. You learned their typical use cases and why you should try to keep your composables stateless. Hoisting state is a tool to achieve that. We covered this important topic in the second main section. I also showed you that you can make your composable functions more reusable by passing logic as parameters, rather than implementing it inside the composable. The previous section explored the integration of a Compose UI hierarchy in activities related to how to retain user input. We looked at the differences between `remember {}` and `rememberSaveable {}`, and I gave you a glimpse of how bigger Compose apps can benefit from `ViewModel` classes.

Chapters 1 to *5* introduced you to various aspects of Jetpack Compose, such as composable functions, state, and layout. *Chapter 6, Building a Real-World App*, will focus on one app, providing you with a bigger picture of how these pieces work together to form a real-world app. We will implement a simple temperature and distances converter, focusing on the app architecture and UI, including theming and navigation.

Questions

1.   What are the key differences between stateless and stateful composable functions?

2.   What does the term *idempotent* mean?

3.   What is a simple way to retain state across configuration changes?

6

Building a Real-World App

The previous chapters explored various aspects of Jetpack Compose. For example, *Chapter 2, Understanding the Declarative Paradigm*, compared the traditional view system to composable functions and explained the benefits of the declarative approach. *Chapter 4, Laying Out UI Elements in Compose*, gave you a solid understanding of important built-in layout composables, such as `Box()`, `Row()`, and `Column()`. In *Chapter 5, Managing State of Your Composable Functions*, we looked at state and learned about the important role it plays in a Compose app.

Now, it's time to see how these key elements work together in a real-world app. In this chapter, you will learn how Compose apps can be themed. We will also look at `Scaffold()`, an integrational UI element that picks up quite a few concepts that were originally related to activities, such as toolbars and menus. Finally, we will learn how to add screen-based navigation.

In this chapter, we will cover the following topics:

- Styling a Compose app
- Integrating toolbars and menus
- Adding navigation

We will start by setting up a custom theme for a Compose app. You can define quite a few colors, shapes, and text styles that the built-in Material composables will use when drawing themselves. I will also show you what to keep in mind when you're adding additional Jetpack components that rely on app themes, such as *Jetpack Core Splashscreen*.

The following section, *Integrating toolbars and menus*, will introduce you to app bars and the options menu. You will also learn how to create snack bars.

In the final main section, *Adding navigation*, I will show you how to structure your app into screens. We will use the Compose version of *Jetpack Navigation* to navigate between them.

Technical requirements

Please refer to the *Technical requirements* section in *Chapter 1, Building Your First Compose App*, for information on how to install and set up Android Studio, as well as how to get the example apps. This chapter includes one example app, `ComposeUnitConverter`, as shown in the following screenshot:

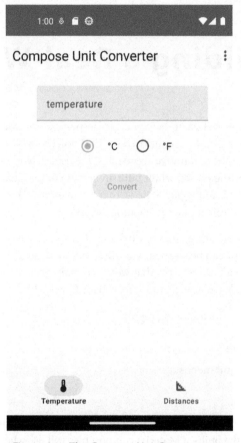

Figure 6.1 – The ComposeUnitConverter app

Styling a Compose app

Most of your Compose UI will likely use the built-in composable functions from the `androidx.compose.material3` package. They implement the design language known as **Material Design** and its successor, **Material You** (which was introduced with Android 12). Material You is the native design language on Android, though it's also available on other platforms. It expands on the idea of a pen, paper, and cards, and it makes heavy use of grid-based layouts, responsive animations, and transitions, as well as padding and depth effects. Material You advocates large buttons and rounded corners. Custom color themes can be generated from the user's wallpaper.

Defining colors, shapes, and text styles

While apps should certainly honor both system and user preferences regarding visual appearance, you may want to add colors, shapes, or text styles that reflect your brand or corporate identity. So, how can you modify the look of the built-in Material composable functions?

The main entry point to Material Theming is `MaterialTheme()`. This composable may receive custom color schemes, shapes, and text styles. If a value is not set, a corresponding default (`MaterialTheme.colorScheme`, `MaterialTheme.typography`, or `MaterialTheme.shapes`) is used. The following theme sets custom colors but leaves the text styles and shapes unchanged:

```
@Composable
fun ComposeUnitConverterTheme(
    darkTheme: Boolean = isSystemInDarkTheme(),
    content: @Composable () -> Unit
) {
    val colorScheme = if (darkTheme) {
        DarkColorPalette
    } else {
        LightColorPalette
    }
    MaterialTheme(
        colorScheme = colorScheme,
        content = content
    )
}
```

The `isSystemInDarkTheme()` composable detects whether the device is currently using a dark theme. Your app should use colors that suit this configuration. My example has two palettes: `DarkColorPalette` and `LightColorPalette`. Here's how the latter is defined:

```
private val LightColorPalette = lightColorScheme(
    primary = AndroidGreen,
    secondary = Orange,
)
```

`lightColorScheme()` is a top-level function inside the `androidx.compose.material3` package. It provides a complete color definition for the Material color specification. You can find more information about this at `https://m3.material.io/styles/color/the-color-system/key-colors-tones`. `LightColorPalette` overrides the default values for `primary` and `secondary`. All the others (such as `background`, `surface`, and `onPrimary`) remain unchanged.

`primary` will be displayed most frequently across your app's screens and components. With `secondary`, you can accentuate and distinguish your app.

> **Tip**
> Material composables typically receive their default colors from composable functions called `colors()`, which belong to their accompanying ...`Defaults` objects. For example, `RadioButton()` invokes `RadioButtonDefaults.colors()` if no `colors` parameter is passed to `RadioButton()`. By looking at these `colors()` functions, you can find out which color attribute you can set in your theme.

You may be wondering how I defined, for example, `AndroidGreen`. The simplest way to achieve this is as follows:

```
val AndroidGreen = Color(0xFF3DDC84)
```

This works great if your app does not require other libraries or components that rely on the traditional Android theming system. We will turn to such scenarios in the *Using resource-based themes* section. Besides colors, `MaterialTheme()` allows you to provide alternative shapes. Let's have a look.

Shapes direct attention and communicate state. The shape scale defines the style of the corners. This ranges in roundedness from square to fully circular. The different sizes of shapes are as follows:

- Extra small (used for autocomplete menus, select menus, snackbars, standard menus, and text fields, for example)
- Small (chips use this shape by default)
- Medium (cards and small floating action buttons)
- Large (floating action buttons, extended floating action buttons, and navigation drawers)
- Extra large (used by large floating action buttons)

To pass an alternative set of shapes to `MaterialTheme()`, which will customize the shape system for all components, you instantiate `androidx.compose.material3.Shapes` and provide implementations of the `androidx.compose.foundation.shape.CornerBasedShape` abstract class for the categories you want to modify (`extraSmall`, `small`, `medium`, `large`, and `extraLarge`). `AbsoluteCutCornerShape`, `CutCornerShape`, `AbsoluteRoundedCornerShape`, and `RoundedCornerShape` are direct subclasses of `CornerBasedShape`.

The following screenshot shows a button with cut corners. While this makes the button look less familiar, it gives your app a distinctive look and may help you emphasize your brand. On the other hand, users expect a consistent look across apps; therefore, please consider whether this level of distinction is really needed.

Figure 6.2 – A button with cut corners

Here is how to make a button with cut corners:

```
@Composable
@Preview
fun CutCornerShapeDemo() {
  MaterialTheme(
    shapes = Shapes(small = CutCornerShape(8.dp)),
  ) {
    Button(
      onClick = {},
      shape = MaterialTheme.shapes.small
    ) {
      Text(text = "Click me")
    }
  }
}
```

By default, buttons use the shape style `full`, which cannot be passed as a `Shapes` parameter. Therefore, you need to set `shape` to `MaterialTheme.shapes.small` when invoking `Button()`.

To alter the text styles that are used by Material composable functions, you need to pass an instance of `androidx.compose.material3.Typography` to `MaterialTheme()`. `Typography` receives quite a few parameters, including `headlineLarge`, `titleMedium`, `bodySmall`, `labelLarge`, and `displaySmall`. They can be grouped into five categories (`display…`, `headline…`, `title…`, `body…`, and `label…`) and three sizes (`…Small`, `…Medium`, and `…Large`). All of these are instances of `androidx.compose.ui.text.TextStyle`. If you do not pass a value for a parameter, a default is used. Here's how to apply `Typography` to your app:

```
@Composable
fun ComposeUnitConverterTheme(
  darkTheme: Boolean = isSystemInDarkTheme(),
  content: @Composable () -> Unit
```

```
) {
  ...
  MaterialTheme(
    ...,
    typography = Typography(
      labelLarge = MaterialTheme.typography.labelLarge.copy
      (
        fontSize = 22.sp
      )
    ),
    ...
  )
}
```

This increases the font size of composables that use `labelLarge`, such as buttons, to 22 scale-independent pixels.

But how do you set the theme? To make sure that your complete Compose UI uses it, you should invoke your theme as early as possible:

```
class ComposeUnitConverterActivity : ComponentActivity() {
  override fun onCreate(savedInstanceState: Bundle?) {
    super.onCreate(savedInstanceState)
    val factory = …
    setContent {
      ComposeUnitConverter(factory)
    }
  }
}
```

In my example, `ComposeUnitConverter()` is the root of the app's composable UI hierarchy since it is invoked inside `setContent {}`:

```
@Composable
fun ComposeUnitConverter(factory: ViewModelFactory) {
  …
  ComposeUnitConverterTheme {
    Scaffold( ...
```

`ComposeUnitConverter()` immediately delegates to `ComposeUnitConverterTheme {}`, which receives the remaining UI as its content. `Scaffold()` is a skeleton for real-world Compose user interfaces. We will be taking a closer look at this in the *Integrating toolbars and menus* section.

If you need to style parts of your app differently, you can nest themes by overriding your parent theme (see *Figure 6.3*). Let's see how this works:

```
@Composable
@Preview
fun MaterialThemeDemo() {
  MaterialTheme(
    typography = Typography(
      headlineLarge = TextStyle(color = Color.Red)
    )
  ) {
    Row {
      Text(
        text = "Hello",
        style = MaterialTheme.typography.headlineLarge
      )
      Spacer(modifier = Modifier.width(2.dp))
      MaterialTheme(
        typography = Typography(
          headlineLarge = TextStyle(color = Color.Blue)
        )
      ) {
        Text(
          text = "Compose",
          style = MaterialTheme.typography.headlineLarge
        )
      }
    }
  }
}
```

In the preceding code snippet, the base theme configures any text that is styled as `headlineLarge` so that it appears in red. The second `Text()` uses a nested theme that styles `headlineLarge` to appear in blue. So, it overrides the parent theme:

Figure 6.3 – Nesting themes

> **Please note**
>
> All the parts of your app must have a consistent look. Consequently, you should use nested themes carefully.

In the next section, we will continue exploring styles and themes. We look at how themes are set in the manifest file, as well as how libraries may influence the way you define your Compose theme.

Using resource-based themes

App styling and theming has been present on Android since API level 1. It is based on resource files. Conceptually, there is a distinction between styles and themes. A **style** is a collection of attributes that specify the appearance (font color, font size, or background color) of a single View. Consequently, styles do not matter for composable functions. A **theme** is also a collection of attributes, but it's applied to an entire app, activity, or View hierarchy. Many elements of a Compose app are provided by Material composables; for them, a resource-based theme does not matter either. However, themes can apply styles to non-View elements, such as the status bar and window background. This may be relevant for a Compose app.

Styles and themes are declared in XML files inside the res/values directory and are typically named styles.xml and themes.xml, depending on the content. A theme is applied to the application or activity inside the manifest file with the android:theme attribute of the <application /> or <activity /> tag. If none of them receive a theme, ComposeUnitConverter will look as follows:

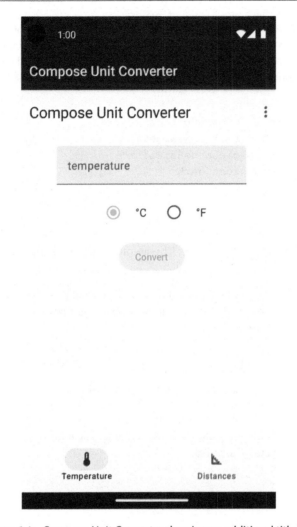

Figure 6.4 – Compose Unit Converter showing an additional title bar

To avoid the unwanted additional title bar, Compose apps should configure a theme without action bars, such as `Theme.Material3.DayNight.NoActionBar`, using `android:theme="@ style/…"` for `<application />` or `<activity />`. This way, `ComposeUnitConverter` looks like *Figure 6.1*. Have you noticed that the status bar has a purple background in this picture?

When Theme.Material3.DayNight is used, the status bar receives its background color from the android:statusBarColor theme attribute. If no value is specified, a default is used. Therefore, to make sure that the status bar is shown in a color that fits the remaining UI elements (our Compose user interface), you should add a file named themes.xml to res/values:

```
<resources>
  <style name="Theme.ComposeUnitConverter"
    parent="Theme.Material3.DayNight">
    <item name="android:statusBarColor">
      @color/android_green_dark
    </item>
  </style>
</resources>
```

In the manifest file, the value of android:theme must then be changed to "@style/Theme.ComposeUnitConverter".

@color/android_green_dark represents a color. Instead of this expression, you could also pass the value directly; for example, #FF20B261. It is, however, best practice to store it in a file named colors.xml inside res/values:

```
<resources>
  <color name="android_green_dark">#FF20B261</color>
  <color name="orange_dark">#FFCC8400</color>
</resources>
```

This way, you can assign a different value to the dark theme. The following version of themes.xml should be put in res/values-night:

```
<resources>
  <style name="Theme.ComposeUnitConverter"
    parent="Theme.Material3.DayNight">
    <item name="android:statusBarColor">@color/orange_dark
    </item>
  </style>
</resources>
```

The status bar now has a background color that fits the remaining UI elements. However, we need to define colors in two places: colors.xml and the Compose theme. Fortunately, this is rather easy to fix. Usually, we pass a literal:

```
val AndroidGreenDark = Color(0xFF20B261)
```

Instead of doing this, we should obtain the value from the resources. The `colorResource()` composable function belongs to the `androidx.compose.ui.res` package. It returns the color associated with a resource that's identified by an ID.

```
@Composable
fun ComposeUnitConverterTheme(
  darkTheme: Boolean = isSystemInDarkTheme(),
  content: @Composable () -> Unit
) {
  val colors = if (darkTheme) {
    DarkColorPalette
  } else {
    LightColorPalette.copy(secondary = colorResource(
      id = R.color.orange_dark))
  }
  MaterialTheme(
    colors = colors,
    …
```

You saw most of this in the *Defining colors, shapes, and text styles* section. The important difference is that I created a modified version of `LightColorPalette` using `copy()`, which is then passed to `MaterialTheme()`. If you store all the colors inside `colors.xml`, you should create your palettes completely inside your theme composable.

As you have seen, you may need to provide some values for resource-based themes, depending on how heavily you want to brand your app. Additionally, certain non-Compose Jetpack libraries use themes too, such as *Jetpack Splashscreen*. This component makes the advanced splash screen features of Android 12 available on older platforms. The images and colors of the splash screen are configured through theme attributes. The library requires that the theme of the starting activity has `Theme.SplashScreen` as its parent. Additionally, the theme must provide the `postSplashScreenTheme` attribute, which refers to the theme to be used once the splash screen has been dismissed. You can find more information about this library at `https://developer.android.com/reference/kotlin/androidx/core/splashscreen/SplashScreen`.

Tip

To ensure the consistent use of colors, the `colors.xml` file should be the single point of truth in your app if more than one component relies on resource-based themes.

This concludes our look at Compose themes. In the next section, we will turn to an important integrational UI element called Scaffold. `Scaffold()` acts as a frame for your content, providing support to top and bottom bars, navigation, and actions.

Integrating toolbars and menus

Early Android versions did not know about action or app bars. They were introduced with API level 11 (Honeycomb). The options menu, on the other hand, has been around since the beginning, but it was opened by pressing a dedicated hardware button and shown at the bottom of the screen. For Android 3, it moved to the top and became a vertical list. Some elements could be made available permanently as actions. In a way, the options menu and the action bar merged. While all the aspects of the action bar were originally handled by the hosting activity, the `AppCompat` support library introduced an alternative implementation (`getSupportActionBar()`).

Using Scaffold() to structure your screen

Jetpack Compose includes several app bar implementations that follow Material You specifications. They can be added to a Compose UI through `Scaffold()`, a composable function that acts as an app frame or skeleton. The following code snippet is the root of the `ComposeUnitConverter` user interface. It sets up the theme and then delegates it to `Scaffold()`:

```kotlin
@Composable
fun ComposeUnitConverter(factory: ViewModelFactory) {
  val navController = rememberNavController()
  val menuItems = listOf("Item #1", "Item #2")
  val snackbarCoroutineScope = rememberCoroutineScope()
  val snackbarHostState = remember { SnackbarHostState() }
  ComposeUnitConverterTheme {
    Scaffold(
      snackbarHost = { SnackbarHost(snackbarHostState) },
      topBar = {
        ComposeUnitConverterTopBar(menuItems) { s ->
          snackbarCoroutineScope.launch {
            snackbarHostState.showSnackbar(s)
          }
        }
      },
      bottomBar = {
        ComposeUnitConverterBottomBar(navController)
      }
    ) {
      ComposeUnitConverterNavHost(
        navController = navController,
        factory = factory,
        modifier = Modifier.padding(it)
      )
    }
  }
}
```

```
    }
}
```

`Scaffold()` implements the basic Material Design visual layout structure. You can add several other Material composables, such as `TopAppBar()` or `BottomNavigation()`. Google calls this a **slot API** because a composable function is customized by inserting another composable into an area or space (slot) of the parent. Passing an already configured child provides more flexibility than exposing lots of additional configuration parameters.

Have you noticed that my example remembers an instance of `SnackbarHostState`? It is used to show a **snack bar**: a brief temporary message that appears toward the bottom of the screen. As `showSnackbar()` is a suspending function, it must be called from a coroutine or another suspending function. Therefore, we create and remember a `CoroutineScope` using `rememberCoroutineScope()` and invoke its `launch {}` function.

In the next section, I will show you how to create a top app bar with an options menu.

Creating a top app bar

App bars at the top of the screen are implemented using `TopAppBar()`. You can provide a navigation icon, a title, and a list of actions here:

```
@Composable
fun ComposeUnitConverterTopBar(menuItems: List<String>,
onClick: (String) -> Unit) {
  var menuOpened by remember { mutableStateOf(false) }
  TopAppBar(title = {
    Text(text = stringResource(id = R.string.app_name))
  },
    actions = {
      Box {
        IconButton(onClick = {
          menuOpened = true
        }) {
          Icon(Icons.Default.MoreVert, "")
        }
        DropdownMenu(expanded = menuOpened,
          onDismissRequest = {
            menuOpened = false
          }) {
          menuItems.forEachIndexed { index, s ->
            if (index > 0) Divider()
            DropdownMenuItem(
              onClick = {
```

```
                    menuOpened = false
                    onClick(s)
                },
                text = {
                    Text(s)
                })
            }
        }
      }
    }
  )
}
```

TopAppBar() has no specific API for an options menu. Instead, the menu is treated as an ordinary **action**. Actions are typically IconButton() composables. They are displayed at the end of the app bar in a horizontal row. An IconButton() receives an onClick callback and an optional enabled parameter, which controls whether the user can interact with the UI element.

In my example, the callback only sets a Boolean mutable state (menuOpened) to true. This opens the menu. content (usually an icon) is drawn inside the button. The Icon() composable receives an instance of ImageVector and a content description. You can get icon data from the resources, but you should use predefined graphics if possible. My example uses Icons.Default.MoreVert. Next, let's learn how to display a menu.

A Material Design dropdown menu (DropdownMenu()) allows you to display multiple choices compactly. It usually appears when you interact with another element, such as a button. My example places DropdownMenu() in a Box() with an IconButton(), which determines the location on the screen. The expanded parameter makes the menu visible (open) or invisible (closed). onDismissRequest is called when the user requests to dismiss the menu, such as by tapping outside the menu's bounds.

The content should consist of DropdownMenuItem() composables. onClick is called when the corresponding menu item is clicked. Your code must make sure that the menu is closed. If possible, you should pass the domain logic to be executed as a parameter to make your code reusable and stateless. In my example, a snack bar is shown.

This concludes our look at top app bars. In the next section, I will show you how to use BottomNavigation() to navigate to different screens using the Compose version of Jetpack Navigation.

Please note

To use the Compose version of Jetpack Navigation in your app, you must add an implementation dependency of androidx.navigation:navigation-compose to your module-level build.gradle file.

Adding navigation

Scaffold() allows you to put content in a slot at the bottom of the screen using its bottomBar parameter. This can, for example, be a BottomAppBar(). Material Design bottom app bars provide access to a bottom navigation drawer and up to four actions, including a floating action button. ComposeUnitConverter adds BottomNavigation() instead. Material Design bottom navigation bars allow movement between primary destinations in an app.

Defining screens

Conceptually, primary destinations are **screens**, something that, before Jetpack Compose, may have been displayed in separate activities. Here's how screens are defined in ComposeUnitConverter:

```
sealed class ComposeUnitConverterScreen(
  val route: String,
  @StringRes val label: Int,
  val icon: ImageVector
) {
  companion object {
    val screens = listOf(
      Temperature,
      Distances
    )

    const val route_temperature = "temperature"
    const val route_distances = "distances"
  }

  private object Temperature : ComposeUnitConverterScreen(
    route_temperature,
    R.string.temperature,
    Icons.Default.Thermostat
  )

  private object Distances : ComposeUnitConverterScreen(
    route_distances,
    R.string.distances,
    Icons.Default.SquareFoot
  )
}
```

ComposeUnitConverter consists of two screens: Temperature and Distances. route uniquely identifies a screen. label and icon are shown to the user. Let's see how this is done:

```
@Composable
fun ComposeUnitConverterBottomBar(
    navController: NavHostController
) {
  BottomAppBar {
    val navBackStackEntry
      by navController.currentBackStackEntryAsState()
    val currentDestination = navBackStackEntry?.destination
    ComposeUnitConverterScreen.screens.forEach { screen ->
      NavigationBarItem(
        selected = currentDestination?.hierarchy?.any {
          it.route == screen.route } == true,
        onClick = {
          navController.navigate(screen.route) {
            launchSingleTop = true
          }
        },
        label = {
          Text(text = stringResource(id = screen.label))
        },
        icon = {
          Icon(
            imageVector = screen.icon,
            contentDescription =
              stringResource(id = screen.label)
          )
        },
        alwaysShowLabel = true
      )
    }
  }
}
```

The content of BottomNavigation() consists of BottomNavigationItem() items. Each item represents a destination. We can add them with a simple loop:

```
ComposeUnitConverterScreen.screens.forEach { screen ->
```

As you can see, the `label` and `icon` properties of a `ComposeUnitConverterScreen` instance are used during the invocation of `BottomNavigationItem()`. `alwaysShowLabel` controls whether the label is visible when an item is selected. An item will be selected if the corresponding screen is currently displayed. When a `BottomNavigationItem()` is clicked, its `onClick` callback is invoked. My implementation calls `navigate()` on the provided `NavHostController` instance, passing `route` from the corresponding `ComposeUnitConverterScreen` object.

So far, we have defined screens and mapped them to `BottomNavigationItem()` items. When an item is clicked, the app navigates to a given route. But how do routes relate to composable functions? I will show you in the next section.

Using NavHostController and NavHost()

An instance of `NavHostController` allows us to navigate to different screens by calling its `navigate()` function. We can obtain a reference to it inside `ComposeUnitConverter()` by invoking `rememberNavController()` and then passing it to `ComposeUnitConverterBottomBar()`. The mapping between a route and a composable function is established through `NavHost()`. It belongs to the `androidx.navigation.compose` package. Here's how this composable is invoked:

```
@Composable
fun ComposeUnitConverterNavHost(
  navController: NavHostController,
  factory: ViewModelProvider.Factory?,
  modifier: Modifier
) {
  NavHost(
    navController = navController,
    startDestination =
      ComposeUnitConverterScreen.route_temperature,
    modifier = modifier
  ) {
    composable(
      ComposeUnitConverterScreen.route_temperature
    ) {
      TemperatureConverter(
        viewModel = viewModel(factory = factory)
      )
    }
    composable(ComposeUnitConverterScreen.route_distances) {
      DistancesConverter(
        viewModel = viewModel(factory = factory)
      )
    }
  }
}
```

`NavHost()` receives three parameters:

- A reference to our `NavHostController`
- The route for the start destination
- The builder that was used to construct the navigation graph

Before Jetpack Compose, the navigation graph was usually defined through an XML file. `NavGraphBuilder` provides access to a simple domain-specific language. `composable()` adds a composable function as a destination. Besides the route, you can pass a list of arguments and a list of deep links.

> **Tip**
> A detailed description of Jetpack Navigation is beyond the scope of this book. You can find more information at `https://developer.android.com/guide/navigation`.

Summary

This chapter showcased how key elements of Jetpack Compose work together in a real-world app. You learned how to theme Compose apps and how to keep your Compose theme in sync with resource-based themes using `colorResource()`.

`Scaffold()` acts as an app frame or skeleton. We used its slot API to plug in a top app bar with a menu, as well as a bottom bar to navigate between screens using the Compose version of Jetpack Navigation.

In the next chapter, *Exploring App Architecture*, we will discuss how to separate UI and business logic. We will revisit `ComposeUnitConverter`, this time focusing on its use of ViewModels. But there's more. I will also explain how to make sure your app feels snappy by introducing side effects.

Questions

1. What parts does a Compose theme consist of?
2. How can your app react to changes between light mode and dark mode?
3. What is `Scaffold()` used for and what are its main elements?
4. What are the basic Compose Navigation building blocks and how do they work?

Exploring App Architecture

In *Chapter 6, Building a Real-World App*, we combined several key techniques of Jetpack Compose, including state hoisting, app theming, and navigation, in a real-world example. `ComposeUnitConverter` stores state in a `ViewModel` and eventually persists it using the *Repository* pattern. In this chapter, I will show you how to pass objects to a `ViewModel` upon instantiation and use these objects to load and save data. In *Chapter 3, Exploring the Key Principles of Compose*, we examined features of well-behaved composable functions. Composables should be free of side effects to make them reusable and easy to test. However, there are situations when you need to either react to or initiate state changes that happen outside the scope of a composable function. We will cover this at the end of this chapter.

These are the main sections of this chapter:

- Persisting and retrieving state
- Keeping your composables responsive
- Understanding side effects

We will start by continuing the exploration of the `ViewModel` pattern we began in the *Using ViewModel* section of *Chapter 5, Managing State of Your Composable Functions*. This time, we will add business logic to the `ViewModel` and inject an object that can persist and retrieve data.

The *Keeping your composables responsive* section revisits one of the key requirements of a composable function. As recomposition can occur very often, composables must be as fast as possible. This greatly influences what the code may and may not do. Long-running tasks—for example, complex computations or network calls—should not be invoked synchronously.

The *Understanding side effects* section covers situations where you need to either react to or initiate state changes that happen outside the scope of a composable function. For example, we will be using `LaunchedEffect` to start and stop complex computations.

Technical requirements

Please refer to the *Technical requirements* section of *Chapter 1, Building Your First Compose App*, for information about how to install and set up Android Studio, as well as how to get the example apps.

The *Persisting and retrieving state* and *Keeping your composables responsive* sections further discuss the example `ComposeUnitConverter` app of *Chapter 6, Building a Real-World App*. The *Understanding side effects* section is based on the `EffectDemo` example.

Persisting and retrieving state

State is app data that may change over time. In a Compose app, state is typically represented as instances of `State` or `MutableState`. If such objects are used inside composable functions, a recomposition is triggered upon state changes. If a state is passed to several composables, all of them may be recomposed. This leads to the *state hoisting* principle: state is passed to composable functions rather than being remembered inside them.

> **Please note**
>
> Here, *passed* doesn't necessarily mean using `State<?>` or `MutableState<?>` as parameters of composable functions. As you've seen in many of my examples, you can instead pass the current value of the state as an ordinary data type and the code that you want to be executed upon state changes as a callback.

Often, state is remembered in the composable that is the parent of the ones using the state. An alternative approach is to implement an architectural pattern called **ViewModel**. It is used in many **user interface** (**UI**) frameworks on various platforms. On Android, it has been available since 2017 as part of **Android Architecture Components**.

The general idea of a `ViewModel` is to combine the data and access logic specific to a certain part of an app. Depending on the platform, this may be a screen, a window, a dialog, or another similar top-level container. On Android, it's usually an activity or fragment. The data is **observable**, so UI elements can register and get notified upon changes.

How the observable pattern is implemented depends on the platform. The Android Architecture Components introduced `LiveData` and `MutableLiveData`. In the *Surviving configuration changes* section of *Chapter 5, Managing State of Your Composable Functions*, I showed you how to use them inside a `ViewModel` to store data that survives device rotations, along with how to connect `LiveData` instances to composable functions.

Here's a brief recap: to connect `LiveData` objects to the Compose world, we first obtain a `ViewModel` instance using `androidx.lifecycle.viewmodel.compose.viewModel()`, and then invoke the `observeAsState()` extension function on a property of the `ViewModel`. The returned state is read-only, so if a composable wants to update the property, it must call a setter that needs to be provided by the `ViewModel`.

So far, I have not explained how to persist state and restore it later. To put it another way: where do `ViewModel` instances get the initial values for their data, and what do they do upon changes? Let's find out in the next section.

Injecting objects into a ViewModel

If a `ViewModel` wants to load and save data, it may need to access a database, the local filesystem, or some remote web service. Yet, it should be irrelevant for the `ViewModel` how reading and writing data works behind the scenes. The Android Architecture Components suggest implementing the *Repository* pattern. A repository abstracts the mechanics of loading and saving data and makes it available through a collection-like interface. You can find out more about the Repository pattern at `https://martinfowler.com/eaaCatalog/repository.html`.

You will see shortly what the implementation of a simple repository looks like, but first, I need to show you how to pass objects to a `ViewModel` upon instantiation. `viewModel()` receives a `factory` parameter of type `ViewModelProvider.Factory`. It is used to create `ViewModel` instances. If you pass `null` (the default value), a built-in default factory is used. The following code snippets belong to the `ComposeUnitConverter` app from *Chapter 6, Building a Real-World App*. The app has two screens, so its factory must be able to create `ViewModel` instances for each of them.

Here's what `ViewModelFactory` looks like:

```
class ViewModelFactory(
  private val repository: Repository
) : ViewModelProvider.NewInstanceFactory() {
  override fun <T : ViewModel> create(
    modelClass: Class<T>
  ): T = if (
    modelClass.isAssignableFrom(
      TemperatureViewModel::class.java
    )
  )
    TemperatureViewModel(repository) as T
  else
    DistancesViewModel(repository) as T
}
```

ViewModelFactory extends the ViewModelProvider.NewInstanceFactory class and overrides the create() method, which belongs to the parent Factory interface. The modelClass represents the ViewModel to be created. Therefore, if the following code is true, then we instantiate TemperatureViewModel and pass repository:

```
modelClass.isAssignableFrom(TemperatureViewModel::class.java)
```

This parameter was passed to the constructor of ViewModelFactory. Otherwise, a DistancesViewModel instance is created. Its constructor also receives repository.

> **Tip**
> If your factory needs to differentiate between more ViewModel instances, you will probably use when instead.

Next, let's look at my Repository class to find out how ComposeUnitConverter loads and saves data. You can see this in the following code snippet:

```
class Repository(context: Context) {

  private val prefs =
    PreferenceManager.getDefaultSharedPreferences(context)

  fun getInt(key: String, default: Int) =
    prefs.getInt(key, default)

  fun putInt(key: String, value: Int) {
    prefs.edit().putInt(key, value).apply()
  }

  fun getString(key: String, default: String) =
    prefs?.getString(key, default) ?: default

  fun putString(key: String, value: String) {
    prefs.edit().putString(key, value).apply()
  }
}
```

Repository uses Jetpack Preference. This library is a replacement for the platform classes and interfaces inside the android.preference package, which was deprecated with **application programming interface (API)** level 29.

> **Important note**
>
> Both the platform classes and the library are designed for user settings. You should not use them to access more complex data, larger texts, or images. Record-like data is best kept in an SQLite database, whereas files are ideal for large texts or images.

To use Jetpack Preference, we need to add an implementation dependency to `androidx.preference:preference-ktx` in the module-level `build.gradle` file. `getDefaultSharedPreferences()` requires an instance of `android.content.Context`, which is passed to the constructor of `Repository`.

Before we move on, let's recap what I showed you so far, as follows:

- `TemperatureViewModel` and `DistancesViewModel` receive a `Repository` instance in their constructor.
- `Repository` receives a `Context` object.
- `ViewModel` instances are decoupled from activities. They survive configuration changes.

The last bullet point here has an important consequence regarding the context we can pass to the repository. Please refer to the *Important note regarding Context* in the following *Using the factory* section to learn more.

Using the factory

Here's how both the repository and factory are created:

```
class ComposeUnitConverterActivity : ComponentActivity() {
  override fun onCreate(savedInstanceState: Bundle?) {
    super.onCreate(savedInstanceState)
    val factory =
      ViewModelFactory(Repository(applicationContext))
    setContent {
      ComposeUnitConverter(factory)
    }
  }
}
```

Both `Repository` and `ViewModelFactory` are ordinary objects, so they are simply instantiated and the required parameters passed to them.

> **Important note regarding Context**
>
> It may be tempting to pass `this` (the calling activity) as the context. However, as `ViewModel` instances survive configuration changes (that is, the recreation of an activity), the context may change. If it does, the repository would be accessing a no-longer-available activity. By using `applicationContext`, we make sure that this issue does not occur. An even better approach is to get the default shared preferences *somewhere else* and pass them to the repository. Please refer to the exercise at the end of this chapter to learn more.

`ComposeUnitConverter()` is the root of the composable hierarchy. It passes the factory to `ComposeUnitConverterNavHost()`, which in turn uses it inside `composable {}` as a parameter for the screens, as illustrated in the following code snippet:

```
composable(ComposeUnitConverterScreen.route_temperature) {
  TemperatureConverter(
    viewModel = viewModel(factory = factory)
  )
}
```

In this section, I showed you how to inject a repository object into a `ViewModel` using simple constructor invocation. If your app relies on a **dependency injection** (**DI**) framework, you will need to use its mechanisms (for example, an annotation) instead. However, this is beyond the scope of this book. Next, we will look at how the `ViewModel` uses the repository.

Keeping your composables responsive

When implementing composable functions, you should always keep in mind that their main purpose is to declare the UI and to handle user interactions. Ideally, anything needed to achieve this is passed to the composable, including state and logic (such as click handlers), making it stateless. If state is needed only inside a composable, the function may keep state temporarily using `remember {}`. Such composables are called **stateful**. If data is kept in a `ViewModel`, composables must interact with it. So, the `ViewModel` code must be fast, too.

Communicating with ViewModel instances

Data inside a ViewModel should be observable. ComposeUnitConverter uses StateFlow and MutableStateFlow from the kotlinx.coroutines.flow package to achieve this. You can choose other implementations of the *Observer* pattern, provided there is a way to obtain State or MutableState instances that are updated upon changes in the ViewModel. This, however, is beyond the scope of this book. TemperatureViewModel is the ViewModel for the TemperatureConverter() composable function. Let's look at its implementation:

```
class TemperatureViewModel(
  private val repository: Repository
) : ViewModel() {

  private val _scale: MutableStateFlow<Int> =
    MutableStateFlow(
      repository.getInt("scale", R.string.celsius)
    )

  val scale: StateFlow<Int>
    get() = _scale

  fun setScale(value: Int) {
    _scale.value = value
    repository.putInt("scale", value)
  }

  private val _temperature: MutableStateFlow<String> =
    MutableStateFlow(
      repository.getString("temperature", "")
    )

  val temperature: StateFlow<String>
    get() = _temperature

  fun getTemperatureAsFloat(): Float =
      _temperature.value.let {
    return try {
      it.toFloat()
    } catch (e: NumberFormatException) {
      Float.NaN
    }
  }

  fun setTemperature(value: String) {
```

```
    _temperature.value = value
    repository.putString("temperature", value)
}

fun convert() = getTemperatureAsFloat().let {
  if (!it.isNaN())
    if (_scale.value == R.string.celsius)
      (it * 1.8F) + 32F
    else
      (it - 32F) / 1.8F
  else
    Float.NaN
  }
}
```

ViewModel instances present their data through pairs of variables, as follows:

- A public read-only property (temperature, scale)
- A private writeable backing variable (_temperature, _scale)

Properties are not changed by assigning a new value but by invoking some setter functions (setTemperature(), setScale()). The reasoning is that mutable data should not be exposed to the outside. You can find more information about this in the *Using ViewModel* section of *Chapter 5, Managing State of Your Composable Functions.*

There may be additional functions that can be invoked by the composable—for example, logic to convert a temperature from °C to °F (convert()) should not be part of the composable code. The same applies to format conversions (from String to Float). These are best kept in the ViewModel.

Here's how the ViewModel is used from a composable function:

```
@Composable
fun TemperatureConverter(viewModel: TemperatureViewModel) {
  val strCelsius = stringResource(id = R.string.celsius)
  val strFahrenheit =
    stringResource(id = R.string.fahrenheit)
  val currentValue =
    viewModel.temperature.collectAsStateWithLifecycle()
  val scale = viewModel.scale.collectAsStateWithLifecycle()
  var result by remember { mutableStateOf("") }
  val calc = {
    val temp = viewModel.convert()
    result = if (temp.isNaN())
      ""
```

```
    else
      "$temp${
        if (scale.value == R.string.celsius)
          strFahrenheit
        else strCelsius
      }"
}
val enabled by remember(currentValue.value) {
  mutableStateOf
  (
    !viewModel.getTemperatureAsFloat().isNaN()
  )
}
Column(
  modifier = Modifier
    .fillMaxSize()
    .padding(16.dp),
  horizontalAlignment = Alignment.CenterHorizontally
) {
  TemperatureTextField(
    temperature = currentValue,
    modifier = Modifier.padding(bottom = 16.dp),
    callback = calc,
    viewModel = viewModel
  )
  TemperatureScaleButtonGroup(
    selected = scale,
    modifier = Modifier.padding(bottom = 16.dp)
  ) { resId: Int ->
    viewModel.setScale(resId)
  }
  Button(
    onClick = calc,
    enabled = enabled
  ) {
    Text(text = stringResource(id = R.string.convert))
  }
  if (result.isNotEmpty()) {
    Text(
      text = result,
      style = MaterialTheme.typography.headlineSmall
    )
  }
```

```
    }
  }
```

Have you noticed that `TemperatureConverter()` receives its `ViewModel` as a parameter?

> **Tip**
>
> You should provide a default value (`viewModel()`) for preview and testability, if possible. However, this doesn't work if the `ViewModel` requires a repository (as in my example) or other constructor values.

`State` instances are obtained by invoking the `collectAsStateWithLifecycle()` extension function of `ViewModel` properties (`temperature` and `scale`), which are `StateFlow` instances.

The code assigned to `calc` is executed when either the **Convert** or **Done** buttons of the virtual keyboard are pressed. It creates a string representing the converted temperature, including a scale, and assigns it to `result`, a state being used in a `Text()` composable. Please note that the `calc` lambda expression calls the `convert()` function of `ViewModel` function to get the converted temperature. You should always try to remove business logic from composables and instead put it inside the `ViewModel`.

So far, I have showed you how to observe (or collect) changes in the `ViewModel` and how to invoke logic inside it. There is one piece left: changing a property. In the preceding code snippet, `TemperatureTextField()` receives the `ViewModel`. Let's see what it does with it here:

```
@Composable
fun TemperatureTextField(
  temperature: State<String>,
  modifier: Modifier = Modifier,
  callback: () -> Unit,
  viewModel: TemperatureViewModel
) {
  TextField(
    value = temperature.value,
    onValueChange = {
      viewModel.setTemperature(it)
    },
    ...
  )
}
```

Whenever the text changes, `setTemperature()` is invoked with the new value. Please recall that the setter does the following:

```
_temperature.value = value
```

The `ViewModel` updates the value of the `_temperature` (`MutableStateFlow`) backing variable. As the `temperature` public property references `_temperature`, its observers (in my example, the state returned by `collectAsStateWithLifecycle()` in `TemperatureConverter()`) are notified. This triggers a recomposition.

In this section, we focused on how communication flows between composable functions and `ViewModel` instances. Next, we examine what can go wrong if the `ViewModel` breaks the contract with the composable and what you can do to prevent this.

Handling long-running tasks

Composable functions actively interact with a `ViewModel` by setting new values for properties (`setTemperature()`) and by invoking functions that implement business logic (`convert()`). As recompositions can occur frequently, these functions may be called very often. Consequently, they must return very fast. This is the case for simple arithmetic, such as converting between °C and °F.

On the other hand, some algorithms may become increasingly time-consuming for certain inputs. Here's an example: Fibonacci numbers can be computed recursively and iteratively. While a recursive algorithm is simpler to implement, it takes much longer for large numbers. If a synchronous function call does not return in a timely fashion, it may affect how the user perceives your app. You can test this by adding `while (true) ;` as the first line of code inside `convert()`. If you then run `ComposeUnitConverter`, enter some number, and press **Convert**, the app will no longer respond.

> **Important note**
> Potentially long-running tasks must be implemented asynchronously.

To avoid situations where the app is not responding because a computation takes too much time, you must decouple the computation from delivering the result. This is done with just a few steps, as follows:

1. Provide the result as an observable property.

2. Compute the result using a coroutine or a Kotlin Flow.

3. Once the computation is finished, update the `result` property.

Here's an example implementation taken from `DistancesViewModel`:

```
private val _convertedDistance: MutableStateFlow<Float> =
  MutableStateFlow(Float.NaN)

val convertedDistance: StateFlow<Float>
  get() = _convertedDistance

fun convert() {
```

```
getDistanceAsFloat().let {
  viewModelScope.launch {
    _convertedDistance.value = if (!it.isNaN())
      if (_unit.value == R.string.meter)
        it * 0.00062137F
      else
        it / 0.00062137F
    else
      Float.NaN
  }
 }
}
```

viewModelScope is available via an implementation dependency to androidx.
lifecycle:lifecycle-viewmodel-ktx in the module-level build.gradle file.
convert() spawns a coroutine, which will update the value of _convertedDistance
once the computation is finished. Composable functions can observe changes by invoking
collectAsStateWithLifecycle() on the convertedDistance public property. But
how do you access convertedDistance and convert()?

Let's find out. Here's a code snippet from DistancesConverter.kt:

```
val convertedValue by
  viewModel.convertedDistance.collectAsStateWithLifecycle()
val result by remember(convertedValue) {
  mutableStateOf(
    if (convertedValue.isNaN())
      ""
    else
      "$convertedValue ${
        if (unit.value == R.string.meter)
          strMile
        else strMeter
      }"
  )
}
val calc = {
  viewModel.convert()
}
```

`result` receives the text to be output once a distance has been converted, so it should update itself whenever `convertedValue` changes. Therefore, I pass `convertedValue` as a key to `remember {}`. Whenever the key changes, the `mutableStateOf()` lambda expression is recomputed, so `result` gets updated. `calc` is invoked when either the **Convert** or **Done** buttons are pressed on the virtual keyboard. It spawns an asynchronous operation, which eventually will update `convertedValue`.

In this section, I have often used the term *computation*. Computation does not only mean arithmetic. Accessing databases, files, or web services may also consume considerable resources and be time-consuming. Such operations must be executed asynchronously. Please keep in mind that long-running tasks may not be part of the `ViewModel` itself but be invoked from it (for example, a repository). Consequently, such code must be fast too. My `Repository` implementation accesses the `Preferences` API synchronously for simplicity. Strictly speaking, even such basic operations should be asynchronous.

> **Tip**
>
> Jetpack DataStore allows you to store key-value pairs or typed objects with protocol buffers. It uses Kotlin coroutines and Flow to store data asynchronously. You can find more information about Jetpack DataStore at `https://developer.android.com/topic/libraries/architecture/datastore`.

This concludes our look at the communication between composable functions and `ViewModel` instances. In the next section, I will introduce you to composables that do not emit UI elements but cause side effects to run when a composition completes.

Understanding side effects

In the *Using Scaffold() to structure your screen* section of *Chapter 6*, *Building a Real-World App*, I showed you how to display a snack bar using `rememberCoroutineScope {}` and `snackbarHostState.showSnackbar()`. As `showSnackbar()` is a suspending function, it must be called from a coroutine or another suspending function. Therefore, we created and remembered `CoroutineScope` using `rememberCoroutineScope()` and invoked its `launch {}` function.

Invoking suspending functions

The `LaunchedEffect()` composable is an alternative approach for spawning a suspending function. To see how it works, let's look at the `LaunchedEffectDemo()` composable. It belongs to the `EffectDemo` example, as illustrated in the following screenshot:

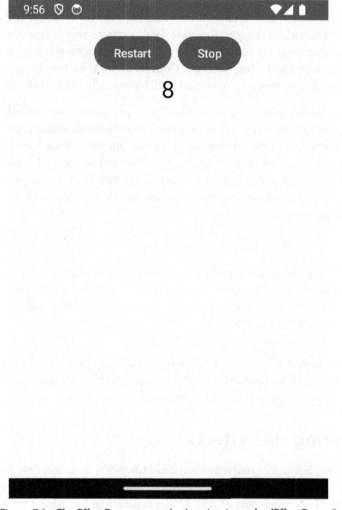

Figure 7.1 – The EffectDemo example showing LaunchedEffectDemo()

LaunchedEffectDemo() implements a counter. Once the **Start** button has been clicked, a counter is incremented every second. Clicking on **Restart** resets the counter. **Stop** terminates it. The code to achieve this is illustrated in the following snippet:

```
@Composable
fun LaunchedEffectDemo() {
  var clickCount by rememberSaveable { mutableStateOf(0) }
  var counter by rememberSaveable { mutableStateOf(0) }
  Column(
    modifier = Modifier
      .fillMaxSize()
```

```
        .padding(16.dp),
    horizontalAlignment = Alignment.CenterHorizontally
) {
    Row {
      Button(onClick = {
        clickCount += 1
      }) {
        Text(
          text = if (clickCount == 0)
            stringResource(id = R.string.start)
          else
            stringResource(id = R.string.restart)
        )
      }
      Spacer(modifier = Modifier.width(8.dp))
      Button(enabled = clickCount > 0,
        onClick = {
          clickCount = 0
        }) {
        Text(text = stringResource(id = R.string.stop))
      }
      if (clickCount > 0) {
        // Code from section
        // Cleaning up with DisposableEffect()
        // will be placed here
        LaunchedEffect(clickCount) {
          counter = 0
          while (isActive) {
            counter += 1
            delay(1000)
          }
        }
      }
    }
    Text(
      text = "$counter",
      style = MaterialTheme.typography.headlineMedium
    )
  }
}
```

clickCount counts how often **Start** or **Restart** has been clicked. **Stop** resets it to 0. A value greater than 0 indicates that another remembered variable (counter) should be increased every second. This is done by a suspending function that is passed to LaunchedEffect(). This composable is used to safely call suspend functions from inside a composable. Let's see how it works.

When LaunchedEffect() enters the composition (if (clickCount > 0) ...), it launches a coroutine with the block of code passed as a parameter. The coroutine will be canceled if LaunchedEffect() leaves the composition (clickCount <= 0). Have you noticed that it receives one parameter? If LaunchedEffect() is recomposed with different keys (my example uses just one, but you can pass more if needed), the existing coroutine will be canceled and a new one is started.

As you have seen, LaunchedEffect() makes it easy to start and restart asynchronous tasks. The corresponding coroutines are cleaned up automatically. But what if you need to do some additional housekeeping (such as unregistering listeners) when keys change or when the composable leaves the composition? Let's find out in the next section.

Cleaning up with DisposableEffect()

The DisposableEffect() composable function runs code when its key changes. Additionally, you can pass a lambda expression for cleanup purposes. It will be executed when the DisposableEffect() function leaves the composition. The code is illustrated in the following snippet:

```
DisposableEffect(clickCount) {
  println("init: clickCount is $clickCount")
  onDispose {
    println("dispose: clickCount is $clickCount")
  }
}
```

A message starting with init: will be printed each time clickCount changes (meaning when either **Start** or **Restart** are clicked). A message starting with dispose: will appear when clickCount changes or when DisposableEffect() leaves the composition.

Important note

DisposableEffect(] *must* include an onDispose {} clause as the final statement in its block.

I have given you two hands-on examples that use side effects in a Compose app. The Effect APIs contain several other useful composables—for example, you can use SideEffect() to publish Compose state to non-Compose parts of your app, and produceState() allows you to convert non-Compose state into State instances.

You can find additional information about the `Effect` APIs at https://developer.android.
com/jetpack/compose/side-effects.

Summary

This chapter covered additional aspects of the `ComposeUnitConverter` example. We continued the exploration of the `ViewModel` pattern we began looking at in the *Using ViewModel* section of *Chapter 5, Managing State of Your Composable Functions*. This time, we added business logic to the `ViewModel` and injected an object that can persist and retrieve data.

The *Keeping your composables responsive* section revisited one of the key requirements of a composable function. Recomposition can occur very often, therefore composables must be as fast as possible, which in turn dictates what the code inside them can and cannot do. I showed you how a simple loop can cause a Compose app to stop responding, and how coroutines are used to counteract this.

In the final main section, *Understanding side effects*, we examined so-called side effects and used `LaunchedEffect` and `DisposableEffect` to implement a simple counter.

In *Chapter 8, Working with Animations*, you will learn how to show and hide UI elements with animations. We will spice up transitions through visual effects and use animation to visualize state changes.

Questions

1. Why can it become necessary to inject an object into your ViewModel?

2. ViewModels do not expose mutable data, but only read-only properties. How is changing the data implemented?

3. Why is it considered a bad practice to keep long-running code in a composable function?

4. What can `LaunchedEffect` and `DisposableEffect` be used for?

Exercise

Passing wrong (being too short-lived) `Context` instances to ViewModels or repositories can lead to unexpected behavior during runtime. By using `applicationContext`, *ComposeUnitConverter* makes sure this doesn't happen. However, in production apps, you should try not to pass the `Context`, but instead the object that uses the context. Let's refactor *ComposeUnitConverter* so that the `Repository` class constructor receives a *SharedPreferences* instance. Where do you need to put `PreferenceManager.getDefaultSharedPreferences()` and what is important to keep in mind? Finally, which other code do you need to adapt once you have refactored the `Repository` class?

Part 3:
Advanced Topics

This part focuses on how to improve the quality of Compose apps, such as by enhancing their visual appeal through animations. It also illustrates how and why to test composable functions, and how to mix composables with old-fashioned Views. Finally, it explains how to make apps look great on foldables and large screens and introduces the Compose Multiplatform framework to leverage your Compose skills beyond Android.

We will cover the following chapters in this part:

- *Chapter 8, Working with Animations*
- *Chapter 9, Exploring Interoperability APIs*
- *Chapter 10, Testing and Debugging Compose Apps*
- *Chapter 11, Developing for Different Form Factors*
- *Chapter 12, Bringing Your Compose UI to Other Platforms*

8

Working with Animations

In the previous chapters, I introduced you to many technical aspects of Jetpack Compose and showed you how to write well-behaving and good-looking apps. Now, adding animations and transitions will make your apps really shine! Compose simplifies the process of adding animation effects greatly compared to the old View-based approach.

In this chapter, you will learn important animation-related application programming interfaces, see animations of single and multiple properties, look at transitions between composables in action, and understand the relationship between state changes and visual interactions.

The main sections of this chapter are as follows:

- Using animation to visualize state changes

- Showing and hiding UI elements with animations

- Spicing up transitions through visual effects

We start by using animations to visualize state changes. Think of a simple use case: clicking a button might change the color of a UI object. However, just switching between colors feels somewhat abrupt, whereas a gradual change is much more visually pleasing. Also, if you want to change several values during the animation, Jetpack Compose can do that easily, too. I'll introduce you to the `updateTransition()` composable, which is used in such scenarios.

The *Showing and hiding UI elements with animations* section introduces you to the `AnimatedVisibility()` composable function. It allows you to apply enter and exit transitions, which will be played back while the content appears or disappears. We will also animate size changes and learn about the corresponding `animateContentSize()` modifier.

In the *Spicing up transitions through visual effects* section, we will be using the `Crossfade()` composable to switch between two layouts with a crossfade animation. Furthermore, you will learn about `AnimationSpec`. This interface represents the specification of an animation. A take on infinite animations concludes the section.

Technical requirements

Please refer to the *Technical requirements* section in *Chapter 1, Building Your First Compose App*, for information about how to install and set up Android Studio, as well as how to get the example apps. This chapter covers the `AnimationDemo` example.

Using animation to visualize state changes

An app's state is app data that may change over time. In a Compose app, state (for example, a color) is represented by `State` or `MutableState` instances. State changes trigger recompositions. The composable `StateChangeDemo()` shows a button and a box. Clicking the button toggles the color of the box between red and white by changing state:

```
@Composable
fun StateChangeDemo() {
  var toggled by remember {
    mutableStateOf(false)
  }
  val color = if (toggled)
    Color.White
  else
    Color.Red
  Column(
    modifier = Modifier
      .padding(16.dp),
    horizontalAlignment = Alignment.CenterHorizontally
  ) {
    Button(onClick = {
      toggled = !toggled
    }) {
      Text(
        stringResource(R.string.toggle)
      )
    }
    Box(
      modifier = Modifier
        .padding(top = 32.dp)
        .background(color = color)
        .size(128.dp)
    )
  }
}
```

In this example, `color` is a simple immutable variable. It is set each time `toggled` (a mutable `Boolean` state) changes. This happens inside `onClick`. As `color` is used with a modifier applied to `Box()` (`background(color = color)`), clicking the button changes the box color.

If you try the code, the change feels very sudden and abrupt. This is because white and red are not very similar colors. Using an animation will make the change much more pleasant. Let's see how this works.

Animating single value changes

To animate a color, you can use the built-in `animateColorAsState()` composable. Just replace the `val color = if (toggled) ...` assignment inside `StateDemo()` with the following code block. If you want to try it out, you can have a look at the `SingleValueAnimationDemo()` composable. It's part of the `AnimationDemo` example app:

```
val color by animateColorAsState(
  targetValue = if (toggled)
    Color.White
  else
    Color.Red
)
```

`animateColorAsState()` returns a `State<Color>` instance. Whenever `targetValue` changes, the animation will run automatically. If the change occurs while the animation is in progress, the ongoing animation will adjust to match the new target value.

> **Tip**
> Using the `by` keyword, you can access the color state like you can with ordinary variables.

You can provide an optional listener to get notified when the animation is finished. The following line of code prints the color that matches the new state:

```
finishedListener = { color -> println(color)}
```

To customize your animation, you can pass an instance of `AnimationSpec<Color>` to `animateColorAsState()`. The default value is `colorDefaultSpring`, a private value in `SingleValueAnimation.kt`:

```
private val colorDefaultSpring = spring<Color>()
```

`spring()` is a top-level function in `AnimationSpec.kt` (which belongs to the `android.compose.animation` package). It receives a damping ratio, a **stiffness**, and a visibility threshold. The following line of code makes the color animation very soft:

```
animationSpec = spring(stiffness = Spring.StiffnessVeryLow)
```

`spring()` returns `SpringSpec`. This class implements the `FiniteAnimationSpec` interface, which in turn extends `AnimationSpec`. This interface defines the specification of an animation, which includes the data type to be animated and the animation configuration. In this case, it is a spring metaphor, though there are others. We will be returning to this interface in the *Spicing up transitions through visual effects* section. Next, we look at animating multiple value changes.

Animating multiple value changes

In this section, I will show you how to animate several values at once upon a state change. The setup is similar to `StateDemo()` and `SingleValueAnimationDemo()`: a `Column()` composable contains a `Button()` composable and a `Box()` composable. However, this time, the content of the box is `Text()`. The button toggles a state, which starts the animation. The following version of `MultipleValuesAnimationDemo()` does not yet contain an animation. It will be inserted below the comment reading `FIXME: animation setup missing`:

```
@Composable
fun MultipleValuesAnimationDemo() {
  var toggled by remember {
    mutableStateOf(false)
  }
  // FIXME: animation setup missing
  Column(
    modifier = Modifier
      .padding(16.dp),
    horizontalAlignment = Alignment.CenterHorizontally
  ) {
    Button(onClick = {
      toggled = !toggled
    }) {
      Text(
        stringResource(R.string.toggle)
      )
    }
    Box(
      contentAlignment = Alignment.Center,
      modifier = Modifier
        .padding(top = 32.dp)
```

```
      .border(
        width = borderWidth,
        color = Color.Black
      )
      .size(128.dp)
  ) {
    Text(
      text = stringResource(id = R.string.app_name),
      modifier = Modifier.rotate(degrees = degrees)
    )
  }
 }
}
```

The `Box()` shows a black border, whose width is controlled by `borderWidth`. To apply borders to your composable functions, just add the `border()` modifier. The child of the box, `Text()`, is rotated. You can achieve this with the `rotate()` modifier. The `degrees` variable holds the angle. `degrees` and `borderWidth` will change during the animation. Here's how this is done:

```
val transition = updateTransition(
  targetState = toggled,
  label = "toggledTransition"
)
val borderWidth by transition.animateDp(
  label = "borderWidthTransition"
) { state ->
  if (state)
    10.dp
  else
    1.dp
}
val degrees by transition.animateFloat(
  label = "degreesTransition"
) { state ->
  if (state) -90F
  else
    0F
}
```

The updateTransition() composable function configures and returns a Transition. When targetState changes, the transition will run all of its child animations toward their target values. The label parameter is used to differentiate different transitions in Android Studio. While it is optional, please consider setting it because the transition can then be better inspected in the **Animation Preview**. Please refer to the *Exercise* section at the end of this chapter for more information about previewing animations.

Child animations are added using animate...() functions. They are not part of a Transition instance but are extension functions. animateDp() adds an animation based on density-independent pixels.

In my example, it controls the border width. animateFloat() creates a Float animation. This function is ideal for changing the rotation of Text(), which is a Float value. There are more animate...() functions, which operate on other data types. For example, animateInt() works with Int values. animateOffset() animates an Offset instance. You can find them in the Transition.kt file, which belongs to the androidx.compose.animation.core package.

Transition instances provide several properties reflecting the status of a transition. For example, isRunning indicates whether any animation in the transition is currently running. segment contains the initial state and the target state of the ongoing transition. The current state of the transition is available through currentState. This will be the initial state until the transition is finished. Then, currentState is set to the target state.

As you have seen, it is very easy to use state changes to trigger animations. So far, these animations have modified the visual appearance of one or more composable functions. In the next section, I will show you how to apply animations while showing or hiding UI elements.

Showing and hiding UI elements with animations

Your user interface will often contain information that need not be visible all the time. For example, in an address book, you may want to show only key attributes of a contact and present detailed information upon request, typically after a button click. However, just showing and hiding the additional data feels sudden and abrupt. Using animations leads to a more pleasant experience, so let's investigate this more.

Understanding AnimatedVisibility()

In this section, we will look at the AnimatedVisibilityDemo() composable function. Like StateDemo(), SingleValueAnimationDemo(), and MultipleValuesAnimationDemo(), it uses a Column(), which contains a Button() and a Box(). This part of the code is simple and straightforward, so there is no need to repeat it in print. The button toggles a state, which starts the animation. Let's see how this works:

```
AnimatedVisibility(
    visible = visible,
    enter = slideInHorizontally(),
```

```
    exit = slideOutVertically()
) {
  Box(
    modifier = Modifier
      .padding(top = 32.dp)
      .background(color = Color.Red)
      .size(128.dp)
  )
}
```

The box is wrapped in `AnimatedVisibility()`. This built-in composable function animates the appearance and disappearance of its content when the `visible` parameter changes. You can specify different `EnterTransition` and `ExitTransition` instances. In my example, the box enters by sliding in horizontally and exits by sliding out vertically.

Currently, there are four transition types:

- Fade

- Expand and shrink

- Slide

- Scale

They can be combined using +:

```
enter = slideInHorizontally() + fadeIn(),
```

The combination order doesn't matter, as the animations start simultaneously.

If you do not pass a value for `enter`, the content will default to fading in while expanding vertically. Omitting `exit` will cause the content to fade out while shrinking vertically.

In this section, I showed you how to animate the appearance and disappearance of content. A variation of this is to visualize size changes (if either `width`, `height`, or both are `0`, the UI element is no longer visible). Let's find out how to do this in the following section.

Animating size changes

Sometimes you want to change the amount of space a UI element requires onscreen. Think of text fields: in compact mode, your app should show only a few lines, while in detail mode it might display 10 or more lines. The `SizeChangeAnimationDemo()` example composable in *Figure 8.1* uses a slider to control the `maxLines` value of `Text()`:

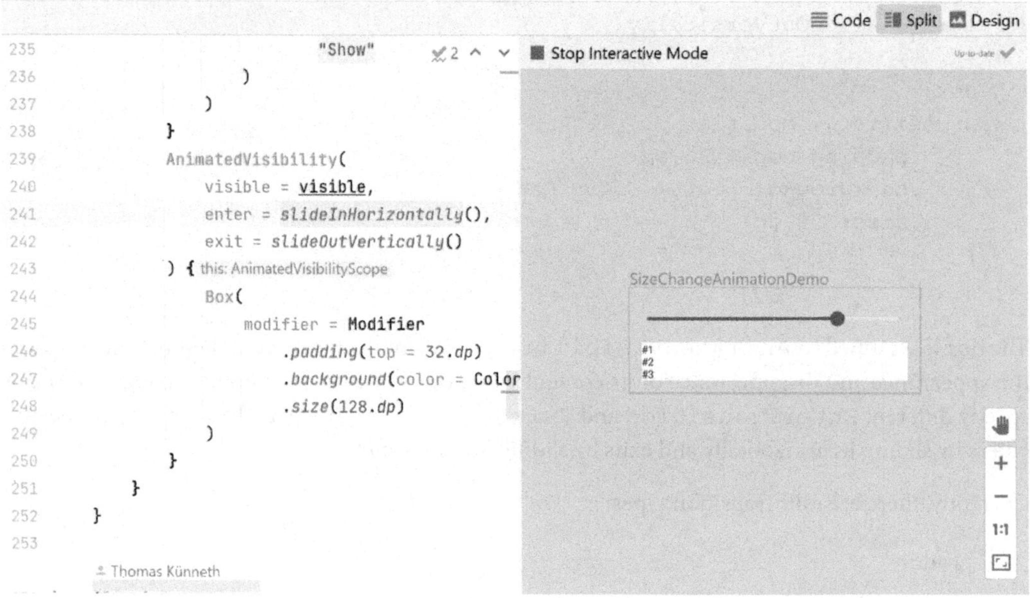

Figure 8.1 – SizeChangeAnimationDemo() in Android Studio split view

The general setup follows the examples from the previous sections: a `Column()` acts as a container for some composable functions, in this case, a `Slider()` and a `Text()`. A state change triggers the animation. Here is the code:

```
@Composable
fun SizeChangeAnimationDemo() {
  var size by remember { mutableStateOf(1F) }
  Column(
    modifier = Modifier
      .padding(16.dp)
  ) {
    Slider(
      value = size,
      valueRange = (1F..4F),
      steps = 3,
      onValueChange = {
        size = it
      },
      modifier = Modifier.padding(bottom = 8.dp)
    )
    Text(
      text = stringResource(id = R.string.lines),
```

```
    modifier = Modifier
      .fillMaxWidth()
      .background(Color.White)
      .animateContentSize(),
    maxLines = size.toInt(),
    color = Color.Blue
  )
 }
}
```

`size` is a mutable `Float` state. It is passed to `Slider()` as its default value. When the slider is moved, `onValueChange {}` is invoked. The lambda expression receives the new value, which is assigned to `size`. The `Text()` composable uses the state as a value for `maxLines`.

The animation is handled by the `animateContentSize()` modifier. It belongs to the `androidx.compose.animation` package. The modifier expects two optional parameters: `animationSpec` and `finishedListener`. I introduced both briefly in the *Animating single value changes* section. `animationSpec` defaults to `spring()`. If you want the lines to appear all at once after some delay, you can add the following:

```
animationSpec = snap(1000)
```

A snap animation immediately switches the animating value to the end value. You pass the number of milliseconds to wait before the animation runs. It defaults to 0. Now, `snap()` returns an instance of `SnapSpec`, an implementation of `AnimationSpec`. We will look at this interface in the *Spicing up transitions through visual effects* section.

The default value of `finishedListener` is `null`. You can provide an implementation if you want your app to get notified when the size change animation is finished. Both the initial value and the final size are passed to the listener. If the animation is interrupted, the initial value will be the size at the point of interruption. This helps to determine the direction of the size change.

This concludes our look at showing and hiding UI elements with animations. In the next section, we focus on exchanging parts of the user interface. For example, we will be using `Crossfade()` to switch between two composable functions with a crossfade animation.

Spicing up transitions through visual effects

So far, I have shown you animations that modify certain aspects of a UI element, such as its color, size, or visibility. However, sometimes you may want to exchange parts of your user interface. This is where `Crossfade()` comes in handy. It allows you to switch between two composable functions with a crossfade animation. Let's look at the `CrossfadeAnimationDemo()` composable in *Figure 8.2* to see how this works:

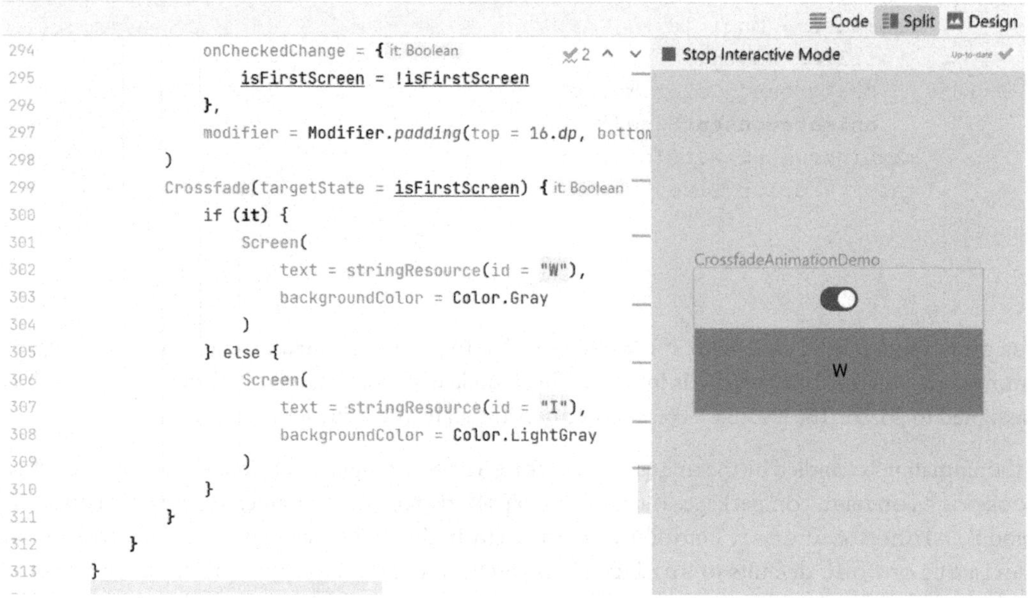

```
                                                      ≡ Code  ⋮⋮ Split  ▨ Design
294          onCheckedChange = { it: Boolean        ✗ 2  ∧  ∨  ■ Stop Interactive Mode          Up-to-date ✓
295              isFirstScreen = !isFirstScreen
296          },
297          modifier = Modifier.padding(top = 16.dp, bottom
298      )
299      Crossfade(targetState = isFirstScreen) { it: Boolean
300          if (it) {
301              Screen(
302                  text = stringResource(id = "W"),
303                  backgroundColor = Color.Gray
304              )
305          } else {
306              Screen(
307                  text = stringResource(id = "I"),
308                  backgroundColor = Color.LightGray
309              )
310          }
311      }
312  }
313 }
```

Figure 8.2 – CrossfadeAnimationDemo() in Android Studio split view

A switch toggles between two screens. As we are focusing on animation, I kept the `Screen()` composable very simple. Here's how it is implemented:

```
@Composable
fun Screen(
  text: String,
  backgroundColor: Color = Color.White
) {
  Box(
    modifier = Modifier
      .fillMaxSize()
      .background(color = backgroundColor),
    contentAlignment = Alignment.Center
  ) {
    Text(
      text = text,
      style = MaterialTheme.typography.headlineSmall
    )
  }
}
```

As you can see, it is just a box with a customizable background color, and there is text styled as a small headline centered inside.

Crossfading composable functions

Like most examples in this chapter, `CrossfadeAnimationDemo()` uses a `Column()` as the root element. The column contains a switch and the screen to display. The one that is shown depends on a mutable `Boolean` state:

```
@Composable
fun CrossfadeAnimationDemo() {
  var isFirstScreen by remember { mutableStateOf(true) }
  Column(
    modifier = Modifier
      .fillMaxWidth()
      .height(192.dp),
    horizontalAlignment = Alignment.CenterHorizontally
  ) {
    Switch(
      checked = isFirstScreen,
      onCheckedChange = {
        isFirstScreen = !isFirstScreen
      },
      modifier = Modifier.padding(top = 16.dp,
                                  bottom = 16.dp)
    )
    Crossfade(targetState = isFirstScreen) {
      if (it) {
        Screen(
          text = stringResource(id = R.string.letter_w),
          backgroundColor = Color.Gray
        )
      } else {
        Screen(
          text = stringResource(id = R.string.letter_i),
          backgroundColor = Color.LightGray
        )
      }
    }
  }
}
```

The onCheckedChange lambda expression of Switch() toggles isFirstScreen. This state is passed to Crossfade() as the targetState parameter. Like in the other animations I've shown you so far, it triggers the animation every time the value changes. Specifically, the content called with the old value will fade out, while the content called with the new one will fade in.

Crossfade() receives an optional animationSpec of type FiniteAnimationSpec<Float>. It defaults to tween(). This function returns a TweenSpec instance configured with the given duration, delay, and easing curve. The parameters default to DefaultDurationMillis (300 ms), 0, and FastOutSlowInEasing. The easing curve is represented by instances of CubicBezierEasing. This class models third-order Bézier curves. Its constructor receives four parameters:

- The *x* and *y* coordinates of the first control point
- The *x* and *y* coordinates of the second control point

The documentation explains that the line through the point (0, 0) and the first control point is tangent to the easing at the point (0, 0), and that the line through the point (1, 1) and the second control point is tangent to the easing at the point (1, 1). CubicBezierEasing is an implementation of the Easing interface (the androidx.compose.animation.core package). Besides FastOutSlowInEasing, you can choose from three other predefined curves to customize your animation: LinearOutSlowInEasing, FastOutLinearInEasing, and LinearEasing.

As Crossfade() receives an animationSpec of type FiniteAnimationSpec<Float>, you can, for example, pass the following code to use a spring animation with very low stiffness:

```
animationSpec = spring(stiffness = Spring.StiffnessVeryLow)
```

In the next section, we will look at how the different specifications of an animation are related.

Understanding animation specifications

AnimationSpec is the base interface for defining animation specifications. It stores the data type to be animated and the animation configuration. Its only function, vectorize(), returns a VectorizedAnimationSpec instance with the given TwoWayConverter, which converts a given type to and from AnimationVector.

The animation system operates on AnimationVector instances. VectorizedAnimationSpec describes how these vectors should be animated; for example, they may simply interpolate between the start and end values (as you have seen with TweenSpec), show no animation at all (SnapSpec), or apply spring physics to produce the motion (SpringSpec).

The FiniteAnimationSpec interface extends AnimationSpec. It is directly implemented by the RepeatableSpec and SpringSpec classes. It overrides vectorize() to return VectorizedFiniteAnimationSpec. Now, FiniteAnimationSpec is the parent of the interface DurationBasedAnimationSpec, which overrides vectorize() to return VectorizedDurationBasedAnimationSpec. Then, DurationBasedAnimationSpec is implemented by the TweenSpec, SnapSpec, and KeyframesSpec classes.

To create a KeyframesSpec instance, you can invoke the keyframes() function and pass an initialization function for the animation. After the duration of the animation, you pass mappings of the animating value at a given amount of time in milliseconds:

```
animationSpec = keyframes {
    durationMillis = 8000
    0f at 0
    1f at 2000
    0f at 4000
    1f at 6000
}
```

In this example, the animation takes eight seconds, which is longer than you'd ever practically use, but it allows you to observe the changes. If you apply the code snippet to CrossfadeAnimationDemo(), you will notice that each letter is visible twice during the animation.

So far, we have looked at finite animations. What if you want an animation to continue forever? Jetpack Compose does this through the CircularProgressIndicator() and LinearProgressIndicator() composables. InfiniteRepeatableSpec repeats the provided animation until it is canceled manually.

When used with transitions or other animation composables, the animation will stop when the composable is removed from the compose tree. InfiniteRepeatableSpec implements AnimationSpec. The constructor expects two arguments: animation and repeatMode. The RepeatMode enum class defines two values: Restart and Reverse. The default value for repeatMode is RepeatMode.Restart, meaning each repeat restarts from the beginning.

You can use infiniteRepeatable() to create an InfiniteRepeatableSpec instance. My InfiniteRepeatableDemo() example composable in *Figure 8.3* shows you how to do this:

Figure 8.3 – Android Studio showing InfiniteRepeatableDemo()

The composable rotates a piece of text clockwise from 0 to 359 degrees. Then, the animation restarts. Text() is centered inside Box():

```
@Composable
fun InfiniteRepeatableDemo() {
  val infiniteTransition = rememberInfiniteTransition()
  val degrees by infiniteTransition.animateFloat(
    initialValue = 0F,
    targetValue = 359F,
    animationSpec = infiniteRepeatable(
      animation = keyframes {
        durationMillis = 1500
        0F at 0
        359F at 1500
      },
      repeatMode = RepeatMode.Restart
    )
  )
  Box(
    modifier = Modifier
      .fillMaxWidth()
      .height(192.dp),
    contentAlignment = Alignment.Center
```

```
  ) {
    Text(
      text = stringResource(id = R.string.app_name),
      modifier = Modifier.rotate(degrees = degrees)
    )
  }
}
```

To create a potentially infinite animation, you first need to remember an infinite transition using `rememberInfiniteTransition()` and then invoke `animateFloat()` on the transition instance. This returns `State<Float>`, which is used with the `rotate()` modifier. The result of `infiniteRepeatable()` (an instance of `InfiniteRepeatableSpec`) is passed to `animateFloat()` as its `animationSpec` parameter.

The animation itself is based on keyframes. We need to define only two frames, the first representing the start and the second representing the end angle. If you want the text to return to its initial angle rather than rotate continuously, you can change the optional `repeatMode` parameter of `infiniteRepeatable()` to `RepeatMode.Reverse`. Its default value is `RepeatMode.Restart`.

If you do so, you should add short delays to the beginning and the end. `keyframes  {}` should look like this:

```
keyframes {
    durationMillis = 2000
    0F at 500
    359F at 1500
}
```

This concludes our look at animation specifications. To finish this chapter, let me briefly summarize what you have learned and what you can expect in the next chapter.

Summary

This chapter showed you how easy it is to use Jetpack Compose to enrich your apps with animations and transitions. We started by using simple animations to visualize state changes. For example, I introduced you to `animateColorAsState()`. We then used `updateTransition()` to obtain `Transition` instances and invoked extension functions, such as `animateDp()` and `animateFloat()` to animate several values based on state changes simultaneously.

The *Showing and hiding UI elements with animations* section introduced you to the `AnimatedVisibility()` composable function, which allows you to apply enter and exit transitions. They are played back while the content appears or disappears. You also learned how to animate size changes using the `animateContentSize()` modifier.

In the final main section, *Spicing up transitions through visual effects*, we used the `Crossfade()` composable function to switch between two layouts with a crossfade animation. Furthermore, you learned about `AnimationSpec` and related classes and interfaces. I concluded the section with a take on infinite animations.

In *Chapter 9*, *Exploring Interoperability APIs*, you will learn how to mix old-fashioned views and composable functions. We will once again return to ViewModels as a means of sharing data between both worlds. I will also show you how to integrate third-party libs in your Compose app.

Exercise

When adding animations to your app, you should make sure that they behave the way you want them to. Android Studio allows you to examine every frame of an animation in the **Animation Preview**. If a composable function with animations can be inspected using the **Animation Preview**, you will spot an icon labeled **Start Animation Preview** (*Figure 8.4*). Which APIs are supported depends on your Android Studio version.

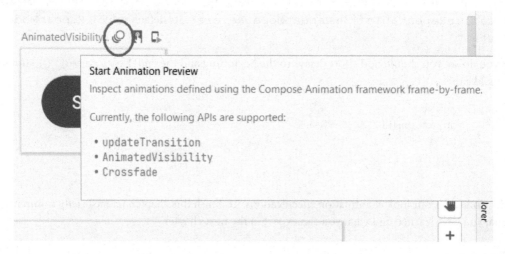

Figure 8.4 – Launching the Animation Preview

Let's try this cool feature. Please open the `CrossfadeAnimationDemo()` composable in the Animation Preview (*Figure 8.5*)

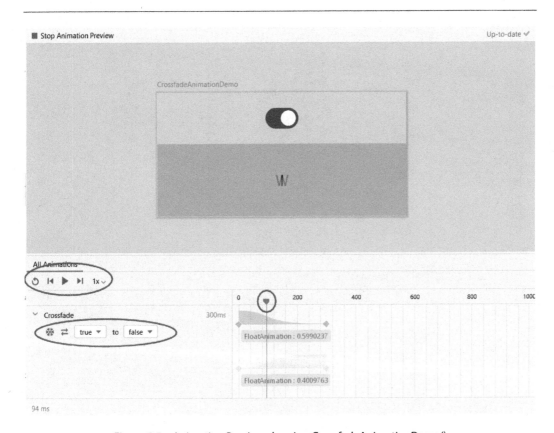

Figure 8.5 – Animation Preview showing CrossfadeAnimationDemo()

You can then inspect every frame by moving the handle in the timeline, change the animation parameters (which become visible after unfolding the corresponding animation), and start and stop all animations at once.

9

Exploring Interoperability APIs

The aim of this book is to show you how to develop beautiful, fast, and maintainable Jetpack Compose apps. The previous chapters helped you get familiar with the core techniques and principles, as well as important interfaces, classes, packages, and—of course—composable functions. The remaining chapters cover topics beyond a successful adoption of Android's new declarative user interface toolkit.

In this chapter, we are going to look at `AndroidView()`, `AndroidViewBinding()`, and `ComposeView` as the interoperability **application programming interfaces** (**APIs**) of Jetpack Compose. The main sections we will cover are the following:

- Showing Views in a Compose app
- Sharing data between Views and composable functions
- Embedding composables in View hierarchies

We start by looking at how to show a traditional View hierarchy in a Compose app. Imagine you have written a custom component (which, under the hood, consists of several UI elements), such as an image picker, a color chooser, or a camera preview. Instead of rewriting your component with Jetpack Compose, you can save your investment by simply reusing it. A lot of third-party libraries are still written in Views, so I will show you how to use them in Compose apps.

Once you have embedded a View in a Compose app, you need to share data between the View and your composable functions. The *Sharing data between Views and composable functions* section explains how to do this with ViewModels.

Often, you may not want to rewrite an app from scratch but rather to migrate it to Jetpack Compose gradually, replacing View hierarchies with composable functions step by step. The final main section, *Embedding composables in View hierarchies*, discusses how to include a Compose hierarchy in existing View-based apps.

Technical requirements

Please refer to the *Technical requirements* section of *Chapter 1, Building Your First Compose App*, for information on how to install and set up Android Studio, as well as how to get the example apps. This chapter covers the `ZxingDemo` and `InteropDemo` example apps.

Showing Views in a Compose app

Imagine you have written a View-based custom component for one of your previous apps—for example, an image picker, a color chooser, or a camera preview—or you would like to include a third-party library such as *Zebra Crossing* (*ZXing*) to scan **Quick Response** (**QR**) codes and barcodes. To incorporate them into a Compose app, you need to add the View (or the root of a View hierarchy) to your composable functions. Let's see how this works.

Adding custom components to a Compose app

The *ZxingDemo* example, shown in the following screenshot, uses the *ZXing Android Embedded* barcode scanner library for Android, which is based on the ZXing decoder. It is released under the terms of the Apache-2.0 License and is hosted on GitHub (`https://github.com/journeyapps/zxing-android-embedded`):

Figure 9.1 – The ZxingDemo example app

My example continuously scans for barcodes and QR codes. The decorated barcode view is provided by the library. If the scanner engine provides a result, the corresponding text is shown as an overlay using Text().

To use *ZXing Android Embedded*, you need to add an implementation dependency to your module-level build.gradle file, as follows:

```
implementation 'com.journeyapps:zxing-android-embedded:4.3.0'
```

The scanner accesses the camera and (optionally) the device vibrator. The app must request at least the android.permission.WAKE_LOCK and android.permission.CAMERA permissions in the manifest, and the android.permission.CAMERA permission during runtime:

```
class ZxingDemoActivity : ComponentActivity() {
  private lateinit var barcodeView: DecoratedBarcodeView

  ...

  private val requestPermission = registerForActivityResult
  (
    ActivityResultContracts.RequestPermission()
  ) {
    isGranted -> if (isGranted) { barcodeView.resume() }
  }
  ...

  override fun onResume() {
    super.onResume()
    requestPermission.launch(Manifest.permission.CAMERA)
  }

  override fun onPause() {
    super.onPause()
    barcodeView.pause()
  }
  ...
}
```

My implementation uses ActivityResultContracts.RequestPermission, which replaces the old approach overriding onRequestPermissionsResult(). Also, depending on the lifecycle of the activity, the scanner must be paused and resumed. For the sake of simplicity, I use a lateinit variable named barcodeView and invoke barcodeView.pause() and barcodeView.resume() when needed.

> **Please note**
>
> While there is nothing wrong in using `lateinit`, you need to make sure that the corresponding variable is accessed only after it has been properly initialized. Your users will experience crashes during runtime otherwise. My example makes sure that no such crashes occur.

Next, I will show you how to initialize the scanner library. This involves inflating a layout file (named `layout.xml`). Let's have a look at it:

```xml
<?xml version="1.0" encoding="utf-8"?>
<com.journeyapps.barcodescanner.DecoratedBarcodeView
  xmlns:android="http://schemas.android.com/apk/res/
    android"
  android:id="@+id/barcode_scanner"
  android:layout_width="match_parent"
  android:layout_height="match_parent"
  android:layout_alignParentTop="true" />
```

The layout consists of only one element, `DecoratedBarcodeView`. It is configured to fill all available space. The following code snippet is part of `onCreate()`. Please remember that `barcodeView` is accessed in some lifecycle functions such as `onPause()`, and is therefore a `lateinit` property:

```kotlin
val root = layoutInflater.inflate(R.layout.layout, null)
barcodeView = root.findViewById(R.id.barcode_scanner)
val formats = listOf(BarcodeFormat.QR_CODE,
  BarcodeFormat.CODE_39)
barcodeView.barcodeView.decoderFactory =
  DefaultDecoderFactory(formats)
barcodeView.initializeFromIntent(intent)
val callback = object : BarcodeCallback {
  override fun barcodeResult(result: BarcodeResult) {
    if (result.text == null || result.text == text.value) {
      return
    }
    text.value = result.text
  }
}
barcodeView.decodeContinuous(callback)
```

First, `layout.xml` is inflated and assigned to `root`. We need `root` to get a reference to the Barcode View using `findViewById()`. After that, `barcodeView` is initialized (`initializeFromIntent()`) and configured (by setting a decoder factory). Finally, the continuous scanning process is started using `decodeContinuous()`. The `callback` lambda expression is invoked every time a new scan result is available. The `text` variable is defined as follows:

```kotlin
private val text = MutableStateFlow("")
```

I am using `MutableStateFlow` because it can easily be collected as state. Before I show you how to access it inside a composable function, let's briefly recap, as follows:

- We have set up and activated the scanner library

- When the library detects a barcode or a QR code, it updates the value of a `MutableStateFlow` instance

- We defined and initialized two `View` instances—`root` and `barcodeView`

Now it's time to show you how to access the state obtained from the ViewModel inside a composable:

```
setContent {
  with(text.collectAsStateWithLifecycle()) {
    ZxingDemo(
      root = root,
      value = value
    )
  }
}
```

The value of the state (we get the state with `collectAsStateWithLifecycle()`) and `root` are passed to the `ZxingDemo()` composable. Inside `ZxingDemo()`, we display `value` using `Text()`. The `root` parameter is used to include the View hierarchy in the Compose UI. The corresponding code is illustrated in the following snippet:

```
@Composable
fun ZxingDemo(root: View, value: String) {
  Box(
    modifier = Modifier.fillMaxSize(),
    contentAlignment = Alignment.TopCenter
  ) {
    AndroidView(modifier = Modifier.fillMaxSize(),
      factory = {
        root
      }
    )
    if (value.isNotBlank()) {
      Text(
        modifier = Modifier.padding(16.dp),
        text = value,
        color = Color.White,
        style = MaterialTheme.typography.headlineMedium
      )
```

```
        }
      }
    }
```

The UI consists of a `Box()` composable with two children, `AndroidView()` and `Text()`. `AndroidView()` receives a `factory` block, which just returns `root` (the View hierarchy containing the scanner viewfinder). The `Text()` composable shows the last scan result, if `value` is not blank.

The `factory` block is called exactly once, to obtain the View to be composed. It will always be invoked on the UI thread, so you can set View properties as needed. In my example, this is not needed, as all initialization has already been done in `onCreate()`. Configuring the barcode scanner should not be done in a composable, because preparing the camera and preview is potentially time-consuming. Also, parts of the component tree are accessed on the activity level, therefore references to children (`barcodeView`) are needed anyway.

Besides `factory`, you can pass an additional lambda code block to `AndroidView()` via the `update` parameter. Its default value is `NoOpUpdate`. The lambda will be invoked during a recomposition. Its main task is to update `View` properties. We will look at using `update` in the *Inflating View hierarchies with AndroidViewBinding()* section.

In this section, I have shown you how to include a View hierarchy in your Compose app using `AndroidView()`. This composable function is one of the important pieces of the Jetpack Compose interoperability APIs. We used `layoutInflater.inflate()` to inflate the component tree and `findViewById()` to access one of its children. Modern View-based apps try to avoid `findViewById()` and use *View Binding* instead. In the next section, you will learn how to combine View Binding and composable functions.

Inflating View hierarchies with AndroidViewBinding()

Traditionally, activities held references to Views in `lateinit` properties if the corresponding components needed to be modified in different functions. The *Inflating layout files* section of *Chapter 2, Understanding the Declarative Paradigm*, discussed some issues with this approach and introduced View Binding as a solution. It was adopted by many apps. Therefore, if you want to migrate an existing app to Jetpack Compose, you likely need to combine **View Binding** and composable functions. This section explains how to achieve that.

The following screenshot shows the *InteropDemo* example app:

Figure 9.2 – The InteropDemo example app showing ComposeActivity

The *InteropDemo* example consists of two activities. One (`ViewActivity`) integrates a composable function in a `View` hierarchy. We will turn to this in the *Embedding composables in View hierarchies* section. The second one, `ComposeActivity`, does the opposite: it inflates a `View` hierarchy using View Binding and shows the component tree inside a `Column()` composable. Let's take a look at the following code block:

```
class ComposeActivity : ComponentActivity() {
  override fun onCreate(savedInstanceState: Bundle?) {
    super.onCreate(savedInstanceState)
    val viewModel: InteropDemoViewModel by viewModels()
    viewModel.setSliderValue(intent.getFloatExtra(KEY, 0F))
    setContent {
      ViewIntegrationDemo(viewModel) {
        val i = Intent(
          this,
```

```
            ViewActivity::class.java
        )
        i.putExtra(KEY, viewModel.sliderValue.value)
        startActivity(i)
      }
    }
  }
}
```

The root composable is called `ViewIntegrationDemo()`. It receives a ViewModel and a lambda expression. The ViewModel is used to share data between the Compose and the `View` hierarchies, which I will discuss in the *Sharing data between Views and composable functions* section. The lambda expression starts `ViewActivity` and passes a value from the ViewModel (`sliderValue`). Next, let's have a look at `ViewIntegrationDemo()`:

```
@Composable
fun ViewIntegrationDemo(viewModel: InteropDemoViewModel,
                        onClick: () -> Unit) {
  val sliderValueState =
    viewModel.sliderValue.collectAsStateWithLifecycle()
  Scaffold( ... ) { padding ->
    Column( ... ) {
      Slider( ... )
      AndroidViewBinding(
        modifier = Modifier.fillMaxWidth(),
        factory = CustomBinding::inflate
      ) {
        // Here Views will be updated
      }
    }
  }
}
```

`Scaffold()` is an important integrational composable function. It structures a Compose screen. Besides the top and bottom bars, it contains some content—in this case, a `Column()` composable with two children, `Slider()` and `AndroidViewBinding()`. The slider gets its current value from a ViewModel and propagates changes back to it. You will learn more about that in the *Revisiting ViewModels* section.

To use `AndroidViewBinding()` in your app, add the following implementation dependency to your `build.gradle` file:

```
dependencies {
    ...
    implementation "androidx.compose.ui:ui-viewbinding"
}
```

`AndroidViewBinding()` is similar to `AndroidView()`. A `factory` block creates a View hierarchy to be composed. `CustomBinding::inflate` inflates the layout from the `custom.xml` file represented by `CustomBinding` and returns an instance of this type. The class is created and updated during builds. It provides constants that reflect the contents of a layout file named `custom.xml`. Here is an abridged version:

```xml
<?xml version="1.0" encoding="utf-8"?>
<androidx.constraintlayout.widget.ConstraintLayout
  xmlns:android="http://schemas.android.com/apk/res/
    android"
  xmlns:app="http://schemas.android.com/apk/res-auto"
  android:layout_width="match_parent"
  android:layout_height="match_parent">

  <com.google.android.material.textview.MaterialTextView
    android:id="@+id/textView"
    ... />

  <com.google.android.material.button.MaterialButton
    android:id="@+id/button"
    ...
    android:text="@string/view_activity"
    ...
    app:layout_constraintTop_toBottomOf="@id/textView" />

</androidx.constraintlayout.widget.ConstraintLayout>
```

This `ConstraintLayout` has two children, a `MaterialTextView` and a `MaterialButton`. A button click invokes the lambda expression passed to `ViewIntegrationDemo()`. The text field receives the current slider value. This is done in the `update` block. The following code belongs below the `// Here Views will be updated` comment inside `ViewIntegrationDemo()`:

```
textView.text = sliderValueState.value.toString()
button.setOnClickListener {
  onClick()
}
```

You may be wondering where `textView` and `button` are defined, and why they can be accessed immediately. The `update` block is invoked right after the layout is inflated. It is an extension function of the type whose instance is returned by `inflate`—in my example, `CustomBinding`. Because the **identifiers (IDs)** of the button and the text field in `custom.xml` are `button` and `textView`, there are corresponding variables in `CustomBinding`.

The `update` block is also invoked when a value being used inside it (`sliderValueState.value`) changes. In the next section, we look at when and where such changes are triggered.

Sharing data between Views and composable functions

State is app data that may change over time. Recomposition occurs when state being used by a composable changes. To achieve something similar in the traditional View world, we need to store data in a way that changes to it can be observed. There are many implementations of the *Observable* pattern. The Android Architecture Components (and subsequent Jetpack versions) include `LiveData` and `MutableLiveData`. Both have been used frequently inside ViewModels to store state outside activities, but are increasingly often replaced by other techniques, such as `StateFlow` and `MutableStateFlow`.

Revisiting ViewModels

I introduced you to ViewModels in the *Surviving configuration changes* section of *Chapter 5, Managing State of Your Composable Functions*, and the *Persisting and retrieving state* section of *Chapter 7, Exploring App Architecture*. Before we look at how to use ViewModels to synchronize data between Views and composable functions, let's briefly recap the key techniques, as follows:

- To create or get an instance of a ViewModel, use the top-level `viewModels()` function, which belongs to the `androidx.activity` package
- To observe `StateFlow` instances as Compose state, invoke the `collectAsStateWithLifecycle()` extension function on a ViewModel property inside a composable function
- To change a ViewModel property, invoke the corresponding setter

Please make sure to add the implementation dependencies of the following files as needed:

```
def lifecycle_version = …
implementation "androidx.lifecycle:lifecycle-viewmodel-ktx:$lifecycle_
version"
implementation "androidx.lifecycle:lifecycle-runtime-
compose:$lifecycle_version"
implementation "androidx.lifecycle:lifecycle-viewmodel-
compose:$lifecycle_version"
```

Now that we have refamiliarized ourselves with the key techniques related to ViewModels, let's look at how the synchronization between Views and composable functions works. *Synchronization* means that a composable function and the code related to a View observe the same ViewModel property and may trigger changes on that property. Triggering changes is usually done by invoking a setter. For a `Slider()` composable, it could look like this:

```
Slider(
  modifier = Modifier.fillMaxWidth(),
  onValueChange = {
    viewModel.setSliderValue(it)
  },
  value = sliderValueState.value
)
```

This example also shows the readout inside a composable (`sliderValueState.value`). Here is how `sliderValueState` has been defined:

```
val sliderValueState =
  viewModel.sliderValue.collectAsStateWithLifecycle()
```

Next, let's look at traditional (non-Compose) code using View Binding. The following examples are part of `ViewActivity`, which belongs to the *InteropDemo* example.

Combining View Binding and ViewModels

Activities taking advantage of View Binding usually have a `lateinit` property named `binding`, as illustrated in the following code snippet:

```
private lateinit var binding: LayoutBinding
…
binding = LayoutBinding.inflate(layoutInflater)
```

`LayoutBinding.inflate()` returns an instance of `LayoutBinding`. The root of the component tree can then be accessed using `binding.root`. It is passed to `setContentView()`. Here is an abridged version of the corresponding layout file (`layout.xml`):

```
<?xml version="1.0" encoding="utf-8"?>
<androidx.coordinatorlayout.widget.CoordinatorLayout
  xmlns:android="http://schemas.android.com/apk/res/
    android"
  xmlns:app="http://schemas.android.com/apk/res-auto"
  android:layout_width="match_parent"
  android:layout_height="match_parent">

  <androidx.core.widget.NestedScrollView ...>
```

```xml
<androidx.constraintlayout.widget.ConstraintLayout ...>
  <com.google.android.material.slider.Slider
    android:id="@+id/slider"
    ... />

  <androidx.compose.ui.platform.ComposeView
    android:id="@+id/compose_view"
    ...
    app:layout_constraintTop_toBottomOf="@id/slider" />
</androidx.constraintlayout.widget.ConstraintLayout>

</androidx.core.widget.NestedScrollView>

<com.google.android.material.appbar.AppBarLayout ... >
  <com.google.android.material.appbar.MaterialToolbar
    ... />
</com.google.android.material.appbar.AppBarLayout>
</androidx.coordinatorlayout.widget.CoordinatorLayout>
```

ConstraintLayout contains a com.google.android.material.slider.Slider
and a ComposeView (which is discussed in detail in the following section). The ID of the slider is
slider, so LayoutBinding contains an equally named variable. We can therefore link the slider
to the ViewModel as follows:

```
lifecycleScope.launch {
  lifecycle.repeatOnLifecycle(Lifecycle.State.STARTED) {
    viewModel.sliderValue.collect {
      binding.slider.value = it
    }
  }
}
```

The block passed to collect() is invoked when the value stored in sliderValue changes. By
updating binding.slider.value, we change the position of the slider handle, which means
we update the slider. But how do we update the ViewModel upon slider interactions?

```
binding.slider.addOnChangeListener { _, value, _ ->
  viewModel.setSliderValue(value) }
```

The block passed to addOnChangeListener() is invoked when the user drags the slider handle.
By calling setSliderValue() we update the ViewModel, which in turn triggers updates on
observers—for example, our composable functions.

In this section, I familiarized you with the steps needed to tie composable functions and traditional Views to a ViewModel property. When the property is changed, all observers are called, which leads to the update of both the composable and View. In the following section, we continue our look at the `InteropDemo` example. This time, I will show you how to embed composables into a View hierarchy. This is important if an existing app is to be migrated to Jetpack Compose step by step.

Embedding composables in View hierarchies

As you have seen, integrating Views in composable functions is simple and straightforward using `AndroidView()` and `AndroidViewBinding()`. But what about the other way round? Often, you may not want to rewrite an existing (View-based) app from scratch but migrate it to Jetpack Compose gradually, replacing View hierarchies with composable functions step by step. Depending on the complexity of the activity, it may make sense to start with small composables that reflect portions of the UI and incorporate them into the remaining layout.

The `androidx.compose.ui.platform.ComposeView` view makes composables available inside classic layouts. The class extends `AbstractComposeView`, which has `ViewGroup` as its parent. Once the layout that includes it has been inflated, you can configure the `ComposeView` as follows:

```
binding.composeView.run {
  setViewCompositionStrategy(
      ViewCompositionStrategy.DisposeOnDetachedFromWindow)
  setContent {
    …
  }
}
```

`setContent()` sets the content (a Compose hierarchy) for this view. We'll turn to this soon. An initial composition will occur when the view is attached to a window, or when `createComposition()` is called. While `setContent()` is defined in `ComposeView`, `createComposition()` belongs to `AbstractComposeView`. It performs the initial composition for this view. Typically, you do not need to invoke this function directly. `setViewCompositionStrategy()` configures how to manage the disposal of the View's internal composition. You can choose from a couple of strategies, for example:

- `DisposeOnDetachedFromWindow` (the default): The composition is disposed whenever the view becomes detached from a window. This is preferred for simple scenarios, as in my example.

- `DisposeOnViewTreeLifecycleDestroyed` or `DisposeOnLifecycleDestroyed`: If your view is shown inside a fragment or a component with a known `LifecycleOwner`, you should use one of these two strategies. This, however, is a topic beyond the scope of this book.

The following code creates state based on the `sliderValue` property of the ViewModel and passes the value to `ComposeDemo()`:

```
val sliderValue =
    viewModel.sliderValue.collectAsStateWithLifecycle()
sliderValue.value.let {
  ComposeDemo(it) {
  val i = Intent(
    context,
    ComposeActivity::class.java
  )
  i.putExtra(KEY, it)
  startActivity(i)
  }
}
```

The composable also receives a block that launches `ComposeActivity` and passes the current slider value to it. Next, let's look at `ComposeDemo()`:

```
@Composable
fun ComposeDemo(value: Float, onClick: () -> Unit) {
  Column(
    modifier = Modifier
      .fillMaxSize(),
    horizontalAlignment = Alignment.CenterHorizontally
  ) {
    Box(
      modifier = Modifier
        .fillMaxWidth()
        .background
        (
          MaterialTheme.colorScheme.secondaryContainer
        )
        .height(64.dp),
      contentAlignment = Alignment.Center
    ) {
      Text(
        text = value.toString()
      )
    }
    OutlinedButton(
      onClick = onClick,
      modifier = Modifier.padding(top = 16.dp)
    ) {
```

```
    Text(
      text = stringResource(id =
        R.string.compose_activity)
    )
  }
 }
}
```

As illustrated in the following screenshot, `ComposeDemo()` puts `Box()` (which contains `Text()`) and `Button()` inside `Column()`, in order to resemble `ComposeActivity`. Wrapping `Text()` inside `Box()` is necessary to vertically center the text inside an area with a particular height. A click on the button invokes the `onClick` lambda expression. `Text()` just shows the `value` parameter:

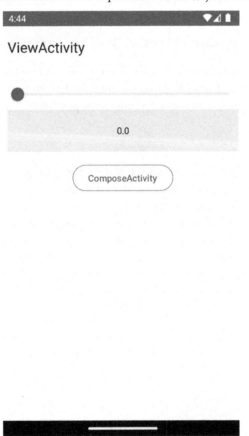

Figure 9.3 – The InteropDemo example app showing ViewActivity

Before closing out this chapter, let me recap some important steps you need to take to include a Compose hierarchy in a layout, as follows:

- Add `androidx.compose.ui.platform.ComposeView` to the layout
- Decide on `ViewCompositionStrategy`, depending on where the layout is shown (activity, fragment, …)
- Set the content using `setContent {}`
- Obtain a reference to the `ViewModel` by invoking `viewModels()`
- Register listeners to relevant Views and update the `ViewModel` upon changes
- Inside composable functions, create state by invoking `collectAsStateWithLifecycle()` on ViewModel properties as needed
- Inside composables, update the ViewModel by invoking the corresponding setters

The Jetpack Compose interoperability APIs allow for the seamless two-way integration of composable functions and `View` hierarchies. They help you use libraries that rely on Views and ease the transition to Compose by making a gradual, fine-grained migration possible.

Summary

In this chapter, we looked at the interoperability APIs of Jetpack Compose, which allow you to mix composable functions and traditional Views. We started by incorporating a traditional View hierarchy from a third-party library in a Compose app, using `AndroidView()`. As recent apps favor View Binding over the direct use of `findViewById()`, I also showed you how to embed layouts in a composable with View Binding and `AndroidViewBinding()`. Once you have embedded a `View` in a Compose UI, you need to share data between the two worlds. The *Sharing data between Views and composable functions* section explained how to achieve this with ViewModels. The final main section, *Embedding composables in View hierarchies*, discussed how to include a Compose UI in existing apps using `ComposeView`.

Chapter 10, Testing and Debugging Compose Apps, focuses on testing your Compose apps. You will learn how to use `ComposeTestRule` and `AndroidComposeTestRule`. Also, I will introduce you to the *Semantics tree*.

Questions

1. Why might it be desirable to mix Views and Compose hierarchies?
2. What are the similarities between `AndroidView()` and `AndroidViewBinding()`? In which aspect are they different?
3. What role do ViewModels play with regard to synchronizing between Views and Compose hierarchies?

10

Testing and Debugging Compose Apps

Programming is a very creative process. Implementing great-looking **user interfaces (UIs)** with slick animations is pure fun with Jetpack Compose. However, making an outstanding app involves more than just writing code. Testing and debugging are equally important because no matter how carefully you design and implement your app, bugs and glitches are inevitable, at least in non-trivial programs. Yet there is nothing to fear, as there are powerful tools you can wield to check whether your code is acting as intended.

This chapter introduces you to these tools. The main sections included are listed here:

- Setting up and writing tests
- Understanding semantics
- Debugging Compose apps

In the first main section, I will walk you through important terms and techniques regarding testing. We will set up the infrastructure, write a simple unit test, and then turn to Compose specifics—for example, `createComposeRule()` and `createAndroidComposeRule()`.

The *Understanding semantics* section builds on these foundations. We will look at how composable functions are selected—or found—in a test, and why making your app accessible also helps to write better tests. You will also learn about actions and assertions.

Failing tests often hint at bugs unless, of course, the failure is intentional. If you suspect the code being checked by a test is buggy, a debugging session is due. The final main section, *Debugging Compose apps*, explains how to examine your Compose code. We will be revisiting the Semantics tree, discussed in the *Understanding semantics* section. Finally, I will show you how to take advantage of `InspectorInfo` and `InspectorValueInfo`.

Technical requirements

Please refer to the *Technical requirements* section of *Chapter 1, Building Your First Compose App*, for information about how to install and set up Android Studio, as well as how to get the sample apps. This chapter covers the `TestingAndDebuggingDemo` sample.

Setting up and writing tests

As a software developer, you probably enjoy writing code. Seeing an app gain functionality feels very rewarding, probably more than writing tests—or worse, finding bugs—yet testing and debugging are essential. Eventually, your code will contain bugs, because all non-trivial programs do. To make your developer life easier, you need to familiarize yourself with writing tests and debugging your own and others' code. Testing an app has various facets that correspond to different types of tests, as outlined here:

- **Unit test**: You need to make sure that the business logic works as expected. This, for example, means that formulas and calculations always produce correct results.

- **Integration tests**: Are all building blocks of the app properly integrated? Depending on what the app does, this may include accessing remote services, talking to a database, or reading and writing files on the device.

- **UI tests**: Is the UI accurate? Are all UI elements visible on all supported screen sizes? Do they always show the right values? Do interactions such as button clicks or slider movements trigger the intended function? And something very important: Are all parts of the app accessible?

The number of tests varies among types. It has long been claimed that, ideally, most of your tests should be unit tests, followed by integration tests. This leads to the perception of a **test pyramid**, with unit tests being its foundation and UI tests the tip. As with all metaphors, the test pyramid has received both support and harsh criticism. If you want to learn more about it, and testing strategies in general, please refer to the *Further reading* section at the end of this chapter. Jetpack Compose tests are UI tests. So, while you likely write many corresponding test cases, testing the underlying business logic using unit tests may well be even more important.

To make testing reliable, comprehensible, and reproducible, automation is used. In the next section, I will show you how to write unit tests using the *JUnit 4* testing framework.

Implementing unit tests

Units are small, isolated pieces of code—usually a function, method, subroutine, or property, depending on the programming language. Let's look at a simple Kotlin function in the following code snippet:

```kotlin
fun isEven(num: Int): Boolean {
  val div2 = num / 2
  return (div2 * 2) == num
}
```

`isEven()` determines if the passed `Int` value is even. If this is the case, the function returns `true`; otherwise, it returns `false`. The algorithm is based on the fact that only even `Int` values can be divided by 2 without a remainder. Assuming we use the function often, we certainly want to make sure that the result is always correct. But how do we do that (how do we test that)? To verify `isEven()` exhaustively, we would need to check every possible input value, ranging from `Int.MIN_VALUE` to `Int.MAX_VALUE`. Even on fast computers, this may take some time. Part of the art of writing good unit tests is to identify all important boundaries and transitions. Regarding `isEven()`, these might be the following ones:

- `Int.MIN_VALUE` and `Int.MAX_VALUE`

- One negative even and one negative odd `Int` value

- One positive even and one positive odd `Int` value

To write and execute tests, you should add the following dependencies to your module-level `build.gradle` properties file. They allow you to use JUnit and Espresso:

```
dependencies {
  implementation platform(
    'androidx.compose:compose-bom:2023.06.01')
  ...
  androidTestImplementation
    "androidx.compose.ui:ui-test-junit4:1.4.3"
  debugImplementation
    "androidx.compose.ui:ui-test-manifest"
  ...
  androidTestImplementation 'androidx.test.ext:junit:1.1.5'
  // optional
  testImplementation 'junit:junit:4.13.2'
  androidTestImplementation
    'androidx.test.espresso:espresso-core:3.5.1'
}
```

`androidx.test.ext:junit` is the basis for testing your app. `androidx.compose.ui:ui-test-manifest` adds necessary properties to the debug manifest. Finally, `androidx.compose.ui:ui-test-junit4` provides Compose testing integration with JUnit 4.

Depending on which types of tests you will be adding to your app project, some of the preceding dependencies will be optional. For example, `androidx.test.espresso` is needed only if your app also contains old-fashioned views you wish to test (such as in interoperability scenarios).

Unit tests are executed on your development machine. Test classes are placed inside the `app/src/test/java` directory and are available through the **Project** tool window, as illustrated in the following screenshot. The Android Studio project assistant configures your projects accordingly and creates a test class, which I have renamed `SimpleUnitTest`:

Figure 10.1 – Unit tests in the Android Studio Project tool window

Let's look at the class in the following code snippet:

```
package
  eu.thomaskuenneth.composebook.testinganddebuggingdemo

import org.junit.After
import org.junit.Assert.assertEquals
import org.junit.Before
import org.junit.BeforeClass
import org.junit.Test

class SimpleUnitTest {

  companion object {
    @BeforeClass
    @JvmStatic
    fun setupAll() {
      println("Setting things up")
    }
  }

  @Before
  fun setup() {
```

```kotlin
    println("Setup test")
}


@After
fun teardown() {
  println("Clean up test")
}


@Test
fun testListOfInts() {
  val nums = listOf(Int.MIN_VALUE,
                    -3, -2, 2, 3, Int.MAX_VALUE)
  val results = listOf(true, false, true, true,
                       false, false)
  nums.forEachIndexed { index, num ->
    val result = isEven(num)
    println("isEven($num) returns $result")
    assertEquals(result, results[index])
  }
}
}
```

A test class contains one or more tests. A **test** (also called a **test case**) is an ordinary Kotlin function, annotated with @Test. It checks certain well-defined situations, conditions, or criteria. Tests should be isolated, which means they should not rely on previous ones.

My example function, testListOfInts(), tests if isEven() returns correct results for six input values, which are stored in nums. The results list contains the correct answers. They are compared with the return value of the corresponding call to isEven(). Such checks are based on **assertions**. An assertion formulates expected behavior. If an assertion is not met, the test fails.

If you need something to be done before or after each test, you can implement functions and annotate them with @Before or @After. You can achieve something similar using @Rule. We will be looking at this in the following section. To run code before all tests, you need to implement a companion object with a function annotated with @BeforeClass and @JvmStatic. @AfterClass is useful for cleanup purposes after all tests have been run.

You can run a unit test by right-clicking on the test class in the **Project** tool window and choosing **Run '…'** in this context menu. Once a launch configuration for the test class has been created, you can also run the tests using the menu bar and the toolbar.

Test results are presented in the **Run** tool window, as illustrated in the following screenshot:

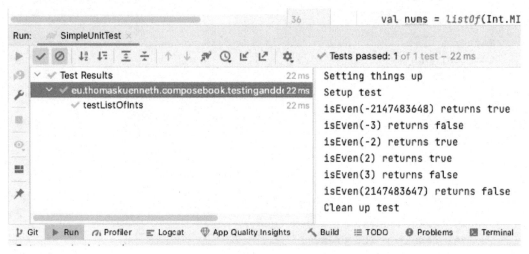

Figure 10.2 – Test results in the Android Studio Run tool window

Although the test passes, my implementation of isEven() may still not be flawless. While the test checks the upper and lower bounds, it leaves the transition between negative and positive numbers untested, because the nums list in testListOfInts() doesn't contain 0. Let's correct this and add another test, as follows:

```
@Test
fun testIsEvenZero() {
    assertEquals(true, isEven(0))
}
```

Fortunately, this test passes, too.

> **Important note**
>
> Pay close attention to the parameters a unit receives and the result it produces. Always test boundaries and transitions. Make sure to cover all code paths (if possible) and watch for pitfalls such as exceptions due to invalid arguments (for example, division by zero or wrong number formats).

Please remember that composable functions are top-level Kotlin functions, so they are prime candidates for unit tests. Let's see how this works. In the next section, you will learn to test a simple Compose UI.

Testing composable functions

The `SimpleButtonDemo()` composable (which belongs to the `TestingAndDebuggingDemo` sample) shows a box with a button centered inside. Clicking the button for the first time changes its text from **A** to **B**. Subsequent clicks toggle between **B** and **A**. The code is illustrated in the following snippet:

```
@Composable
fun SimpleButtonDemo() {
  val a = stringResource(id = R.string.a)
  val b = stringResource(id = R.string.b)
  var text by remember { mutableStateOf(a) }
  Box(
    modifier = Modifier.fillMaxSize(),
    contentAlignment = Alignment.Center
  ) {
    Button(onClick = {
      text = if (text == a) b else a
    }) {
      Text(text = text)
    }
  }
}
```

The text is stored as a mutable `String` state. It is changed inside the `onClick` block and used as a parameter for the `Text()` composable. If we want to test `SimpleButtonDemo()`, we may need to check the following:

- **Initial state of the UI**: Is the initial button text **A**?

- **Behavior**: Does the first button click change the text to **B**?

  Do subsequent clicks toggle between **B** and **A**?

Here's what a simple test class looks like:

```
@RunWith(AndroidJUnit4::class)
class SimpleInstrumentedTest {

  @get:Rule
  var name = TestName()

  @get:Rule
  val rule = createComposeRule()

  @Before
  fun setup() {
```

```
      rule.setContent {
        SimpleButtonDemo()
      }
    }
    ...
  }
```

Unlike the `SimpleUnitTest` class from the *Implementing unit tests* section, its source code is stored inside the `app/src/androidTest/java` directory (contrary to .../`test`/... for ordinary unit tests). `SimpleInstrumentedTest` is an **instrumented test**.

Contrary to plain unit tests, instrumented tests are not executed locally on the development machine, but on the Android Emulator or a real device, because they need Android-specific functionality to run. Instrumented tests are available through the **Project** tool window, as illustrated in the following screenshot:

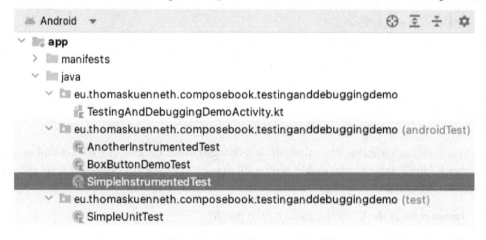

Figure 10.3 – Instrumented tests in the Android Studio Project tool window

You can run an instrumented test by right-clicking on the test class in the **Project** tool window and choosing **Run '...'**. Once a launch configuration for the test class has been created, you can also run the tests using the menu bar and the toolbar. Test results are presented in the **Run** tool window, as illustrated in the following screenshot:

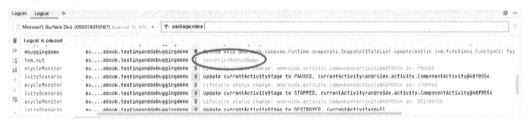

Run:	SimpleInstrumentedTest				
Status		1 passed 1 tests, 5 s 746 ms			
Filter tests:					
Tests			Duration	6.7_Horizontal_Fold-in_API_33	
✓ Test Results			987 ms	1/1	
✓ SimpleInstrumentedTest			987 ms	1/1	
✓ testInitialLetterIsA			987 ms	✓	

Git ▶ Run ⌔ Profiler ≡ Logcat ⊕ App Quality Insights ⚒ Build ≔ TODO ❶ Problems ▣ Terminal

Figure 10.4 – Instrumented test results in the Android Studio Run tool window

JUnit **rules** allow you to run some code alongside a test case. In a way, this is like having `@Before` and `@After` annotations in your test class. There are several predefined rules—for example, the `TestName` rule can provide the current test name inside a test method, as follows:

```
@get:Rule
var name = TestName()

...

@Test
fun testPrintMethodName() {
    println(name.methodName)
}
```

When the `testPrintMethodName()` function runs, it prints its name. You can see the output in **Logcat** (*Figure 10.5*):

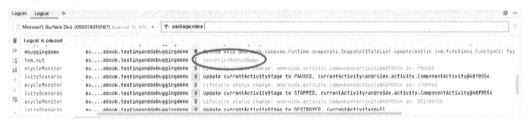

Figure 10.5 – Output of the testPrintMethodName() function in Logcat

Please remember—you need to apply the `@Rule` annotation to the property getter by adding `get:`. Failing to do so will result in a `ValidationError (The @Rule '...' must be public)` message during execution.

Compose tests are based on rules. `createComposeRule()` returns an implementation of the `ComposeContentTestRule` interface, which extends `ComposeTestRule`. This interface in turn extends `org.junit.rules.TestRule`. Each `TestRule` instance implements `apply()`. This method receives `Statement` and returns the same, a modified, or completely new `Statement`. However, writing your own test rules is beyond the scope of this book. To learn more, please refer to the *Further reading* section at the end of this chapter.

Which implementation of the `ComposeContentTestRule` interface `createComposeRule()` returns depends on the platform. It is `AndroidComposeTestRule<ComponentActivity>` on Android. That is why you should add a dependency to `androidx.compose.ui:ui-test-manifest` in the module-level `build.gradle` file. Otherwise, you may need to manually add a reference to `ComponentActivity` in the manifest file.

`createAndroidComposeRule()` allows you to create `AndroidComposeTestRule` for activity classes other than `ComponentActivity`. This is useful if you require the functionality of this activity in a test. On Compose for Desktop or Web, `createComposeRule()` may return different implementations of `ComposeContentTestRule`, depending on where the Compose UI is hosted. To help make your tests platform-independent, use `createComposeRule()` whenever possible.

Your test cases use (among others) methods provided by `ComposeContentTestRule` implementations. For example, `setContent()` sets the composable function to act as the content of the current screen—that is, the UI to be tested. `setContent()` should be called exactly once per test. To achieve this, just invoke it in a function annotated with `@Before`.

> **Important note**
>
> If you want to reuse your tests among platforms, try to rely only on methods defined in the `ComposeContentTestRule`, `ComposeContentTestRule`, and `TestRule` interfaces. Avoid calling functions from the implementation.

Next, let's look at `testInitialLetterIsA()`. This test case checks if the initial button text is **A**:

```
@Test
fun testInitialLetterIsA() {
  rule.onNodeWithText("A").assertExists()
}
```

To do so, the test must find the button, get its text, and compare it to `"A"`. `onNodeWithText()` tries to find a composable (more precisely, a *semantics node*) with a given text. The comparison is done with the `assertExists()` assertion. `assertExists()` checks if a matching node is present in the current UI. If so, the test passes. Otherwise, it fails. `onNodeWithText()` is called a **finder**. Finders work on **semantics nodes**. You will learn more about these in the following section.

Understanding semantics

Unlike the traditional view system, Jetpack Compose does not use references to identify individual UI elements. Please remember that such references are needed in an imperative approach to modify the component tree during runtime. But this is not how Compose works—instead, we declare how the UI should look based on state. Yet, to test if a particular composable looks and behaves as expected, we need to find it among all other children of a Compose hierarchy.

This is where the **semantics tree** comes into play. As the name implies, *semantics* give meaning to a UI element or element hierarchies. The semantics tree is generated alongside the UI hierarchy, which it describes using attributes such as `Role`, `Text`, and `Actions`. It is used for accessibility and testing.

In the previous section, I showed you a simple test case that checks if a button text matches a given string. Here is another test case. `testLetterAfterButtonClickIsB()` performs a click on the button to see if the button text changes as expected:

```
@Test
fun testLetterAfterButtonClickIsB() {
  rule.onNodeWithText("A")
    .performClick()
  rule.onNode(matcher = hasClickAction())
    .assert(hasText("B"))
}
```

Again, we start by finding the button using `onNodeWithText().performClick()` (this is called an **action**) clicks it. `Assert(hasText("B"))` checks if the button text is **B** afterward. But what does `rule.onNode(matcher = hasClickAction())` do, and why do we need it? Clicking on the button changes our Compose hierarchy (the button text is changed). This changes the semantics tree. Depending on the internal implementation of this tree, the old node may no longer be there. So, we need to find the text of the button again so that we can assert the new value. `hasClickAction()` is called a **matcher**—it finds nodes that match a certain condition.

Assertions determine if a test passes or fails. `onNodeWithText()` (an extension function of `SemanticsNodeInteractionsProvider`) returns a `SemanticsNodeInteraction` semantics node. The `SemanticsNodeInteractionsProvider` interface is the main entry point into testing and is typically implemented by a test rule. It defines two methods, as follows:

- `onNode()` finds and returns a semantics node (`SemanticsNodeInteraction`) that matches the given condition.

- `onAllNodes()` finds all semantics nodes that match the given condition. It returns a `SemanticsNodeInteractionCollection` instance.

Both are called finders because they return (*find*) semantics nodes matching certain conditions.

Working with semantics nodes

To see what the semantics node we tested with `testLetterAfterButtonClickIsB()` from the previous section looks like, you can add the following expression after `.assert(...)`:

```
.printToLog(this::class.java.simpleName)
```

The result is visible in **Logcat**, as illustrated in the following screenshot:

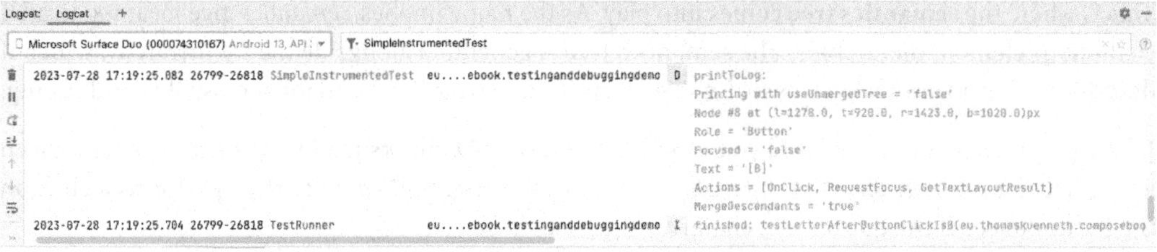

Figure 10.6 – A semantics node in Logcat

`SemanticsNodeInteraction` represents a semantics node. You can interact with a node by performing actions such as `performClick()` or assertions such as `assertHasClickAction()`, or you can navigate to other nodes such as `onChildren()`. Such functions are extension functions of `SemanticsNodeInteraction`. `SemanticsNodeInteractionCollection` is a collection of semantics nodes.

Let's look at another finder function, `onNodeWithContentDescription()`. We will be using it to test if `Image()` is part of the current UI. The code to be tested (the `ImageDemo()` composable function) is illustrated in the following snippet:

```
@Composable
fun ImageDemo() {
  Image(
    painter = painterResource(id =
      R.drawable.ic_baseline_airport_shuttle_24),
    contentDescription = stringResource(id =
      R.string.airport_shuttle),
    contentScale = ContentScale.FillBounds,
    modifier = Modifier
      .size(width = 128.dp, height = 128.dp)
      .background(Color.Blue)
  )
}
```

`Image()` shows a vector drawable on top of a blue background. Please note that we are setting the size of the image to 128 density-independent pixels. The size itself is arbitrary, but we will be using it later in a test case.

If the UI of your app contains images, you should add **content descriptions** for them in most cases. Content descriptions are used, for example, by **accessibility** software to describe to visually impaired people what is currently presented on screen. So, by adding them, you greatly enhance the usability. Additionally, content descriptions help in finding composables. You can see these being used in the following test class:

```
@RunWith(AndroidJUnit4::class)
class AnotherInstrumentedTest {

  @get:Rule
  val rule = createComposeRule()

  @Test
  fun testImage() {
    var contentDescription = ""
    rule.setContent {
      ImageDemo()
      contentDescription = stringResource(id =
                              R.string.airport_shuttle)
    }
    rule.onNodeWithContentDescription(contentDescription)
      .assertWidthIsEqualTo(128.dp)
  }
}
```

`testImage()` first sets the content (`ImageDemo()`). It then finds a semantics node with the given content description using `onNodeWithContentDescription()`. Finally, `assertWidthIsEqualTo()` checks if the width of the UI element represented by this node is 128 density-independent pixels wide.

> **Note**
> Have you noticed that I used `stringResource()` to obtain the content description? Hardcoded values can lead to subtle bugs in tests (for example, spelling errors or typos). To avoid them, try to write your tests in a way that they access the same values as the code being tested. But please keep in mind that under the hood, `stringResource()` relies on Android resources. So, the test case is platform-specific.

Using onNodeWithText() and onNodeWithContentDescription() makes it easy to find composable functions that contain texts and images. But what if you need to find the semantics node for something else—for example, a Box()? The following example, BoxButtonDemo(), shows a Box() with a Button() centered inside. Clicking the button toggles the background color of the box from white to light gray and back:

```
val COLOR1 = Color.White
val COLOR2 = Color.LightGray
const val TAG1 = "BoxButtonDemo"

@Composable
fun BoxButtonDemo() {
  var color by remember { mutableStateOf(COLOR1) }
  Box(
    modifier = Modifier
      .fillMaxSize()
      .testTag(TAG1)
      .background(color = color),
    contentAlignment = Alignment.Center
  ) {
    Button(onClick = {
      color = if (color == COLOR1)
        COLOR2
      else
        COLOR1
    }) {
      Text(text = stringResource(id = R.string.toggle))
    }
  }
}
```

To be able to find the box in a test case, we tag it using the testTag() modifier and apply a tag. We can then check if the box is present, as follows:

```
@RunWith(AndroidJUnit4::class)
class BoxButtonDemoTest {

  @get:Rule
  val rule = createComposeRule()

  @Test
  fun testHasTestTag() {
    rule.setContent {
      BoxButtonDemo()
```

```
    }
    rule.onNode(hasTestTag(TAG1))
        .assertExists()
    }


    …
}
```

The onNode() finder receives a hasTestTag() matcher. Matchers find nodes that meet certain criteria. hasTestTag() finds a node with the given test tag. There are several predefined matchers. For example, isEnabled() returns whether the node is enabled, and isToggleable() returns true if the node can be toggled.

The assertExists() assertion expects that a node matching the conditions was found. You can use assertDoesNotExist() to check if no matching node was found.

> **Tip**
> Google provides a testing cheat sheet at https://developer.android.com/jetpack/compose/testing-cheatsheet. It nicely groups finders, matchers, actions, and assertions.

Another interesting test is to check the background color of the box because it changes upon button clicks. But how do we do that? Following previous examples, you may expect a hasBackgroundColor() matcher. Unfortunately, there currently is none. Tests can rely only on what is available through the semantics tree, yet if it does not contain the information we need, we can easily add it. I will show you how in the following section.

Adding custom semantics properties

If you want to expose additional information to tests, you can create custom semantics properties. This requires the following:

- Defining SemanticsPropertyKey
- Making it available using SemanticsPropertyReceiver

You can see these in use in the following code snippet. It is part of TestingAndDebuggingDemoActivity.kt:

```
val BackgroundColorKey =
    SemanticsPropertyKey<Color>("BackgroundColor")
var SemanticsPropertyReceiver.backgroundColor by
    BackgroundColorKey

@Composable
```

```
fun BoxButtonDemo() {
  ...
  Box(
    modifier = ...
      .semantics { backgroundColor = color }
      .background(color = color),
    ...
```

With `SemanticsPropertyKey`, you can set key-value pairs in semantics blocks in a type-safe way. Each key has one statically defined value type—in my example, this is `Color`. `SemanticsPropertyReceiver` is the scope provided by `semantics { }` blocks. It is intended for setting key-value pairs via extension functions. Here's how to access the custom semantic property in a test case:

```
@Test
fun testBoxInitialBackgroundColorIsColor1() {
  rule.setContent {
    BoxButtonDemo()
  }
  rule.onNode(SemanticsMatcher.expectValue(
    BackgroundColorKey, COLOR1))
    .assertExists()
}
```

The test checks if the initial background color is COLOR1. As usual, we find a node that matches a certain condition and assert that it exists. `expectValue()` checks whether the value of the given key is equal to the expected value.

Adding custom values to the semantics tree can be of great help when writing tests. However, please carefully consider whether you really need to rely on `SemanticsPropertyKey`. The semantics tree is also used by the accessibility framework and tools, so it is vital to not pollute the semantics tree with irrelevant information. A solution is to rethink the testing strategy. Instead of testing *if the initial background color of the box is white*, we may just test if the value we pass to the `background()` function represents white.

This concludes the sections on testing composable functions. In the following section, we look at debugging Compose apps.

Debugging Compose apps

The title of this section, *Debugging Compose apps*, may indicate major differences to debugging traditional `View`-based apps. Fortunately, this is not the case. On Android, all composable hierarchies are wrapped inside `androidx.compose.ui.platform.ComposeView`. This happens indirectly if you invoke the `setContent { }` extension function of `ComponentActivity` or if you deliberately include a composable hierarchy inside a layout (see *Chapter 9, Exploring Interoperability APIs*). Either way, in the end, `ComposeView` is displayed on screen—for example, inside an Activity or a Fragment. Therefore, all aspects regarding the basic building blocks of an Android app (activity, fragment, service, broadcast receiver, intent, and content provider) remain the same.

Of course, any UI framework advocates specific debugging habits. For example, the `View` system requires watching for `null` references. Also, you need to make sure that changes in state reliably trigger updates of the component tree. Fortunately, neither is relevant for Jetpack Compose. As composables are Kotlin functions, you can follow the creation of the composable hierarchy by stepping through the code and examining `State` when needed.

To closely examine the visual representation of your composable functions during runtime, you can use the **Layout Inspector** feature of Android Studio, as illustrated in the following screenshot. Once you have deployed your app on the Android Emulator or a real device, open the tool with **Layout Inspector** in the **Tools** menu:

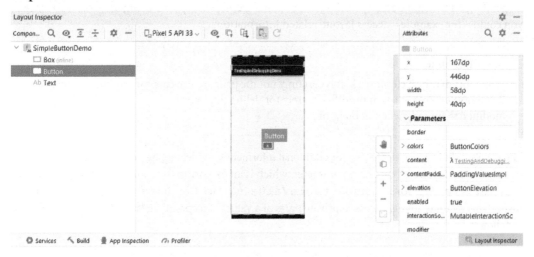

Figure 10.7 – The Layout Inspector feature in Android Studio

You can select a composable to inspect using the tree on the left-hand side of the Android Studio main window. Important attributes are presented on the right. The center of the tool window contains a configurable, zoomable preview. You can also enable a **three-dimensional** (**3D**) mode. This allows you to visually inspect the hierarchy by clicking and dragging to rotate the layout.

If you want to log important values of a composable for debugging purposes, you can easily achieve this with modifiers. The following section shows you how to do this.

Using custom modifiers for logging and debugging

As I explained in the *Modifying behavior* section of *Chapter 3, Exploring the Key Principles of Compose*, a modifier is an ordered, immutable collection of modifier elements. Modifiers can change the look and behavior of Compose UI elements. You create custom modifiers by implementing an extension function of `Modifier`. The following code snippet uses the `DrawScope` interface to print the size of a composable:

```
fun Modifier.simpleDebug() = then(object : DrawModifier {
  override fun ContentDrawScope.draw() {
    println("width=${size.width}, height=${size.height}")
    drawContent()
  }
})
```

Depending on which interface you choose, you can log different aspects. Using `LayoutModifier`, you could—for example—access layout-related information.

> **Important note**
>
> While this may be a clever trick, it is certainly not the primary use case for modifiers. Therefore, if you implement a custom modifier merely for debugging purposes, you should add it to the modifier chain only when debugging.

There is also a built-in feature to provide additional information for debugging purposes. Several modifiers can receive an `inspectorInfo` parameter, which is an extension function of `InspectorInfo`. This class is a builder for an `InspectableValue` interface (this interface defines a value that is inspectable by tools, giving access to private parts of a value). `InspectorInfo` has three properties, as follows:

- `name` (provides `nameFallback` for `InspectableValue`)
- `value` (provides `valueOverride` for `InspectableValue`)
- `properties` (provides `inspectableElements` for `InspectableValue`)

To understand how `inspectorInfo` is used, let's look in the following screenshot at the implementation of the `semantics { }` modifier, which adds semantics key-value pairs for testing and accessibility. Please refer to the *Adding custom semantics properties* section for details:

```
107    fun Modifier.semantics(
108        mergeDescendants: Boolean = false,
109        properties: (SemanticsPropertyReceiver.() -> Unit)
110    ): Modifier = this then SemanticsModifierCore(
111        mergeDescendants = mergeDescendants,
112        clearAndSetSemantics = false,
113        properties = properties,
114        inspectorInfo = debugInspectorInfo { this: InspectorInfo
115            name = "semantics"
116            this.properties["mergeDescendants"] = mergeDescendants
117            this.properties["properties"] = properties
118        }
119    )
```

Figure 10.8 – Source code of the semantics {} modifier

semantics {} adds a SemanticsModifierCore instance to the modifier chain. This internal class implements the SemanticsModifier interface, which extends Modifier.Element (also an interface). SemanticsModifierCore also extends InspectorValueInfo, which in turn implements InspectableValue. InspectorValueInfo provides an important property: inspectableElements keeps a Sequence of ValueElements.

To turn on debug inspector information, you must set the isDebugInspectorInfoEnabled global top-level variable in the androidx.compose.ui.platform package to true. Then, you can access and print debug inspector information—for example, inside tests:

```
@RunWith(AndroidJUnit4::class)
class ModifierTest {

  @Before
  fun setup() {
    isDebugInspectorInfoEnabled = true
  }

  @After
  fun teardown() {
    isDebugInspectorInfoEnabled = false
  }

  @Test
  fun testModifierInspectableValue() {
    val modifier = Modifier.semantics {
      backgroundColor = Color.White }
```

```
    assertEquals(modifier.foldIn(0) { i, _ -> i + 1 }, 1)
    with(modifier as InspectableValue) {
      assertEquals(nameFallback, "semantics")
    }
  }
}
```

We define a modifier chain that has one element. Therefore, we can cast it to `InspectableValue`. The first assertion makes sure that there is indeed only one modifier element present. The second one checks for the name of the value. Depending on how you populate `inspectorInfo` when creating your modifier, you may want to check other conditions.

Summary

In this chapter, we looked at important terms and techniques regarding testing. In the first main section, we set up the infrastructure, wrote and ran a simple unit test locally on the development machine, and then turned to Compose specifics. I introduced you to `createComposeRule()` and `createAndroidComposeRule()`.

Next, we looked at how composable functions are found in a Compose hierarchy, and why making your app accessible also helps in writing better tests. You also learned about actions and assertions. Finally, we added custom entries to the semantics tree.

The final main section explained how to debug a Compose app. We revisited the semantics tree, and I showed you how to take advantage of `InspectorInfo` and `InspectorValueInfo` to debug and test custom modifiers.

Android has always embraced different form factors and device classes. Wouldn't it be great to bring your Jetpack Compose apps to tables and foldables? In *Chapter 11, Developing for Different Form Factors*, I will show you what's special about large screens and why it takes a bit of an effort you make your app really shine there.

Further reading

- This book assumes a basic understanding of how to test Android apps. To learn more, please refer to *Test apps on Android* at `https://developer.android.com/training/testing`.

- *JUnit in Action* by *Catalin Tudose* (*Manning Publications, 2020, ISBN 978-1617297045*) is a thorough introduction to the latest version of the JUnit testing framework.

- If you want to learn more about test automation, you may want to look at *Complete Guide to Test Automation: Techniques, Practices, and Patterns for Building and Maintaining Effective Software Projects* by *Arnon Axelrod* (*Apress, 2018, ISBN 978-1484238318*).

- To get an insight into the test pyramid metaphor, you may want to refer to *The Practical Test Pyramid* by *Ham Vocke*, available at `https://martinfowler.com/articles/practical-test-pyramid.html`.

Questions

1. What is the difference between unit tests and instrumented tests? In which scenarios do you use both?

2. What is the general layout of test classes, and which annotations are typically involved?

3. What is a semantics tree? How can you contribute to it?

11

Developing for Different Form Factors

This book shows you how to write beautiful, fast, and maintainable Jetpack Compose apps. In *Chapters 1 to 3*, I introduced you to the fundamentals of Jetpack Compose, and explained the core techniques and principles, as well as important interfaces, classes, packages, and, of course, composable functions. *Chapters 4 to 7* focused on building Compose **user interfaces** (**UIs**). You learned how to manage the state and navigate to different screens. We also explored the ViewModel and Repository patterns. *Chapters 8 to 10* covered advanced topics such as animation, interoperability, testing, and debugging.

You hopefully enjoyed digging through all of this and may thus be asking yourself what's left to tackle. The remaining two chapters show you how to bring Compose UIs to devices other than smartphones. We'll start with foldables and tablets. The final chapter helps you leverage your Jetpack Compose skills beyond Android. Wouldn't it be great to see your app on other platforms, such as iOS and desktop? With Compose Multiplatform, you can. *Chapter 12, Bringing Your Compose UI to Different Platforms*, will help you take the first steps.

In this chapter, you will learn how to make the most of the available screen real estate using Window Size Classes, Jetpack WindowManager, and Canonical Layouts. The main sections are as follows:

- Understanding different form factors

- Using Jetpack WindowManager

- Organizing the screen content

We'll start by investigating how screen sizes, form factors, and hardware features influence the app layout. I will introduce you to Window Size Classes and explain how they help structure your user interface and how to compute them during runtime.

Relying solely on Window Size Classes is not enough to create awesome layouts for tablets *and* foldables. The second main section, *Using Jetpack WindowManager*, discusses such scenarios. I will show you how to query hardware features such as hinge orientation and device posture and explain how this helps to finetune your user interface.

Finally, the *Organizing the screen content* section explains a Material Design concept called Canonical Layouts. You will learn which Canonical Layouts have been defined so far and in which scenarios they work best.

Technical requirements

Please refer to the *Technical requirements* section in *Chapter 1, Building Your First Compose App*, for information about how to install and set up Android Studio, as well as how to get the sample apps. This chapter covers the `WindowSizeClassDemo` sample.

Understanding different form factors

Android has always been great at supporting different screen sizes, pixel densities, and aspect ratios. These criteria contribute to two terms, **form factor** and **device class**. The latter assigns hardware to broad categories, such as smartphones, tablets, foldables, TVs, and watches. Smartwatches have tiny screens. We need to consider carefully what content should be displayed. Television sets feature huge screens but are watched from a greater distance and are operated with remote controls; we need to make sure content remains readable and easily navigable.

Smartphones usually have smaller screens than foldables, which in turn have displays smaller than or like tablets. All are held in our hands and can be rotated. That's where the form factor becomes important: it describes the size, shape, and *natural orientation* (the way we hold it most of the time) of a device. Smartphones typically are more tall than wide, resembling a portrait. Tablets may favor portrait or landscape (the latter term meaning being wider than tall). Closed foldables usually are held in portrait mode. When opened, they become landscape devices, although they are not rotated. Some devices have a horizontally running hinge. They need to be opened to reveal their main display, which is not particularly large but roughly matches the size of a smartphone. Being foldable does not necessarily mean having a large screen.

Preparing for adaptive layouts

At this point, you may be wondering whether the device class or form factor can help us decide how to lay out the UI. Devices can be rotated, folded, and unfolded at any time. We therefore must not assume they are held in their natural orientation. Here are two examples:

- While we may be using a smartphone in portrait mode most of the time, we will likely rotate it when taking a picture
- Even if a tablet has a portrait form factor, we will likely rotate it while watching a movie because movies are wider than they are tall

Some Android features change the location and size of the area available to your app without *any* orientation or posture change; for example, see the following:

- Picture-in-picture mode

- Multi-window mode

- Resizable windows

These affect the *app window size.*

> **Important**
>
> Do not make assumptions about the available screen real estate based on device classes and form factors. Instead, rely on the app window size and react to events sent by the system.

In the subsequent sections, I will show you how to do that, but first, I need to elaborate on what happens when you don't. *Figure 11.1* shows the *WindowSizeDemo* sample on a smartphone in portrait mode (the device is held in its natural orientation).

Figure 11.1 – The WindowSizeClassDemo sample in portrait mode

The vertical list is easy to navigate, provides just the right amount of content, and does not waste screen space. Let's have a look at the code:

```kotlin
class WindowSizeClassDemoActivity : ComponentActivity() {
  override fun onCreate(savedInstanceState: Bundle?) {
    super.onCreate(savedInstanceState)
    setContent {
      MaterialTheme(
        colorScheme = defaultColorScheme()
      ) {
        // In subsequent sections we'll add code here
        WindowSizeClassDemoScreen()
      }
    }
  }
}
```

The `WindowSizeClassDemoActivity` activity class is short and straightforward: inside `setContent  {}`, we set up a Material theme and invoke a composable called `WindowSizeClassDemoScreen()`. Have you spotted the comment regarding the code to be added later? This refers to making the UI adaptive. The color scheme is received from a composable function called `defaultColorScheme()`:

```kotlin
@Composable
fun defaultColorScheme() = with(isSystemInDarkTheme()) {
  val hasDynamicColor =
        Build.VERSION.SDK_INT >= Build.VERSION_CODES.S
  val context = LocalContext.current
  when (this) {
    true -> if (hasDynamicColor) {
      dynamicDarkColorScheme(context)
    } else {
      darkColorScheme()
    }

    false -> if (hasDynamicColor) {
      dynamicLightColorScheme(context)
    } else {
      lightColorScheme()
    }
  }
}
```

`defaultColorScheme()` makes sure your app honors light mode, dark mode, and (on systems supporting this feature) dynamic colors. Next, let's look at `WindowSizeClassDemoScreen()`. Here is its implementation:

```
@OptIn(ExperimentalMaterial3Api::class)
@Composable
fun WindowSizeClassDemoScreen() {
  val scrollBehavior =
         TopAppBarDefaults.pinnedScrollBehavior()
  Scaffold(modifier = Modifier
    .fillMaxSize()
    .nestedScroll(scrollBehavior.nestedScrollConnection),
    topBar = {
      TopAppBar(
        title = {
          Text(text = stringResource(id =
                  R.string.app_name))
        },
        scrollBehavior = scrollBehavior
      )
    }) {
    val list = (1..42).toList()
    SimpleScreen(
      paddingValues = it,
      list = list
    )
  }
}
```

It shows a `Scaffold()` with a `TopAppBar()` and a content composable named `SimpleScreen()`. The top app bar is configured to change its background color when the list is scrolled through. This is achieved by passing `scrollBehavior` to `TopAppBar()` and the `nestedScroll()` modifier to `Scaffold()`. Next, let's look at `SimpleScreen()`:

```
@Composable
fun SimpleScreen(
  paddingValues: PaddingValues,
  list: List<Int>
) {
  NumbersList(
    paddingValues = paddingValues,
    list = list
  )
}
```

`SimpleScreen()` receives a list of `Int` values, which represent the data to be visualized, and `paddingValues`. We will apply the `PaddingValues` instance to the `Scaffold()` content root via `Modifier.padding()` in order to properly offset the top and bottom bars. This happens inside `NumbersList()`:

```
@Composable
fun NumbersList(
  paddingValues: PaddingValues, list: List<Int>
) {
  LazyColumn(
    modifier = Modifier.padding(paddingValues =
                paddingValues),
    verticalArrangement = Arrangement.spacedBy(8.dp)
  ) {
    items(
      items = list
    ) {
      NumbersItem(it)
    }
  }
}
```

`NumbersList()` uses `LazyColumn()` to show the list of `Int` values as a vertically scrolling list. Each item is rendered using the `NumbersItem()` composable:

```
@Composable
private fun NumbersItem(number: Int) {
  Text(
    modifier = Modifier
      .fillMaxWidth()
      .padding(vertical = 8.dp, horizontal = 16.dp)
      .border(width = 1.dp,
              color =
              MaterialTheme.colorScheme.primary),
    text = number.toString(),
    style = MaterialTheme.typography.displayLarge,
    textAlign = TextAlign.Center
  )
}
```

`NumbersItem()` just shows a large body of text that is centered inside a colored border one density-independent pixel wide. Before we move on, let's briefly recap. We used a vertically scrolling list to show several items, which looks great in portrait mode, but what happens if we rotate the smartphone? Let's find out in the following section.

Enhancing the UI

Figure 11.2 shows the *WindowSizeClassDemo* sample running on a smartphone rotated to landscape mode.

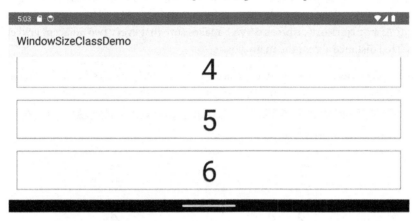

Figure 11.2 – The WindowSizeClassDemo sample in landscape mode

Obviously, the vertical list no longer seems right. That's because there is a lot of empty space inside each list item. Also, the user only sees a few rows. There are several ways to enhance the user experience. One that is easy to implement is switching to a grid. Here's the corresponding composable function:

```
@Composable
fun NumbersGrid(
  paddingValues: PaddingValues,
  list: List<Int>,
  columns: Int = 2
) {
  LazyVerticalGrid(
    columns = GridCells.Fixed(columns),
    modifier = Modifier.padding(paddingValues =
              paddingValues),
    verticalArrangement = Arrangement.spacedBy(8.dp)
  ) {
    items(
      items = list
    ) {
      NumbersItem(number = it)
    }
  }
}
```

Its general structure resembles `NumbersList()`. The content of `LazyVerticalGrid()` is an extension function of `LazyGridScope`, so we can invoke items(), passing the list of `Int` values. `GridCells.Fixed` keeps the size of the columns equal. Like in `NumbersList()`, we set padding using `paddingValues` (which came from `Scaffold()`). Have you noticed the vertical arrangement? `Arrangement.spacedBy()` makes sure that every two adjacent grid elements are spaced by a fixed distance across the main axis.

To use the new composable, we just need to replace the call to `NumbersList()` in `SimpleScreen()` with `NumbersGrid()`. The app will then look as it does in *Figure 11.3* when in landscape mode.

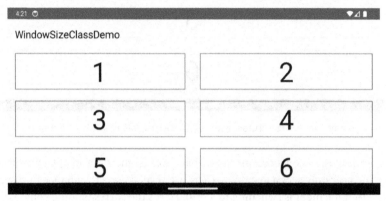

Figure 11.3 – The NumbersGrid() composable in landscape mode

This looks much better than the stretched list items we used before. However, when the app is rotated back to portrait mode, it will still show the grid with two columns. What we need to do instead is display either `NumbersList()` or `NumbersGrid()`, but how do we decide which one? Please recall that we should not consider screen size, posture, or orientation changes but instead rely on the app window size.

In the following section, I will introduce you to Window Size Classes and explain how they help make your app layout adaptive.

Introducing Window Size Classes

Adaptive layouts react to changes in the app window size. Such changes can occur for various reasons, for example, a foldable device being opened (unfolded), or a smartphone being brought into landscape mode.

`View`-based apps can utilize so-called resource qualifiers to signal, for example, that a layout file should be used for displays whose smallest width is at least 600 density-independent pixels (which, by the way, matches a 7-inch tablet). This is done by adding a suffix to the `values` directory name, for example, `res/layout-sw600dp/`. The available qualifiers define a couple of common display sizes. At runtime, the system determines which layout matches the actual hardware closest and uses that one.

Jetpack Compose doesn't rely on layout files. Although any Compose UI hierarchy is hosted by a `ComposeView` instance, that object is not inflated from XML but instantiated inside `setContent {}`. So, we cannot easily use resource qualifiers. Well, we could by providing layout files that contained `<ComposeView …/>` and invoking `setContentView()`; but this is not the endorsed procedure and it fortunately is not necessary.

Like layout-related resource qualifiers, **window size classes** are a set of viewport breakpoints. They categorize the display area available to your app as *compact*, *medium*, or *expanded*. Width and height are classified separately. *Figure 11.4* shows an app running on the Microsoft Surface Duo foldable when folded.

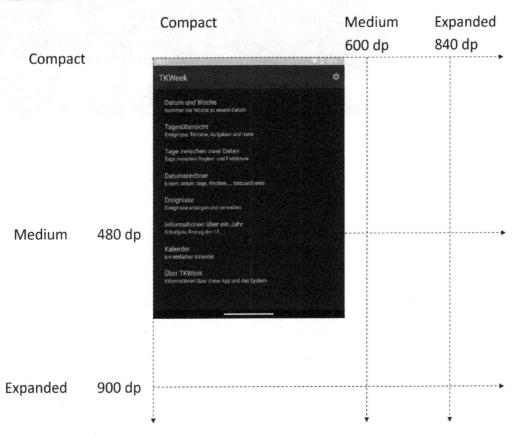

Figure 11.4 – An app running on a foldable device when folded

Your app has two window size classes – horizontal and vertical. They are independent of each other. So, while the horizontal window size class may be compact, while the vertical one could be medium. Please note that the two values will be swapped when the device is rotated by 90 degrees. Next, let's look at what happens when a foldable device is opened.

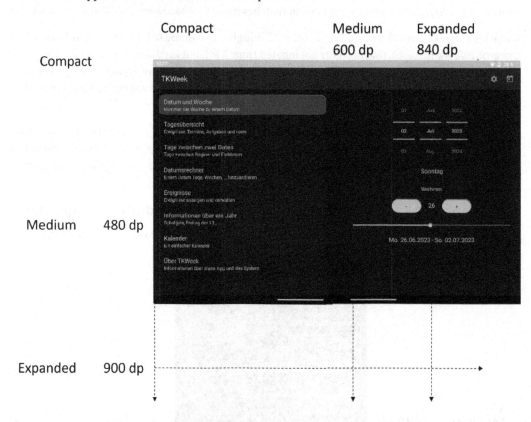

Figure 11.5 – An app running on a foldable device when unfolded

While the vertical window size class remains the same, the horizontal one becomes expanded. Please recall that besides foldable-specific posture changes, a couple of other events can lead to app window size changes, and therefore changes to the horizontal or vertical window size class. You can read more about this in the *Preparing for adaptive layouts* section.

It is often argued that the available app window width is more important than the available height due to the possibility of vertical scrolling. I encourage you to take the vertical window size class into account too, when crafting your app layout, because in some scenarios, switching to a two-row layout will provide a better user experience. I will give you an example in the *Using Jetpack WindowManager* section.

Before we move on, let's quickly recap: window size classes put the horizontal and vertical app window size in one of three buckets – compact, medium, and expanded. The horizontal and vertical window sizes can change independently; therefore, both the horizontal and vertical window size classes can, too.

Let's return to the *WindowSizeClassDemo* sample. Our task is to show either NumbersList() or NumbersGrid(). We will make this decision based on the horizontal window size class. Here's a composable function that achieves this:

```
@Composable
fun AdaptiveScreen(
  paddingValues: PaddingValues,
  list: List<Int>
) {
  with(LocalWindowSizeClass.current) {
    if (widthSizeClass == WindowWidthSizeClass.Compact) {
      NumbersList(
        paddingValues = paddingValues,
        list = list
      )
    } else {
      NumbersGrid(
        paddingValues = paddingValues,
        list = list,
        columns = when (widthSizeClass) {
          WindowWidthSizeClass.Medium -> 2
          else -> 3
        }
      )
    }
  }
}
```

AdaptiveScreen() uses LocalWindowSizeClass.current to obtain a WindowSizeClass instance. This class belongs to the material3-window-size-class library. To use it, we need to add an implementation dependency:

```
implementation "androidx.compose.material3:material3-window-size-
class:1.1.1"
```

`WindowSizeClass` has two properties, `widthSizeClass` and `heightSizeClass`. The decision on whether to show a list or a grid is determined by this condition: `widthSizeClass == WindowWidthSizeClass.Compact`. The horizontal window size class is also used to determine the number of grid columns. If it is medium, we'll use two columns (`WindowWidthSizeClass. Medium -> 2`); otherwise, we use three.

`LocalWindowSizeClass` is a so-called **CompositionLocal**. You have seen in many examples throughout this book that data usually flows down the UI tree to each composable function that requires it using function arguments. This makes the dependencies of composables explicit. However, for widely and frequently used data, it may be unnerving having to pass it to every function. `CompositionLocal` allow data to flow through the UI tree implicitly – the data is *just there*. My example provides a `WindowSizeClass` instance using this technique. It is available through `LocalWindowSizeClass. current`:

```
val LocalWindowSizeClass = compositionLocalOf
  { WindowSizeClass.calculateFromSize(DpSize.Zero) }
```

We first define a `CompositionLocal` key; `compositionLocalOf {}` receives a factory that supplies a default value if no value is *provided* by `CompositionLocalProvider`. You will see shortly what this means. The `WindowSizeClass` companion object function, `calculateFromSize()`, returns a `WindowSizeClass` instance based on a given size in density-independent pixels, here `DpSize.Zero`. Next, let's look at the provider:

```
setContent {
  MaterialTheme(
    colorScheme = defaultColorScheme()
  ) {
    CompositionLocalProvider(
      LocalWindowSizeClass provides
          calculateWindowSizeClass(activity = this)
    ) {
      WindowSizeClassDemoScreen()
    }
  }
}
```

`CompositionLocalProvider()` is a composable function; it therefore must be invoked inside a Compose UI hierarchy. The `provides` infix function belongs to the `ProvidableCompositionLocal` abstract class, which is the return type of `compositionLocalOf()`. I am using `calculateWindowSizeClass()` to create a `WindowSizeClass` instance. The function receives a reference to the activity whose window size class should be calculated.

> **Please note**
>
> CompositionLocals are a great way to implicitly pass data down the Compose UI tree. If you need data only in a few places, it is best to remain explicit and pass it as parameters. You can read more about using this mechanism at `https://developer.android.com/jetpack/compose/compositionlocal`.

In this section, I showed you how to use window size classes to create an adaptive app layout. We achieved this without looking at the device class or form factor. Instead, we relied solely on the app window size. Unfortunately, more complex app layouts may require additional information. In the following section, I will introduce you to a such scenario and explain how to deal with it, using only information provided by the system.

Using Jetpack WindowManager

In the *Understanding different form factors* section, I introduced you to the *WindowSizeClassDemo* sample. The app evolved from always showing one layout (a vertically scrolling list) to utilizing an adaptive layout based on window size classes: depending on the width of the app window, either a list or a two- or three-column grid will be shown. This works great on smartphones and tablets. But how about foldable devices? *Figure 11.6* shows the sample on an unfolded Microsoft Surface Duo.

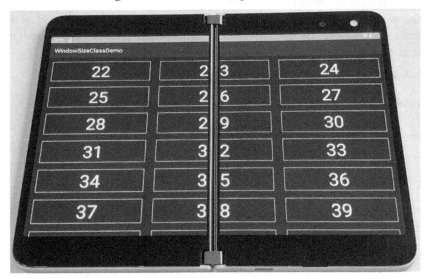

Figure 11.6 – WindowSizeClassDemo running on an unfolded Surface Duo

Foldable devices feature a hinge or fold, which allows the user to switch between two display area sizes. Often, this means it is either *smartphone-sized* or *tablet-sized*. However, there are also products (so-called flip phones) that need to be unfolded to be fully operable. Their screen size resembles smartphones. Consequently, the presence of a hinge does not warrant a certain display area size. Therefore, please avoid building layouts based on conditions such as *is foldable*, *has a hinge*, or *is a tablet*.

Depending on the hardware technology being used, a hinge may obstruct content. In such cases, you should not show important information in the area intersecting with the hinge. How to achieve this depends on your general app layout. You will learn more about global app layout in the *Organizing the screen content* section. Before that, let's look at how to collect information about a hinge or fold using *Jetpack WindowManager*. This library has three main use cases:

- Showing two activities side by side
- Getting window metrics and window size classes
- Getting information related to foldable devices

The first use case, showing two activities side by side, is important to make existing multi-activity apps work great on large screens. This is beyond the scope of this book. What about the second, getting window metrics and window size classes? Didn't we tackle this in the *Introducing Window Size Classes* section? Jetpack WindowManager provides `WindowMetricsCalculator` for obtaining **window metrics**. This is important for both `View`-based and Compose apps because window metrics are used to calculate window size classes. Consequently, `WindowMetricsCalculator` is used inside `calculateWindowSizeClass()` (see *Figure 11.7*).

```
@ExperimentalMaterial3WindowSizeClassApi
@Composable
fun calculateWindowSizeClass(activity: Activity): WindowSizeClass {
    // Observe view configuration changes and recalculate the size class on each change. We can't
    // use Activity#onConfigurationChanged as this will sometimes fail to be called on different
    // API levels, hence why this function needs to be @Composable so we can observe the
    // ComposeView's configuration changes.
    LocalConfiguration.current
    val density = LocalDensity.current
    val metrics = WindowMetricsCalculator.getOrCreate().computeCurrentWindowMetrics(activity)
    val size = with(density) { metrics.bounds.toComposeRect().size.toDpSize() }
    return WindowSizeClass.calculateFromSize(size)
}
```

Figure 11.7 – Source code of calculateWindowSizeClass()

Next, let's focus on the third use case, getting information related to foldable devices. The defining feature of this device class is the **hinge** or **fold**. Which word is used depends on the content being obstructed or separated or not. If it is, we usually say *hinge*. Speaking of a *fold* indicates that its impact on the screen content is less noticeable. The Microsoft Surface Duo has two equal-sized screens, which are connected by a hinge. It can be unfolded up to 360 degrees. The Google Pixel Fold, however, has a fold. Such devices usually can be unfolded up to 180 degrees.

Hinges and folds have a couple of features; among them are the following:

- Orientation

- Location and size

- **Influence on the content**: Obstructing/separating or not

Before I show you how to query them, please recall *Figure 11.6*. If the Surface Duo is unfolded and held in its natural orientation, its hinge runs vertically, and the horizontal window size class is *expanded*; therefore, *WindowSizeClassDemo* shows three columns. The middle one inevitably intersects with the hinge because all the columns are the same width. If the areas to the left and the right of the hinge are equally sized, too, we can lower the impact of the hinge just by making sure that we show an even number of columns.

Here's how to do that. First, we add a dependency to Jetpack WindowManager.

```
dependencies {
  ...
  implementation 'androidx.window:window:1.1.0'
}
```

Second, we make sure that our app receives foldable-related events. This is done like this:

```
class WindowSizeClassDemoActivity : ComponentActivity() {
  override fun onCreate(savedInstanceState: Bundle?) {
    super.onCreate(savedInstanceState)
    lifecycleScope.launch {
      lifecycle.repeatOnLifecycle(
        Lifecycle.State.STARTED
      ) {
        val activity = this@WindowSizeClassDemoActivity
        setContent {
          MaterialTheme(
            colorScheme = defaultColorScheme()
          ) {
            val windowLayoutInfo by
              WindowInfoTracker.getOrCreate(
              context = activity
```

```
        )
        .windowLayoutInfo(activity = activity)
        .collectAsState(initial = null)
      CompositionLocalProvider(
        LocalWindowSizeClass provides
        calculateWindowSizeClass(
          activity = activity
        )) {
        WindowSizeClassDemoScreen(
          windowLayoutInfo = windowLayoutInfo
        )
      }
    }
    }
    }
    }
    }
    }
}
```

We need to wrap setContent {} inside a lifecycle-aware coroutine using launch {} and repeatOnLifecycle {} because foldable-related events are received through an instance of WindowLayoutInfo. Getting it requires us to do the following:

1. Getting an instance of WindowInfoTracker using getOrCreate().

2. Invoking windowLayoutInfo() on it; this returns a flow.

3. Collecting the flow as a state using collectAsState().

The third step is to pass the WindowLayoutInfo instance down the Compose UI hierarchy by adding a parameter to WindowSizeClassDemoScreen() and AdaptiveScreen(). I suggest using WindowLayoutInfo? and setting its default value to null to indicate scenarios in which no foldable-related information is present, such as on ordinary smartphones and tablets:

```
@Composable
fun AdaptiveScreen(
  ...,
  windowLayoutInfo: WindowLayoutInfo? = null
) {
  var numColumnsWhenExpanded = 3
  windowLayoutInfo?.displayFeatures?.forEach {
    displayFeature ->
      (displayFeature as FoldingFeature).run {
      if (orientation ==
          FoldingFeature.Orientation.VERTICAL) {
```

```
            numColumnsWhenExpanded = 2
        }
    }
}

with(LocalWindowSizeClass.current) {
    if (widthSizeClass == WindowWidthSizeClass.Compact) {
        ...
    } else {
    NumbersGrid(
        ...,
        columns = when (widthSizeClass) {
            WindowWidthSizeClass.Medium -> 2
            else -> numColumnsWhenExpanded
        }
    )
    }
}
}
```

The enhanced version of `AdaptiveScreen()` stores the number of columns to be displayed when the horizontal window size class is neither `Compact` nor `Medium`, in a variable named numColumnsWhenExpanded. Its initial value is 3. If there is a hinge or fold that runs vertically, numColumnsWhenExpanded becomes 2. Granted, this is a simplistic approach. I will expand on this soon, but first, let me show you how to read hinge and fold features.

Reading hinge and fold features

The `WindowLayoutInfo` class has a property called `displayFeatures`. It's a list containing elements of type `DisplayFeature`. `DisplayFeature` is an interface with a property named bounds. As the name suggests, display features describe a physical feature on a display, such as a fold or hinge. The bounds property contains the bounding rectangle of the feature within the application window, in the window coordinate space. But how is the fold- or hinge-specific information provided?

The `FoldingFeature` interface extends `DisplayFeature`. It provides a couple of properties, for example, `orientation` (`Orientation.VERTICAL` or `Orientation.HORIZONTAL`), `isSeparating` (the window is split into multiple physical areas), `occlusionType` (`OcclusionType.FULL` or `OcclusionType.NONE`), and state (`State.FLAT` or `State.HALF_OPENED`). Please consult the API documentation of these properties for further information, as digging deeper into them unfortunately is beyond the scope of this book.

Which ones you will be querying depends on the purpose of your app. Consider a media player: if the device reports `State.HALF_OPENED` and the hinge is running horizontally, this posture could indicate that one half of the device is lying flat on a desk while the other one is in an upright position. Consequently, your app could show two rows, one containing the media and the other one media controls and additional information. You will learn more about global app layout in the *Organizing the screen content* section.

Before we move on, let's return to something I wrote a little earlier: I considered my example with the `numColumnsWhenExpanded` variable simplistic. Why is that? Each display feature provides its location and size on the screen through the `bounds` property. However, I didn't use it but instead assumed that both display area halves have the same size. To check, we would need the total display size – which you can obtain using `WindowMetricsCalculator`, another Jetpack WindowManager interface – and do some arithmetic. How to calculate, depends on the orientation of the hinge.

Another simplification I made was to ignore the size of the fold or hinge. While having an even number of columns makes sure that most of the grid item content is visible, the rightmost area of items to the left of the fold or hinge and the leftmost area of items to the right of the fold or hinge may still be invisible if the hinge is obstructing them. Fixing this requires support from the composable rendering the grid.

To finish this section, let's recap what we have learned so far. If a device exposes display features, you can query them by iterating over the `displayFeatures` list provided by `windowLayoutInfo()`. Currently, there is only `FoldingFeature`, but future versions of Jetpack WindowManager might provide additional ones. Depending on the horizontal window size class, the *WindowSizeClassDemo* sample uses either a vertically scrolling list or a grid with two or three columns for its global app layout. The final main section of this chapter, *Organizing the screen content*, will dig deeper into this topic.

Organizing the screen content

In the previous sections, I explained that to make your app look great on a wide range of devices, you should build its layout on top of Window Size Classes and foldable-related events emitted by Jetpack WindowManager. But what does *layout* refer to? *Figure 11.8* shows the *ComposeUnitConverter* sample from *Chapters 6* and *7*.

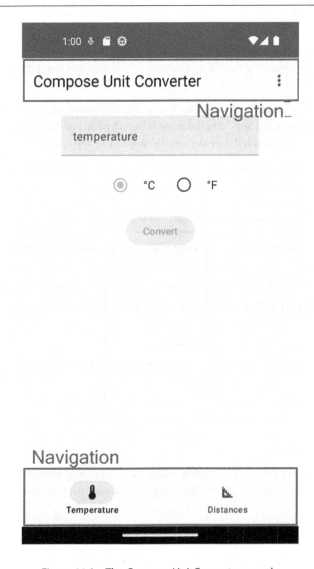

Figure 11.8 – The ComposeUnitConverter sample

There appear to be three areas: the content, bottom navigation, and the top app bar. However, **Material You** (the design language and design system used on Android) puts the latter two in one bucket, *navigation*. Therefore, inside the app window, there are only two major blocks or areas: the content (sometimes referred to as body) and the navigation. How these blocks are laid out is defined in the Material You documentation (`https://m3.material.io/foundations/layout/understanding-layout/overview`). For example, bottom navigation should be used only if the horizontal Window Size Class is `Compact`. Otherwise, display either a navigation rail or a navigation drawer.

> **Please note**
>
> Window Size Classes should be available in most of your composables. Please recall that you can provide them directly by passing them as a parameter or provide them using `CompositionLocal`.

Next, let's focus on the content (or body). Its layout matters the most. After all, the content is the reason why your users open the app. Which layout is best depends on the purpose of the app and the data or information to be presented, but also on the size of the app window.

Google has analyzed lots of apps and has identified three broad app layouts. They are called **Canonical Layouts**. The first one is called **Feed** (see *Figure 11.9*). You already saw it in the *WindowSizeClassDemo* sample.

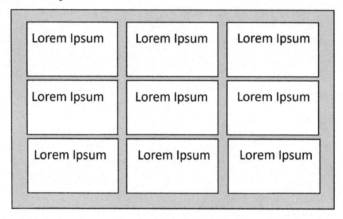

Figure 11.9 – Feed

A feed organizes cards or lists in a grid. It allows users to browse large amounts of content quickly and easily. Example use cases include pictures, business cards, news snippets, and social media entries.

The second Canonical Layout is called **List-detail** (see *Figure 11.10*).

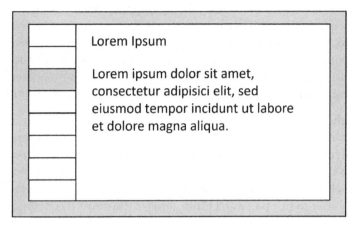

Figure 11.10 – List-detail

List-detail consists of two parts, a scrollable list of items and an item detail containing supplementary information. Example use cases include e-mails, contacts lists, and to-do lists.

The third Canonical Layout is called **Supporting pane** (see *Figure 11.11*).

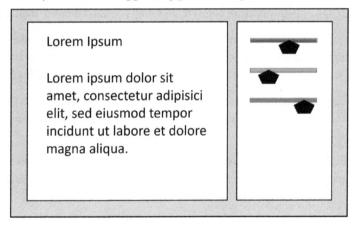

Figure 11.11 – Supporting pane

It consists of a larger primary section for the main app content and a secondary section that supports the main app content. Example use cases include imaging and drawing apps, where the main section contains the picture or graphics, whereas the secondary section offers tools, sliders, or knobs to alter or modify the content.

At this point, you may be asking yourself what's special about Canonical Layouts. Aren't they just **human interaction patterns**? In a way, they are. However, they support Window Size Classes. Here's how: all three are based upon *logical panes*. Feed comprises one such pane, whereas List-detail and Supporting pane consist of two. These panes are called *logical* because they may or may not have representations while the app is running. If the app window size is big enough, both the list and detail can be shown. If not, either the list or detail will be visible. The same applies to Supporting pane. While Feed has only one pane, it can consist of one, two, or more columns – depending on the Window Size Class.

Unfortunately, at the time of writing, there are no ready-to-use composable functions that provide Canonical Layouts. You need to implement them on your own or use additional libraries. Accompanist by Google contains the `TwoPanel()` composable. Please refer to `https://google.github.io/accompanist/adaptive/` for further information. My own library, `compose_adaptive_scaffold`, is also based on the idea of two panes. Like Accompanist, it is open source and available on GitHub. Please refer to `https://github.com/tkuenneth/compose_adaptive_scaffold` for further information.

Summary

In this chapter, you learned how to use Window Size Classes, Jetpack WindowManager, and Canonical Layouts to make sure your app looks great on smartphones, tablets, and foldable devices. First, we investigated how screen sizes, form factors, and hardware features influence app layout. Then, I explained how Window Size Classes help structure your UI, and how you can compute them during runtime.

The second main section, *Using Jetpack WindowManager*, explained why relying solely on Window Size Classes is not enough to create awesome layouts for tablets *and* foldables. You learned how to query hardware features such as hinge orientation and device posture and how this helps fine-tune your UI.

Finally, the *Organizing the screen content* section introduced a Material Design concept called Canonical Layouts. You learned which Canonical Layouts have been defined so far and in which scenarios they work best.

In the final chapter, *Bringing Your Compose UI to Different Platforms*, I will show you how to bring your Jetpack Compose knowledge to systems other than Android, for example, desktop.

Exercise

The *WindowSizeClass* sample makes a few assumptions about hinges and folds. Please modify the app so that it uses `WindowMetricsCalculator` to obtain the display size and then checks whether the areas to the left and the right of the hinge are the same size.

12

Bringing Your Compose UI to Different Platforms

In *Chapter 11, Developing for Different Form Factors*, you learned how to use Window Size Classes, Jetpack WindowManager, and Canonical Layouts to make sure your app looks great on smartphones, tablets, and foldables. We investigated screen sizes, form factors, and hardware features, and understood how they influence app layout. You also learned that Window Size Classes help structure your **user interface (UI)**. Knowing the generalized size of your app window is crucial for finding just the right layout. What *just the right layout* means depends on the purpose of your app. List-detail, Feed, and Supporting panes are great starting points for building the perfect UI. We closed *Chapter 11* by discussing the anatomy of these so-called canonical layouts and learned when they are best used.

In this final chapter, I will show you how to bring your Jetpack Compose knowledge to systems other than Android—for example, the desktop (Windows, Linux, macOS) and the web. The chapter starts with an introduction to Compose Multiplatform and related technologies. After that, we bring one of the sample apps to the desktop. You will also learn about the advantages and challenges of cross-platform apps.

This chapter has three main sections, as follows:

- Introducing Compose Multiplatform
- Building a cross-platform app
- Developing across platforms

In *Introducing Compose Multiplatform*, we set up a project for Android and the desktop. You will learn about the project structure and where you put your source code. Finally, we will run the project on Android and your developer machine.

The second main section, *Building a cross-platform app*, introduces the `expect` and `actual` keywords and explains why you may need to provide different implementations for some functionality.

The *Developing across platforms* section looks at the advantages and challenges of cross-platform development. Additionally, I will show you how to handle multilingual text across platforms.

Technical requirements

Please refer to the *Technical requirements* section of *Chapter 1, Building Your First Compose App*, for information about how to install and set up Android Studio, as well as how to get the sample apps. This section covers the `ComposeMultiplatformDemo` sample. To work with it, you need IntelliJ IDE Community Edition or Ultimnate 2020.3 or later. Installing IntelliJ IDEA is explained at `https://www.jetbrains.com/help/idea/installation-guide.html`.

Introducing Compose Multiplatform

While Jetpack Compose is the new UI toolkit on Android, its underlying ideas and principles make it attractive for other platforms, too. Let's see why this is the case:

- The declarative approach was first implemented on the web
- SwiftUI, Apple's implementation of a declarative UI framework, works well for iPhones, iPads, watches, and macOS devices
- Jetpack Compose UI elements use Material Design, which is designed for different platforms, device categories, and form factors

Most importantly, core concepts such as state and composable functions are not Android-specific. Therefore, if someone provides the toolchain (for example, the Kotlin compiler and the Compose compiler), any platform capable of showing graphics *may* be able to execute Compose apps. Certainly, there is an awful lot of work to be done.

For example, the Compose UI must be hosted *somewhere*. On Android, activities are used. On the web, this would be a browser window. And on the desktop, it will be a window provided by some UI toolkit. Any other functionality (for example, network and file I/O, connectivity, memory management, threading) must be addressed by other libraries or frameworks.

JetBrains, the inventor of Kotlin and IntelliJ, decided to tackle this. In recent years, the company gained a lot of experience in targeting multiple platforms and sharing code among them. With **Kotlin Multiplatform** (**KMP**), you can use a single code base for the business logic of (for example) iOS and Android apps. **Compose Multiplatform** goes even further in aiming to simplify and speed up the development of UIs for mobile, desktop, and web, and to share UI code among them, including Android. Compose Multiplatform is built on top of Kotlin Multiplatform and inherits its project structure, plugins, and concepts.

In the following section, I will show you how to create a Compose Multiplatform app.

Setting up a Compose Multiplatform project

The easiest way to create a new project is usually to run the **New project** wizard. At the time of writing, IntelliJ IDEA provides two relevant templates. Let's have a look:

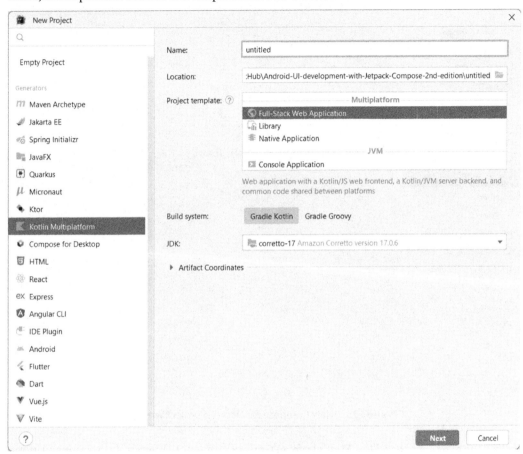

Figure 12.1 – New Kotlin Multiplatform project wizard

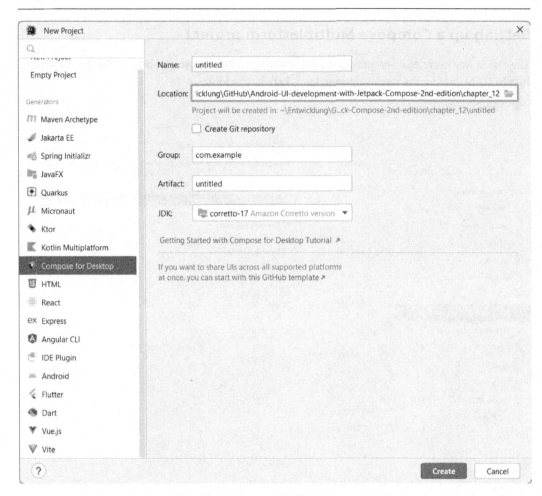

Figure 12.2 – New Compose for Desktop project wizard

At the time of writing, the **Kotlin Multiplatform** template (*Figure 12.1*) can create three multiplatform flavors (a web app, a library, and a native application) and a **Java Virtual Machine**- (**JVM**-) based console app. Unfortunately, no template path will create a project that runs on Android and the desktop. I have chosen to target these platforms because the book is about Android UI development, and you are inevitably using a desktop system for coding.

The **Compose for Desktop** template (*Figure 12.2*) focuses, as its name suggests, on the desktop. If you want to start a new app that runs on Windows, macOS, and Linux, this is just the right template. However, at the time of writing, there's no Android support out of the box in this template. This certainly may change in the future, so you should have a look at the **New project** wizard occasionally. But what do we do right now?

Fortunately, there is a suitable template from JetBrains on GitHub: it is available at `https://github.com/JetBrains/compose-multiplatform-template/tree/main`. On this website, you can either clone the repository or download it as a ZIP file (*Figure 12.3*). As you will be adding your own code, I suggest choosing the zipped version and unzipping it once the download is complete. This way, you can easily initialize a repository using `git init` when needed. The `ComposeMultiplatformDemo` sample, which we will explore in the *Developing across platforms* section, uses this template:

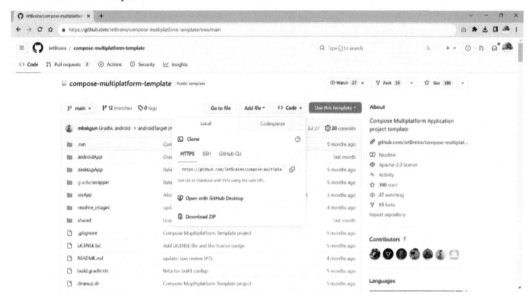

Figure 12.3 – compose-multiplatform-template GitHub repository

Compose Multiplatform requires a recent version of IntelliJ IDEA Community Edition or Ultimate Edition—for example, 2020.3 or later. Setting up IntelliJ is beyond the scope of this book and is not detailed here. Once you have cloned the repository or downloaded and extracted the archive, please open the template from the IntelliJ **Welcome** screen by clicking on **Open** and selecting the base directory in the **Open File or Project** window (*Figure 12.4*).

While your IDE is loading the project, let's look at a couple of important terms. Compose Multiplatform is called a **cross-platform framework**. The underlying idea is to build apps for different platforms from a single code base. Not needing to maintain a set of independent projects—or even teams—is an intriguing prospect (especially when thinking about costs). Consequently, there have been quite a few products that try to achieve this. Among them are Adobe PhoneGap/Apache Cordova, Microsoft Xamarin/MAUI, React Native, and Google Flutter. And there are many more. What differentiates them? What is their unique selling point?

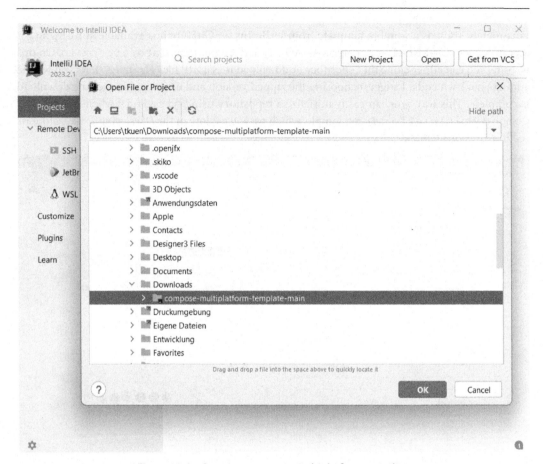

Figure 12.4 – Opening compose-multiplatform-template

All choose a specific set of technologies, tools, and programming languages. Flutter, for example, is based on Dart. React Native relies on JavaScript or TypeScript. And Compose Multiplatform loves Kotlin. Closely tied to the technology stack being used is the *level of integration*. If a framework decides to use—for example—JavaScript, but the platform favors Java or Kotlin, the app code must either be transpiled (converted) or executed in some runtime or container.

For early cross-platform frameworks, this meant that apps were running in a web view. To provide a basic level of platform integration, this container offered a plugin mechanism of some sort. While the apps used JavaScript or TypeScript to invoke the plugins, their implementations required native technology. The app code, the hosting container, and all required plugins were bundled using native mechanisms. So, while essentially developing a web app, you got—for example—an Android **application package** (**APK**) that could be released on Google Play. Such apps are called **hybrid apps**. Regardless of the availability of plugins, hybrid apps remain somewhat isolated because they can only interact with the underlying platform via the hosting container.

Consequently, new cross-platform frameworks seek a much deeper integration—for example, by providing and consuming native artifacts (libraries). You will learn more about this shortly.

Your IDE has surely loaded the project by now, so let's look at its structure (*Figure 12.5*):

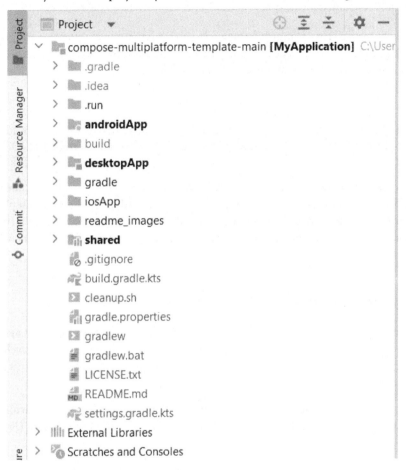

Figure 12.5 – Project structure

You will immediately spot four nodes, as follows:

- `androidApp` is a Kotlin module that builds into an Android app. It depends on the `shared` module and consumes it as an Android library. It uses Gradle as the build system.
- `iosApp` is an Xcode project that builds into an iOS app. It depends on the `shared` module and consumes it as a CocoaPods dependency.

- `desktopApp` is a Kotlin module that builds into a desktop app. It depends on the `shared` module and consumes it as a regular library. It uses Gradle as the build system.

- `shared` is a Kotlin module that contains the logic common for desktop, Android, and iOS apps. It is consumed by the other modules and uses Gradle as the build system.

To really benefit from a cross-platform framework, you want to reuse as much code as possible. This means putting it into `shared` because the code in there is immediately available on all targeted platforms. Consequently, our composable functions will be in `shared`.

> **Note**
>
> Although the template is capable of building iOS apps too, we will focus on Android and the desktop. Please refer to the template's README for more information regarding iOS.

Let's briefly recap. A Compose Multiplatform project contains one shared module for code that is used on all supported platforms, and a couple of platform modules (depending on which platforms are to be supported). Artifacts are provided and consumed using platform-specific means (for example, Android library, CocoaPods dependency, Java Archive). Finally, most modules are built using Gradle.

In the following section, I will show you how to run the sample app.

Running the sample app

In the previous section, I introduced you to the structure of a Compose Multiplatform project. Now, it's time to see it in action. Please make sure you have set up IntelliJ for Android development. To learn more, visit `https://www.jetbrains.com/help/idea/create-your-first-android-application.html`.

To run the app on the Android Emulator or a connected physical device, select **androidApp** in the list of run configurations, choose your target device, and click the green **Play** button (*Figure 12.6*):

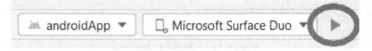

Figure 12.6 – Running the Android app

Figure 12.7 shows the sample app running on a connected physical device:

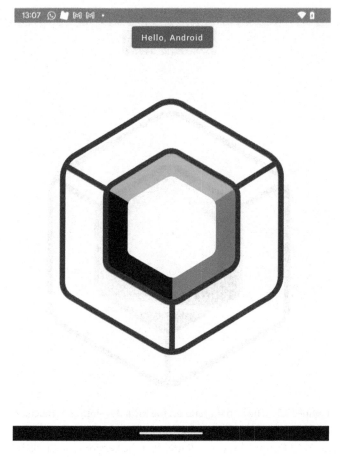

Figure 12.7 – The app running on a connected physical device

To run the app on your local development machine, select **desktopApp** in the list of run configurations, and click the green **Play** button (*Figure 12.8*):

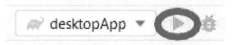

Figure 12.8 – Running the desktop app

Figure 12.9 shows the sample app running on my Windows 11 machine:

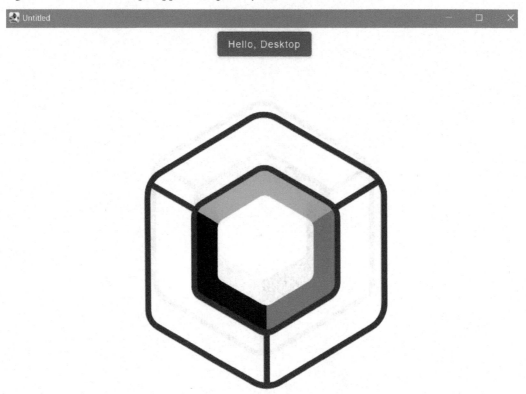

Figure 12.9 – The app running on the local development machine

Comparing *Figure 12.7* and *Figure 12.9*, you will find that the versions look mostly the same. Certainly, the decorations of the app windows differ. They are determined by the underlying platform. But there's another, more subtle deviation: the button text. It contains the platform name.

In the following section, *Building a cross-platform app*, I will explain how to achieve this and why it is important.

Building a cross-platform app

The main goal when using a cross-platform framework is to reuse code. However, there are situations when you want to do different things, depending on the platform. Kotlin Multiplatform and Compose Multiplatform help you achieve this with two new Kotlin keywords, expect and actual. Let's see how they work.

The following code is part of `compose-multiplatform-template`. It's inside `shared/src/commonMain/kotlin/App.kt`:

```kotlin
@Composable
fun App() {
  MaterialTheme {
    var greetingText by remember
      { mutableStateOf("Hello, World!") }
    var showImage by remember { mutableStateOf(false) }
    Column(
      Modifier.fillMaxWidth(),
      horizontalAlignment =
        Alignment.CenterHorizontally) {
      Button(onClick = {
        greetingText = "Hello, ${getPlatformName()}"
        showImage = !showImage
      }) {
        Text(greetingText)
      }
      AnimatedVisibility(showImage) {
        Image(
          painterResource("compose-multiplatform.xml"),
          null
        )
      }
    }
  }
}

expect fun getPlatformName(): String
```

`Column()` contains two children, `Button()` and `Image()`. The image is visible only when `showImage` is `true`. This state changes whenever the button is clicked. The image is shown or hidden using `AnimatedVisibility()`, so it appears and disappears smoothly. The initial button text reads **Hello, World!**. It changes to `"Hello, ${getPlatformName()}"` when the `onClick {}` lambda expression is executed.

The `getPlatformName()` function is declared using `expect`. This keyword signals that somewhere in the project there will be an implementation of this function that adheres to this signature. Consequently, we can invoke the function without knowing anything about its implementation. Here's how an implementation looks:

```kotlin
actual fun getPlatformName(): String = "Android"
```

This line of code is inside `shared/src/androidMain/kotlin/main.android.kt`.

Here's another one:

```
actual fun getPlatformName(): String = "Desktop"
```

You can find it in `shared/src/desktopMain/kotlin/main.desktop.kt`.

The `actual` keyword marks this function as the implementation of a function with the same name and signature.

To summarize, if you want to use something platform-specific (for example, a text, an image, or the result of a computation) in your shared code, a good approach is to define a contract using `expect` and provide implementations using `actual`. Be careful, though, where to put the implementations. If you look at the paths leading to `getPlatformName()`, you may be puzzled to find all three start with `shared/src`. They are in the `shared` module. Shouldn't they be in the `desktopApp` and `androidApp` modules instead? Code put in these two will be visible *only there*: if you move the Android implementation of `getPlatformName()` to `androidApp`, you will receive an error message, as follows:

```
Actual function 'getPlatformName' has no corresponding expected
declaration.
```

The `shared` module is grouped or, depending on your perspective, divided into so-called **source sets**. Have a look here:

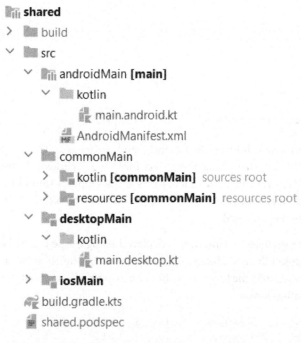

Figure 12.10 – Source sets inside the shared module

There are four source sets (nodes), `androidMain`, `desktopMain`, `iosMain`, and `commonMain`. The first three receive platform-specific code that still needs to be *visible* to the other ones. That's why the `actual` implementations are put there. The fourth, `commonMain`, is truly cross-platform— that's why you find the `expect` declaration there. Source sets are defined in `build.gradle.kts` files. Unfortunately, explaining them fully is beyond the scope of this book, but you can read more at `https://kotlinlang.org/docs/multiplatform-discover-project.html`.

Let's recap. I introduced you to the `expect` and `actual` keywords and showed you where to put the corresponding source code. You should use this mechanism to access a value that is obtained or computed differently, depending on the platform. In the following section, we continue our exploration of Compose Multiplatform. So far, you have seen how to create a composable function that will be shown on Android and iOS. But how is it picked up by platform-specific code?

Accessing composables from platform-specific code

Once you have written your Compose UI, you want to make sure it is displayed on all platforms. Let's see how to achieve this. Please recall from the *Setting up a Compose Multiplatform project* section that the project template includes four modules: `androidApp`, `iosApp`, `desktopApp`, and `shared`. The latter one contains, among other code such as business logic, your composable functions. The first three, on the other hand, represent the app for the corresponding platform. Consequently, anything needed to show a Compose hierarchy on that platform goes there.

On Android, we invoke `setContent {}` inside the `onCreate()` function of an activity to show the UI. Here's what the project template does. You will find the code inside `androidApp/src/androidMain/kotlin/com/myapplication/MainActivity.kt`:

```
class MainActivity : AppCompatActivity() {
  override fun onCreate(savedInstanceState: Bundle?) {
    super.onCreate(savedInstanceState)
    setContent {
      MainView()
    }
  }
}
```

The definition of `MainView()` looks like this:

```
@Composable fun MainView() = App()
```

It is inside `shared/src/androidMain/kotlin/main.android.kt`. If this path feels familiar to you, you are right. This file also contains the Android implementation of `getPlatformName()`.

> **Note**
> The project structure ensures that platform modules can safely reference shared code.

For desktop apps, the entry point is a traditional `main()` function. Here's what it looks like. You can find it inside `desktopApp/src/jvmMain/kotlin/main.kt`:

```
fun main() = application {
    Window(onCloseRequest = ::exitApplication) {
        MainView()
    }
}
```

The `application {}` function makes sure that the app keeps running until all windows are closed and all operations are completed. `Window()` is a composable. It can receive quite a few parameters. Please refer to its documentation to learn more. The `onCloseRequest` lambda will be executed when the user clicks on the **Close** button of the window; `exitApplication` is part of the `ApplicationScope` interface. An implementation is passed to `application {}`.

`MainView()` is the content that will be shown inside the window. Just as for Android, a platform-specific version is just. It is defined inside `shared/src/desktopMain/kotlin/main.desktop.kt`, which is the file that includes the desktop implementation for `getPlatformName()`.

This concludes the second main section, *Building a cross-platform app*. We set up a project that produces apps for Android, iOS, and the desktop, based on a GitHub template by the Compose Multiplatform inventor, JetBrains. You learned about its structure and where to put code such as composable functions that will be shared across platforms. We also saw how platform-specific modules use the shared code.

In the next and final main section, *Developing across platforms*, we will be modifying the template by adding snippets of one of my sample apps. This will help you gain an understanding of both the advantages and limitations of cross-platform frameworks.

Developing across platforms

One of the biggest advantages of a cross-platform framework is that you generate your apps from one code base. This allows you to reuse code and assets (such as images and text). In the previous section, *Building a cross-platform app*, you learned about the project structure of Compose Multiplatform and how you can share a composable function across Android and the desktop. I explained the relationship between the four main modules `androidApp`, `iosApp`, `desktopApp`, and `shared`, and introduced a concept called source sets, which help structure your shared code.

So far, we have focused on reusing *code*. But how about other resources? Usually, apps contain a lot of text that is shown to the user. What's more, this text is often available in different languages. Consequently, changing, adding, or deleting text should apply to all platforms. To put it another way, we don't want copies of text in `androidApp` and `desktopApp`. But how do we do that?

Let's start by copying a few composable functions from the `Hello` sample of *Chapter 1, Building Your First Compose App*, into `shared/src/commonMain/kotlin/App.kt`. This file contains the `App()` composable.

> **Note**
>
> The `ComposeMultiplatformDemo` sample is based on the Compose Multiplatform template that I discussed in the *Introducing Compose Multiplatform* section. My sample contains all the changes I will be describing in this section.

Here's the first code snippet:

```
@Composable
fun App() {
  Hello()
}

@Composable
fun Hello() {
  val name = remember { mutableStateOf("") }
  val nameEntered = remember { mutableStateOf(false) }
  Box(
    modifier = Modifier
      .fillMaxSize()
      .padding(16.dp),
    contentAlignment = Alignment.Center
  ) {
    if (nameEntered.value) {
      Greeting(name.value)
    } else {
      Column(horizontalAlignment =
      Alignment.CenterHorizontally) {
        Welcome()
        TextAndButton(name, nameEntered)
      }
    }
  }
}
```

The `App()` composable is already there; you need to replace it with the new version. Besides missing imports, IntelliJ complains that `Greeting()`, `Welcome()`, and `TextAndButton()` are missing. Let's add them:

```
@Composable
fun Greeting(name: String) {
  Text(
    text = stringResource(id = R.string.hello, name),
    textAlign = TextAlign.Center,
```

```
      style = MaterialTheme.typography.bodyLarge
  )
}

@Composable
fun Welcome() {
  Text(
    text = stringResource(id = R.string.welcome),
    style = MaterialTheme.typography.bodyLarge
  )
}

@Composable
fun TextAndButton(
  name: MutableState<String>,
  nameEntered: MutableState<Boolean>
) {
  Row(modifier = Modifier.padding(top = 8.dp)) {
    TextField(
      value = name.value,
      onValueChange = {
        name.value = it
      },
      placeholder = {
        Text(text = stringResource(id = R.string.hint))
      },
      modifier = Modifier
        .alignByBaseline()
        .weight(1.0F),
      singleLine = true,
      keyboardOptions = KeyboardOptions(
        autoCorrect = false,
        capitalization = KeyboardCapitalization.Words,
      ),
      keyboardActions = KeyboardActions(onAny = {
        nameEntered.value = true
      })
    )
    Button(modifier = Modifier
      .alignByBaseline()
      .padding(8.dp),
      onClick = {
        nameEntered.value = true
```

```
    }) {
    Text(text = stringResource(id = R.string.done))
  }
 }
}
```

Next, let's check if the template is using Material Design version 2, or Material 3. Please have a look inside `shared/build.gradle.kts`. If you spot a block such as the following snippet, you need to apply a tiny change. At the time of writing, this is the case:

```
sourceSets {
  val commonMain by getting {
    dependencies {
      ...
      implementation(compose.material)
      ...
    }
  }
}
```

Replace the highlighted line with the following:

```
implementation(compose.material3)
```

IntelliJ will ask you to load Gradle changes (*Figure 12.11*):

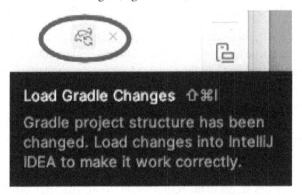

Figure 12.11 – Load Gradle Changes

Please do so by clicking on the corresponding icon. If the file already contains the line printed previously (which means it is using Material 3), no change is needed.

> **Note**
> This book uses Material 3, which contains a couple of name changes. For example, `MaterialTheme.typography.body1` (Material 2) has become `MaterialTheme.typography.bodyLarge`.

After adding all missing imports, two issues remain, as follows:

- `stringResources` is not available
- `R` is not available

The reason for both being unavailable is that they are specific to Android. Putting text in a file called `strings.xml` and using generated constants to reference these string resources is a standard procedure on Android, yet uncommon on other platforms, which have their own best practices for dealing with multilingual text. This is a prime example of the challenges that all cross-platform frameworks face: embrace differences between platforms and, ideally, hide them from the developers. Unfortunately, exploring this in greater detail is beyond the scope of this book. Instead, let's focus on the immediate issue.

We want text to be stored in one central place but also be available in all modules. The `shared` module is visible to `androidApp` and `desktopApp`; therefore, it seems like a good place to put the artifacts. Unfortunately, a couple of questions remain; among them are the following:

- Which format? An XML file, as on Android? Or a properties file, which is common in Java apps?
- How do we reference text? Should we generate IDs as in the `R` class on Android?

Basically, all cross-platform frameworks are backed by a community that provides additional libraries or plugins. Naturally, this is true for Compose Multiplatform/ Kotlin Multiplatform, too. When facing a challenge such as multilingual text handling, please look for a multiplatform library that solves this problem for you before deciding to tackle it on your own. In the following section, we will be using the *Mobile Kotlin resources* library to add text artifacts to the project.

Using Mobile Kotlin resources

Mobile Kotlin resources (**moko-resources**) is a Kotlin Multiplatform/Compose Multiplatform library and Gradle plugin. It provides access to the resources on the desktop, iOS, Android, and the browser, and is released under the terms of the Apache-2.0 license. It's available on GitHub at `https://github.com/icerockdev/moko-resources`.

Let's have a look at how to use it. The first step is to add moko-resources to the project in a couple of places, as follows:

```
// gradle.properties
moko.resources.version=0.23.0
moko.mvvm.version=0.16.0

// build.gradle.kts
plugins {
  ...
  id("dev.icerock.mobile.multiplatform-resources")
    .apply(false)
}

// settings.gradle.kts
pluginManagement {
  repositories {
    ...
  }

  plugins {
    ...
    val mokoResourcesVersion =
            extra["moko.resources.version"] as String
    ...
    id("dev.icerock.mobile.multiplatform-resources")
      .version(mokoResourcesVersion)
  }
}

// shared/build.gradle.kts
plugins {
  ...
  id("dev.icerock.mobile.multiplatform-resources")
}

kotlin {
  android()
  jvm("desktop")
  ...
  sourceSets {
    val commonMain by getting {
      val mokoResourcesVersion =
        extra["moko.resources.version"] as String
```

```
      val mokoMvvmVersion =
        extra["moko.mvvm.version"] as String

      dependencies {
        ...
        api("dev.icerock.moko:resources:${
          mokoResourcesVersion}")
        api("dev.icerock.moko:resources-compose:${
          mokoResourcesVersion}")
        api("dev.icerock.moko:mvvm-compose:
          $mokoMvvmVersion")
      }
    }
    ...
  }
}

multiplatformResources {
  multiplatformResourcesPackage =
    "com.myapplication.common"
}
...
```

Please refer to the moko-resources documentation at `https://github.com/icerockdev/moko-resources#installation` to learn more.

The next step is to provide text. As with Android, the library uses a file called `strings.xml`. Here's how it looks:

```
<?xml version="1.0" encoding="UTF-8" ?>
<resources>
  <string name="welcome">Welcome. What is your
    name?</string>
  <string name="hello">Hello, %1$s.\nNice to meet
    you.</string>
  <string name="done">Done</string>
  <string name="hint">Your name</string>
</resources>
```

Please put it inside `shared/src/commonMain/resources/MR/base/strings.xml`.

The final step is to use the library in code. During builds, moko-resources will create a class named `com.myapplication.common.MR`. As with the R class on Android, it provides references to text defined in `strings.xml` via a property. Its name is `strings`. For example, the `hello` text is identified by `MR.strings.hello`. The code snippet we copied contains `stringResource(id = R.string.hello, name)`. It needs to be replaced by `stringResource(MR.strings.hello, name)`. Please change all other occurrences of `stringResource {}` accordingly.

This section covered a lot. Still, I could only briefly touch on the basics. moko-resources can handle many other artifact types, and it can be customized in many ways—for example, you can specify where to put the MR class. Please refer to its documentation for details.

This concludes the final main section, *Developing across platforms*. We added some code snippets of one of my sample apps to the Compose Multiplatform template, looked at the advantages and challenges of cross-platform frameworks, and incorporated a third-party library to manage string resources.

Summary

In this chapter, I showed you how to expand your Jetpack Compose skills beyond Android. We looked at the *Compose Multiplatform* framework and examined its project structure. `compose-multiplatform-template` from JetBrains is a great start for apps that target Android, iOS, and the desktop. You learned about the new `expect` and `actual` keywords and where to add source code. I also showed you how to incorporate dependencies into third-party libraries. In particular, we added the moko-resources library to provide multilingual text across platforms.

I sincerely hope you enjoyed reading this book. You now have a thorough understanding of the core principles of Jetpack Compose, as well as the important advantages over the traditional Android `View` system. Using a declarative approach makes writing great-looking apps easier than ever. No matter if your apps will remain on Android or you will be embracing other platforms, I can't wait to see what beautiful ideas you are going to turn into code.

Exercise

All desktop platforms (Linux, macOS, and Windows) feature draggable and resizable app windows. In *Chapter 11, Developing for Different Form Factors*, I introduced you to Window Size Classes and explained how they help create a layout that adapts to window size changes. Using a fresh copy of the Compose Multiplatform project template, create a version of the `WindowSizeClassDemo` sample that works on Android and the desktop.

Index

www.packtpub.com

Subscribe to our online digital library for full access to over 7,000 books and videos, as well as industry leading tools to help you plan your personal development and advance your career. For more information, please visit our website.

Why subscribe?

- Spend less time learning and more time coding with practical eBooks and Videos from over 4,000 industry professionals

- Improve your learning with Skill Plans built especially for you

- Get a free eBook or video every month

- Fully searchable for easy access to vital information

- Copy and paste, print, and bookmark content

Did you know that Packt offers eBook versions of every book published, with PDF and ePub files available? You can upgrade to the eBook version at packtpub.com and as a print book customer, you are entitled to a discount on the eBook copy. Get in touch with us at customercare@packtpub.com for more details.

At www.packtpub.com, you can also read a collection of free technical articles, sign up for a range of free newsletters, and receive exclusive discounts and offers on Packt books and eBooks.

Other Books You May Enjoy

If you enjoyed this book, you may be interested in these other books by Packt:

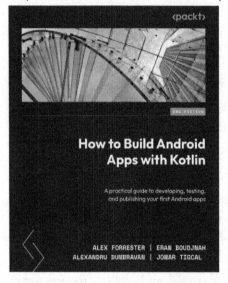

How to Build Android Apps with Kotlin - Second Edition

Alex Forrester, Eran Boudjnah, Alexandru Dumbravan, Jomar Tigcal

ISBN: 978-1-83763-493-4

- Create maintainable and scalable apps using Kotlin
- Understand the Android app development lifecycle
- Simplify app development with Google architecture components
- Use standard libraries for dependency injection and data parsing
- Apply the repository pattern to retrieve data from outside sources
- Build user interfaces using Jetpack Compose
- Explore Android asynchronous programming with Coroutines and the Flow API
- Publish your app on the Google Play store

Kickstart Modern Android Development with Jetpack and Kotlin

Catalin Ghita

ISBN: 978-1-80181-107-1

- Integrate popular Jetpack libraries such as Compose, ViewModel, Hilt, and Navigation into real Android apps with Kotlin
- Apply modern app architecture concepts such as MVVM, dependency injection, and clean architecture
- Explore Android libraries such as Retrofit, Coroutines, and Flow
- Integrate Compose with the rest of the Jetpack libraries or other popular Android libraries
- Work with other Jetpack libraries such as Paging and Room while integrating a real REST API that supports pagination
- Test Compose UI and the application logic through unit tests

Packt is searching for authors like you

If you're interested in becoming an author for Packt, please visit `authors.packtpub.com` and apply today. We have worked with thousands of developers and tech professionals, just like you, to help them share their insight with the global tech community. You can make a general application, apply for a specific hot topic that we are recruiting an author for, or submit your own idea.

Hi!

I am Thomas Künneth, author of *Android UI Development with Jetpack Compose*, I really hope you enjoyed reading this book.

It would really help us (and other potential readers!) if you could leave a review on Amazon sharing your thoughts on *Android UI Development with Jetpack Compose* .

Go to the link below or scan the QR code to leave your review: `https://packt.link/r/1837634254`

Your review will help us to understand what's worked well in this book, and what could be improved upon for future editions, so it really is appreciated.

Best wishes,

Experts
Android

Download a free PDF copy of this book

Thanks for purchasing this book!

Do you like to read on the go but are unable to carry your print books everywhere?

Is your eBook purchase not compatible with the device of your choice?

Don't worry, now with every Packt book you get a DRM-free PDF version of that book at no cost.

Read anywhere, any place, on any device. Search, copy, and paste code from your favorite technical books directly into your application.

The perks don't stop there, you can get exclusive access to discounts, newsletters, and great free content in your inbox daily

Follow these simple steps to get the benefits:

1. Scan the QR code or visit the link below

https://packt.link/free-ebook/9781837634255

2. Submit your proof of purchase
3. That's it! We'll send your free PDF and other benefits to your email directly

Made in the USA
Las Vegas, NV
02 January 2025

15804423R00155